James Bass Mullinger

A History of the University of Cambridge

James Bass Mullinger

A History of the University of Cambridge

ISBN/EAN: 9783337326678

Printed in Europe, USA, Canada, Australia, Japan

Cover: Foto ©ninafisch / pixelio.de

More available books at **www.hansebooks.com**

PREFACE.

ALTHOUGH the present volume appears as one of a series especially designed to illustrate Church History, the writer has not sought to modify the treatment of the subject in order to establish its claim to a place in such a category. The following sketch will suffice to show that it was in the University of Cambridge that the Reformation in England had its real commencement; that it was there that Puritanism first assumed a distinct organisation, and at the same time encountered the most effective resistance; that it was there also that a movement which most materially influenced the religious thought of the seventeenth century,—the teaching of the Cambridge Platonists,—took its rise and made its most important contributions to the cause of freedom and toleration. It is not necessary to refer to yet later movements to prove the close connection which has always existed between the

University and the main current of religious thought and feeling in the country at large,—a connection which becomes more and more apparent in proportion as the history of the former is more closely studied.

But, notwithstanding the intimate relations which have always, in a greater or less degree, been maintained between the University and the nation, a remarkable contrast is to be observed in the character of those relations as they existed in mediæval times and in the first half of the present century. From being at once national and popular, the university had at that time become oligarchical and exclusive; from a recognised training-school for the professions, and a home for all branches of learning, it had dwindled to little more than a seminary for the Church; from a munificent endowment for the poor it had been converted into something like a monopoly of the wealthier classes.

It cannot but be instructive, on the one hand, to note the successive changes and encroachments whereby such a revolution was gradually brought about. It cannot but be of interest, on the other, to observe how, in the latter half of the nineteenth century, the University has once more become national as regards the extent of its action, comprehensive in the range of its studies, and catholic in its sympathies.

In the chapter devoted to the times of the Commonwealth it will be seen (p. 152) that, so early as the seventeenth century, the Head of a Cambridge College ventured to put forward a scheme for creating independent centres of higher education in other English towns. The loss of time, the expense, and the perils attendant in those days upon a journey to either Oxford or Cambridge from the more remote large towns appeared to the author of the scheme sufficient reasons for advocating such a measure. It was, however, precisely these considerations,—suggesting, as they did, that the project, if carried out, would result rather in the creation of independent centres than in the extension of university influence,—which condemned it in the eyes of others.

In the present day, when intercommunication is as rapid and easy as it was then slow and difficult, we have seen the project of William Dell to a great extent realised; and the poor student, who was once under the necessity of journeying laboriously over hill and moor in order to gain the benefits of university instruction, now finds it brought, by the university extension lecturer, almost to his own door. I need offer no apology for having devoted a chapter to some account of this important movement, whereby the university seems destined still further to extend, throughout the nation at large, that influence which, at one time almost lost, it has already more than regained.

In my larger work[1] I have traced in detail, down to the second quarter of the seventeenth century, the subject of which the present volume offers only the outline. From that period down to the commencement of the present half-century, the *Annals of Cambridge*, by C. H. Cooper (vols. iii and iv), and the *Scholæ Academicæ* of the Rev. C. Wordsworth will be found to afford the fullest information. On the architectural development of the University I have touched only incidentally and very slightly, almost all that is ascertainable on the subject being now before the public in a single work, the admirable *Architectural*

---

[1] *The University of Cambridge from the Earliest Times to the Accession of Charles the First.* By J. B. Mullinger, M.A. 2 vols. Cambridge University Press. 1873–83.

PREFACE. ix

History of the University and Colleges of Cambridge, by Willis and Clark, published in 1886.

In the article on " Universities " in the new edition of the *Encyclopædia Britannica* I have endeavoured to give a comparative view of the history of such institutions from their first commencement.

For the chart (see p. 212), exhibiting the numbers of admissions to the B.A. degree from the year 1500 to the present decade, I am indebted to Dr. Venn, by whose kind permission it has been prepared from one drawn by him from the data supplied by the original lists.

J. BASS MULLINGER.

CONTENTS.

PREFACE v

CHAPTER I.

THE EARLIEST UNIVERSITIES—PRÆ-ACADEMIC CAMBRIDGE—
BEGINNINGS OF CAMBRIDGE UNIVERSITY HISTORY.

Original meaning of the term 'university'—Main facts in the history of education subsequent to the fall of the Roman Empire—Distinguishing features of the university movement—The University of Salerno—The study of the Civil Law—The study of the Canon Law—The University of Bologna—The study of logic—The *Sentences* of Peter Lombard—The New Aristotle—Features common to the growth of the early universities—Ely and Cambridge—Oxford and Cambridge—Cambridge early in the twelfth century—The Castle—The Church of St. Giles—St. Benet's Church—First beginnings of the university—Barnwell Priory—The Nunnery of St. Rhadegund—The Hospital of St. John—The School of Pythagoras—Ely and Cambridge—Foundations of the Franciscans and Dominicans—Migrations to Cambridge—Migrations from the university to Northampton and to Stamford—Town and Gown—Destructive fires 1

CHAPTER II.

THE UNIVERSITY IN THE THIRTEENTH AND FOURTEENTH CENTURIES—FOUNDATION OF THE EARLIEST COLLEGES.

Mediæval organisation of the university—The *trivium* or undergraduate course—Grammar, logic, and rhetoric—The *quadrivium*—Course requisite for the theologian—Course requisite for the civilian or canonist—Course requisite for the doctor of medicine—The regents or teachers—Lecturing *ordinarie* and *cursorie*—Duties imposed upon the regents—State of the university in the thirteenth century—Ordinance of Hugh de Balsham—Architectural development of early colleges—The Hospital of St. John—Foundation of Peterhouse—Foundation of Michaelhouse—Foundation of Pembroke Hall—Foundation of Gonville Hall—Foundation of Trinity Hall—Foundation of Corpus Christi College—Foundation of Clare Hall—Foundation of King's Hall—Theories of education exemplified in the foregoing foundations 21

CHAPTER III.

THE UNIVERSITY IN THE FIFTEENTH CENTURY—CHARACTERISTICS OF UNIVERSITY MEDIÆVAL LIFE.

Influence of Lollardism and prevalence of ultramontanism at both universities—Antagonism between the ultramontanist claims and those of the bishops of Ely—The Barnwell Process—Influences unfavourable to free speculation and philosophy—Foundation of Eton College and King's College—Foundation of Queen's College—Foundation of St. Catherine's Hall—Foundation of Jesus College—Character of university instruction at this period—The analytical method—The dialectical method—Subsequent career of the master of arts 50

CONTENTS. xiii

CHAPTER IV.

THE UNIVERSITY AND THE RENAISSANCE.

PAGE

Bishop Fisher—The Lady Margaret—Foundation of Christ's College—Foundation of St. John's College—Bishop Fisher's different statutes for the college—Residence of Erasmus at Cambridge—Richard Croke—Visit of Wolsey—The early Cambridge press 66

CHAPTER V.

THE UNIVERSITY DURING THE REFORMATION.

Præ-Lutheran Reformation movement in Cambridge—Its chief leaders—William Tyndale, Barnes, and Latimer—Influence of Cambridge on Oxford—The university and the Royal Divorce—Election of Thomas Cromwell as chancellor—The Royal Injunctions of 1535—Effects of the dissolution of the monasteries—Leading characters in the university— Thomas Smith and John Cheke—Foundation of the Regius Professorships — Proposed changes in pronunciation of Greek—Foundation of Magdalene College—Designs of the courtiers on the colleges defeated—Foundation of Trinity College—Noteworthy features in its first statutes . . 79

CHAPTER VI.

FROM THE FOUNDATION OF TRINITY COLLEGE TO THE ACCESSION OF ELIZABETH.

Abuses in admission of students into colleges—State of the university as described by Dr. Caius—The statutes of 1549 —Fagius and Bucer appointed professors—State of the study of the Civil Law—Chief incidents of Mary's reign— Refounding of Gonville Hall by Dr. Caius . . . 101

CHAPTER VII.

THE UNIVERSITY DURING THE ELIZABETHAN ERA.

Cambridge more favourable to the Reformation than Oxford —Increase of numbers in the university—Return of the Marian exiles—Changes in the colleges and the university —Thomas Cartwright and rise of the Puritan party— Appointment of Cartwright to the Lady Margaret professorship—Effects of his teaching—John Whitgift—Measures against Cartwright—Enactment of the Elizabethan Statutes —Persecution of Dr. Caius—Death of Archbishop Parker —Increased activity of the Puritans—The *Disciplina* of Walter Travers—Ames, Robert Brown, and John Smith— Foundation of Emmanuel College—Limitation imposed on tenure of fellowships — William Whitaker — Rise of an Arminian party—Arminians and Calvinists—Sir Thomas Smith's Act for the maintenance of colleges—Foundation of Sidney Sussex College—Relations between the university and the town 113

CHAPTER VIII.

FROM THE DEATH OF ELIZABETH TO THE RESTORATION.

Expectations of parties at the accession of James—Influence of Bancroft at Cambridge—University receives the right of returning members to Parliament—Arbitrary rule of colleges —Eminent Heads: Roger Goad, Dr. Neville, Dr. Davenant, John Preston—College plays—Buckingham as chancellor— The university during the Civil War—Imposition of the Solemn League and Covenant—Changes consequent upon its introduction 138

CHAPTER IX.

FROM THE RESTORATION TO THE ACCESSION OF GEORGE I.

Changes at the Restoration—The Crown and the university— Question of mandate degrees—The Cambridge Platonists:

Whichcote, John Smith, Cudworth, and Henry More—
Growth of the study of natural philosophy—Barrow and
Newton—Attempted reformation of discipline—Monmouth
as chancellor—Mandate elections to fellowships—The case
of Alban Francis—Changes consequent upon the accession
of Mary II.—Thomas Baker—Richard Bentley—His efforts
in the cause of science—His improvements at Trinity—
Uffenbach's visit and his impressions—Cotes, Whiston, and
Joshua Barnes—Controversy revived by Whiston . . 155

CHAPTER X.

FROM THE ACCESSION OF GEORGE I. TO THE END OF THE EIGHTEENTH CENTURY.

Later years of Bentley and Newton—Growth of St. Catherine's
College—Dr. Sherlock—Foundation of Regius professorship
of History and of Woodwardian professorship of Geology—
The Tripos: origin of the term and of the institution—The
first Tripos—Proctor's Optimes—Original examination for
the Mathematical Tripos—Subordination of other studies
to mathematics—Richard Porson—Dr. Jebb's proposal of
an annual compulsory examination—Influence of the main
study on Cambridge theology—Edmund Law and William
Paley—Rise of the Evangelical school—Berridge and the
Milners—First publication of the University Calendar . 171

CHAPTER XI.

FROM THE COMMENCEMENT OF THE CENTURY TO THE PRESENT TIME.

Foundation of Downing College—Increase in the numbers of
the university—Institution of the Classical Tripos—Restriction originally imposed on candidates, and its removal
—Sir William Hamilton and Adam Sedgwick on the studies
of the university—Proposed revision of the university statutes—Appointment of the Commission of 1850—Substance

of their Report—Enactment of statutes of 1858—The *Essays on a Liberal Education*—Example set by Trinity College of a reformation of college statutes—Appointment of the Royal Commission of 1872—Memorial to the Prime Minister in 1874—The Universities Act of 1877—Institution of the Law Tripos—The Law and History Tripos—The second Law Tripos—The Historical Tripos—Changes in the same —Changes in the Classical Tripos—Changes in the Theological Tripos—Institution of the Semitic Languages, the Indian Languages, and the Mediæval and Modern Languages Triposes—Foundation of Selwyn College—Foundation of Ridley Hall—Growth of the university during the last quarter of a century 187

CHAPTER XII.

CAMBRIDGE IN RELATION TO NATIONAL EDUCATION.

Institution of the LOCAL EXAMINATIONS — The Syndicate— Original scope of the examinations—Extension of the design to women—Further extension to highest grade schools —The certificates invested with a university value—Inclusion of girls' highest grade schools—The UNIVERSITY EXTENSION MOVEMENT—Scheme of lectures initiated by Professor James Stuart—Adoption of his scheme at Nottingham—Joint-Memorial to the university—Adoption of the scheme by the Cambridge Syndicate—Its remarkable success, and adoption at Oxford, in London, and elsewhere —Method of instruction introduced with the movement —Method of examination—Further development of the scheme—Conference at Cambridge in connection with the movement 213

INDEX 224

Erratum : p. 58, *for* 'Chadworth,' *read* 'Chedworth.'

A HISTORY

OF

ERRATA.

Page 10, line 14, *for* '1109' *read* '1009.'
,,   38, ,, 8, *for* 'religions' *read* 'religious.'
,,   50, ,, ult., *for* 'four' *read* 'two.'
,, 107, ,, 2. there were *three* LL.D.'s between these years, one in 1547, one in 1548, and one in 1549.
,, 152, ,, 2, 3. *for* 'Parker' *read* 'Paske.'
,, 167, ,, 1, *for* 'twenty-three' *read* 'twenty-six.'
,, 184, ,, 12, *for* 'Norrisian' *read* 'Regius.'
,,   ,,   ,, 13, *for* 'senior' *read* 'eighth.'
,,   ,,   ,, 14, *for* 'Regius' *read* 'Norrisian.'

plete the definition,—the most frequent form of expression being *universitas magistrorum et discipulorum* (or *scholarium*), 'a corporation of teachers and scholars.' It was not until the latter part of the fourteenth century that the word *universitas* began to be used by itself to denote a *corporation of teachers and scholars whose existence had been formally recognised by legal authority*,—by far the more common designation of such a body in mediæval times being *studium generale*, of their Report—Enactment of statutes of 1858—The *Essays on a Liberal Education*—Example set by Trinity College of a reformation of college statutes—Appointment of the Royal Commission of 1872—Memorial to the Prime Minister in 1874—The Universities Act of 1877—Institution of the Law Tripos—The Law and History Tripos—The second Law Tripos—The Historical Tripos—Changes in the same —Changes in the Classical Tripos—Changes in the Theological Tripos—Institution of the Semitic Languages, the

———, —— adoption at Oxford, in London, and elsewhere —Method of instruction introduced with the movement —Method of examination—Further development of the scheme—Conference at Cambridge in connection with the movement 213

INDEX 224

Erratum : p. 58, *for* 'Chadworth,' *read* 'Chedworth.'

A HISTORY

OF

THE UNIVERSITY OF CAMBRIDGE.

CHAPTER I.

THE EARLIEST UNIVERSITIES—PRÆ-ACADEMIC CAMBRIDGE—BEGINNINGS OF CAMBRIDGE UNIVERSITY HISTORY.

THE term 'university' (*universitas*) originally denoted nothing more than a community or corporation regarded under its collective aspect. When employed in its modern sense, as denoting a community devoted to learning and education, it required to be supplemented by other words in order to complete the definition,—the most frequent form of expression being *universitas magistrorum et discipulorum* (or *scholarium*), 'a corporation of teachers and scholars.' It was not until the latter part of the fourteenth century that the word *universitas* began to be used by itself to denote a *corporation of teachers and scholars whose existence had been formally recognised by legal authority*,—by far the more common designation of such a body in mediæval times being *studium generale*,

Original meaning of the term 'university.'

or sometimes *studium* alone. It is necessary, however, to bear in mind that universities, in the earlier times, had not infrequently a vigorous virtual existence long before they obtained legal recognition; and it is equally necessary to remember that hostels, halls, and colleges, with complete courses of instruction in all the usual branches of learning, as well as degrees and examinations, were by no means essential features in the mediæval conception of a university.

The conditions under which the first universities came into being will be more clearly understood if we briefly review the chief causes which served to modify alike the theory and the practice of education from the sixth to the twelfth century. Main facts in the history of education subsequent to the fall of the Western Empire. The traditions of pagan education, as preserved in the schools of the Roman Empire, had been almost entirely swept away in the disorganisation that followed upon the barbaric invasions of the fifth and sixth centuries; and when order was in some measure restored, learning had formed those new associations which constitute its main characteristics in the Middle Ages. It was the learning of the monastery and the monastic school, as represented by the rule of St. Benedict and the monastery of Monte Cassino. Or it was the learning of the secular canon and the cathedral school, such as we find it at Arles in Southern Gaul, or at Seville in Spain, or at York in England. The last-named school was indeed the centre from which a great revival throughout Saxon England drew its chief inspiration; and the designs of Gregory the Great, as carried out by Theodorus, Bede, and Alcuin, were attended by important results which lasted until the Danish invasions. Throughout the vast territories ruled by the Franks, on the other hand, learning had everywhere declined under the rule of the Merovingian kings; and it was not until the reign of Charles the Great, who summoned Alcuin of York to his assistance, that a similar revival took place. That revival is especially notable, in that it comprised not only the episcopal and monastic schools throughout the Empire, but was also attended by the introduction of a more secular spirit into learning, such as we find exemplified in the celebrated Palace School, which was founded in connection with the imperial court, and became, for a time, a great centre of literary intercourse. Much of the intellectual activity and care for letters that was thus awakened undoubtedly died out amid the renewal of disorganisation that followed upon the breaking up of the Carolingian Empire and the invasions of the Northmen. Some writers, indeed, go so far as to maintain that no true connection can be traced out between this earlier revival and that which took place in the days of Abélard; and they find in the schools where he taught on the Montagne Ste. Geneviève and in the Isle de la Cité in Paris the commencement, indeed, of the university era, but a commencement altogether independent of the teaching handed down from the days when Alcuin taught in the famous monastery school of St. Martin at Tours.

But whatever may be our conclusion with reference to an obscure and difficult question, it is quite certain that the university movement was essentially a new movement, deriving its chief impulse from forces and conditions which

Distinguishing features of the university movement.

had not previously existed. In exploring the earliest records of most of the older universities, we become aware of three new factors in their intellectual activity which clearly distinguish that activity from anything that had gone before : (1) the introduction of new subjects of study, as embodied in a new or revived literature; (2) the adoption of new methods of teaching, which these subjects rendered necessary; (3) the growing tendency to organisation which accompanied the development and consolidation of the nationalities.

It is a matter of very general agreement that these earlier universities took their rise, for the most part, in endeavours to obtain and provide instruction of a kind beyond the range of the monastic and episcopal schools. The earliest of all, that of Salerno in Italy, for example, which rose in the ninth century, had its origin in a more scientific study of medicine,—the result, in all probability, of a certain intercourse with the Saracens who had recently occupied Sicily ; for, although it has been sought to trace out a connection between the university and the teaching at Monte Cassino, it is more probable that the body of instructors and learners at Salerno represented, in the first instance, a purely secular community.

The University of Salerno.

It was nearly three centuries later, about the commencement of the twelfth century, that Irnerius commenced at Bologna his lectures on the civil law. This instruction, again, was of a kind which the monastery and the cathedral school could not supply, and it also met a new and pressing want. The states of Lombardy were at this time advancing

The study of the civil law.

rapidly in population and in wealth; and the greater complexity of their political relations, their increasing manufactures and commerce, demanded a more definite application of the principles embodied in the codes which had been handed down by Theodosius and Justinian. The distinctly secular character of this new study and its intimate connection with imperial pretensions aroused at first the susceptibilities of the Roman see, and for a time Bologna was regarded by the Church with distrust and even alarm. These sentiments, however, were not of long duration. In the year 1151 the appearance of the *Decretum* of Gratian, largely compiled from spurious documents, invested the studies of the canonist with fresh importance, and the study of the new code gave an impulse to the study of the canon law similar to that which had recently been communicated to the civil law. It was essential that the *Decretum* (on which the Popedom was so largely henceforth to depend for the enforcement of its growing pretensions) should be generally known, recognised, and studied. The wants of the secular student and the wants of the ecclesiastical student were thus brought for a time into notable unison, and from the days of Irnerius, to the close of the thirteenth century, Bologna was the acknowledged centre of instruction in both the civil and the canon law. In the attainment of this pre-eminence she was materially aided by the State. When Barbarossa marched his forces into Italy, on his memorable expedition of 1155, and reasserted those imperial claims which had so long lain dormant, the jurists of

The study of the canon law.

The University of Bologna.

Bologna, professors and students alike, gathered as humble suppliants round the representative of the Empire of the West, and tendered him their allegiance. Frederic, who could not but discern both in them and their profession an aid of no slight value to his own authority, received them graciously. He inquired into their relations with the citizens of Bologna, and when he found that they were often subjected to unjust extortion, he determined to take them under his own protection. He bestowed on them certain immunities and privileges,— rights which were afterwards incorporated in the code of the Empire and extended to the other universities of Italy. These privileges may therefore be regarded as the precedent for that State interference in connection with the university which, however necessary at one time for the protection of an academic community and the freedom of its teachers, has often proved very far from an unmixed benefit, the influence which the civil power was thus enabled to exert being not infrequently wielded for the suppression of that very liberty of thought and inquiry from which the earlier universities derived in no small measure their importance and their fame.

Privileges bestowed on the University by Barbarossa.

The circumstances of the commencement of the University of Paris supply us with a yet more notable illustration of the manner in which the universities first arose. Towards the close of the eleventh century the occurrence of two great theological controversies,—that between Lanfranc and Berengar, and that between Anselm and Roscellinus,— invested the study of logic, or rather of dialectic, with

The study of logic.

a new importance in the eyes of the men of those days. It became a widespread conviction that the intelligent apprehension of spiritual truth depended on a correct use of the traditional methods of argumentation. Dialectic was looked upon as the 'science of sciences'; and when, early in the twelfth century, William of Champeaux opened at Paris a school for the more advanced study of this science, viewed in its practical application as an art, his teaching was attended with a marked success. Among his pupils was the famous Abélard, under whose influence the study of logic made a still more remarkable advance; so that, by the middle of the century, we find John of Salisbury, on his return from Paris to Oxford, relating with astonishment, not unmingled with contempt, how all learned Paris had gone well-nigh mad in its pursuit and practice of the new dialectic.

Another important event still further fanned the new flame. Almost at the same time that John of Salisbury was putting his observations on record, a former pupil of Abélard, named Peter Lombard, who in 1159 had risen to be Bishop of Paris, compiled his memorable volume known as the *Sentences*. It was designed with the view of placing before the student, in as strictly logical a form as practicable, the opinions (*sententiæ*) or tenets of the Fathers and other great doctors of the Church upon the principal and most difficult points in the Christian belief. Conceived as a means of allaying and preventing controversy, it in fact greatly stimulated controversy. The logicians adopted the volume as a recognised storehouse of indisputable major pre-

The Sentences of Peter Lombard.

mises, on which they hung innumerable deductions carried into endless ingenious refinements. It became the theological text-book of the Middle Ages; and on its pages the most eminent of the Schoolmen, in their commentaries *super Sententias*, expended no small share of that marvellous toil and elaborate subtlety which still command the admiration of the student of metaphysical literature.

To these new sources of knowledge and incentives to speculation we must also add the introduction of what is known as the New Aristotle. In the twelfth century nearly all that was known of Aristotle was certain portions of the *Organon* as preserved in the Latin version by Boethius, or as interpreted in a Latin version of the Introduction by Porphyry. But before the close of the thirteenth century the *whole of his extant writings*, in translations either from the Greek or from the Arabic, had become known to Latin Europe.

<small>The New Aristotle.</small>

The relevance of the foregoing facts to university history will be more clearly understood when we recall that the study of this new literature, presenting itself in each branch of what then passed for learning,—that is to say, in the civil and the canon law, in logic, in theology (with Peter Lombard as a text-book), and in hitherto unknown works of Aristotle, and their countless commentators,—was not only the influence which may be said to have called the universities successively into being, but comprised also almost the entire range of the intellectual activity (much greater than is generally supposed) which characterised the universities down to the days of the Renaissance.

<small>Relation between these new studies and the universities.</small>

It is obvious that communities thus attracted together would have, in a great measure, to organise themselves, and the whole question of the organisation of the earlier universities, and the manner in which that organisation was further developed, is one of considerable interest and importance. It is also, it must be added, a question involving points of no little difficulty. As, however, nearly all these early universities were modelled either on Bologna or Paris, they present in common certain general features which admit of no dispute and which may be very briefly indicated. Those two great centres attracted students from nearly all parts of Europe. Of these, the majority were raw and inexperienced youths, who, it is evident, would be apt to fall an easy prey to the extortion of the landlords with whom they lodged, or the traders with whom they dealt,—from extortion, in short, such as that from which Barbarossa is recorded to have sought to protect the students of Bologna. Very early, accordingly, we find students who had come from the same country or province combining together for mutual protection. These societies or confederations were generally known as 'nations.' We find, again, the students,—either in conjunction with their teachers, as at Bologna, or through their teachers, as in Paris,—gradually obtaining State recognition and special privileges. Then, again, we find the teachers themselves, in turn, combining together into 'faculties,'—that is to say, as associates in one and the same branch of learning and instruction. And, finally, we find these several faculties and nations forming themselves into a collective whole,—

Features common to the growth of the early universities.

the UNIVERSITY, with the rector or chancellor at its head.

Turning now to our own country, we find the university movement here in direct connection with the university movement abroad. It had no connection with that earlier learning which made England famous in the days of Bede and Alcuin, but which had sunk to so low an ebb before the Norman Conquest. As on the Seine in the ninth century, so on the Ouse and on the Thames in the tenth and eleventh centuries, there came the Northman, burning and harrying and laying in ruin both the monastery and the church. Oxford was burnt to the ground in 1109, and a like fate overtook Cambridge in the following year. Never since the days which preceded the arrival of Theodorus had learning sunk to a lower depth than in the days of Ethelred the Unready. A considerable revival, it is true, took place in connection with the restored or newly founded Benedictine abbeys, but it reached no higher than the ancient level. And, just as a certain tradition of education had survived in France from the days of Charles the Great and of Alcuin, so at Oxford there was a certain amount of teaching being carried on in the days of Edward the Confessor by the canons of St. Frideswide; and so, at the conventual church at Ely, where King Alfred is said to have received his education, there was a monastic school carrying on a like work. But this traditional unprogressive labour would never have risen to the level of university culture had it not been for those Norman influences which everywhere found their way

The universities of Oxford and Cambridge the result of Norman influences.

Ely and Cambridge.

after the time of Edward the Confessor. And it was on the model of the University of Paris that Oxford and Cambridge were first organised. In the year 1108 Ely was constituted an episcopal see by Pope Paschal II.; its bishop was invested with peculiar privileges, similar to those possessed by some of the great prince-bishops on the Continent; the monks were placed entirely under his control; and as Cambridge lay within his diocese, the relations which, as we shall shortly see, were established between the new episcopate and the university (which rose about a century later) exercised no little influence on Cambridge and its academic history.

Of our two ancient English universities, it is probable that, although both appear to have risen in the twelfth century, Oxford was somewhat the earlier. But the origin of each is recorded only in legend; and in the sixteenth century two antiquarians, representing the two universities, amused the learned world by retailing myths of the foundation of Oxford by King Alfred, and of Cambridge by a fabled Spanish king named Cantaber. Such were the weapons with which Dr. Caius, the founder of Caius College, and Thomas Caius, a fellow of All Souls, carried on the controversy respecting the comparative antiquity of their respective universities. But in the year 1640, when a Bill had been brought into the House of Commons for 'the relief of the King's army and the northern parts,' those members who had received their education at Oxford claimed that in the proviso exempting the two universities Oxford should be placed before Cambridge. They gained their point, and the

Oxford and Cambridge.

priority thus assigned to the former university appears generally to have obtained, in questions of formal procedure, from that time.

As at Bologna, and as at Paris, we find evidence of the existence of flourishing schools long before either university received State recognition. If, indeed, we may credit the very doubtful testimony of Gervase of Canterbury, Vacarius, a famous jurist from Bologna, was teaching the civil law at Oxford so early as the year 1149. But in the year 1209 we have it upon the authority of a far more trustworthy writer, Matthew of Paris, that there were 3000 teachers and scholars in the university; and he further tells us that upon the outbreak of a serious disturbance, which led to the university being for a time deserted, a large number of these betook themselves to Cambridge. It seems, therefore, to be a legitimate inference that both Oxford and Cambridge were recognised centres of study before the commencement of the thirteenth century.

Both universities in existence before the thirteenth century.

Various facts and circumstances, again, lend probability to the belief that, long before the time when we have certain evidence of the existence of Cambridge as a university, the work of instruction was there going on. The *Camboritum* of the Roman period, the *Grantebrycgr* of the Anglo-Saxon Chronicle, the *Grentebrige* of Domesday, must always have been a place of some importance. It was the meeting-place of two great Roman roads,— Akeman Street, running east and west, and the Via Devana, traversing the north and the south. In the new division of Mercia, which took place in the days

Cambridge early in the twelfth century.

of Edward the Elder, the town gave its name to the newly created shire. Confined at first to the rising ground on the left bank of the river, it numbered at the time of the Norman Conquest as many as four hundred houses, of which twenty-seven were pulled down to make way for the castle erected by William the Conqueror. The castles of these days, though often centres of tyranny and oppression, were also of service as strongholds to which the people could resort in times of danger, and the erection of such a structure thus contributed to the sense of security in the neighbourhood. And under the castle walls, with the view, it would seem, of making some atonement for many a deed of violence and wrong, the Norman sheriff, Picot by name, founded the Church of St. Giles, and instituted in connection with it a small body of secular canons. The secular canon was neither a monk nor a friar nor a parish priest, but his duties often led to his taking an active part in the instruction of the community among whom he resided. And it is probable that, in this manner, some educational work was going on in the twelfth century at Cambridge which may have been the nucleus which afterwards developed into the university.

The Castle.

The Church of St. Giles.

Gradually (although the stages of the process cannot now be traced) the town on the north bank, 'the borough,' as it was often termed, overflowed to the other side of the river, and became united with what had before been a distinct village clustering round the ancient præ-Norman Church of St. Benet.

St. Benet's Church.

Such are the main features of præ-academic Cambridge as it presents itself to antiquarian research at the commencement of the twelfth century. There stood the Castle, symbolising in singular conjunction both tyranny and security; there stood the Church of St. Giles, with its canons, who, it is reasonable to suppose, did something for the enlightenment of the inhabitants and the instruction of those designing to enter either the monastery or the Church; there stood the ancient Church of St. Benet, where the long succession of stolid and imperfectly educated Saxon incumbents had probably given place to some more cultured Norman ecclesiastic representing the school of Lanfranc and Anselm.

The year 1112 was marked by the occurrence of an event of considerable importance in connection with the subsequent history of the university. The canons of St. Giles, attended by a large concourse of the clergy and laity, crossed the river, and took up their abode in a new and spacious priory at Barnwell. Their numbers were now considerably augmented, and their foundation was subsequently endowed with the forfeited estates of the tyrannical Picot, whose son, after the father's death, had been compelled to flee the realm on a charge of treason. The priory at Barnwell, which always ranked among the wealthiest of the Cambridge foundations, seems from the first to have been closely associated with the university; and the earliest university exhibitions were those founded by William de Kilkenny, bishop of Ely from 1254 to 1257, for two students of divinity, who

First beginnings of the university.
Origin of the earlier foundations.
Barnwell Priory.

were to receive annually the sum of two marks from the priory. In the year 1133 was founded the nunnery of St. Rhadegund, which, in the reign of Henry VII., was converted into Jesus College; and in 1135 a hospital of Augustinian canons, dedicated to St. John the Evangelist, was founded by Henry Frost, a burgess of the town. The hospital had nothing in common with the modern college, save that it was presided over by a head and supported a certain number of brethren, whose duty it was to receive and tend the sick and to visit the poor and infirm in the neighbourhood. It was, however, a very important foundation, inasmuch as it not only became by conversion in the sixteenth century the College of St. John the Evangelist, but was also, as we shall shortly see, the foundation of which Peterhouse, the earliest Cambridge college, may be said to have been in a certain sense the offshoot.

The nunnery of St. Rhadegund.

The Hospital of St. John.

To some time in the twelfth century we may refer the erection of the mansion known as Merton Hall, which, by a tradition now lost to us, was also styled the 'School of Pythagoras.' It was the residence, it has been conjectured, of some Norman country gentleman, induced probably to fix upon the site by the combined advantages which it offered of proximity to the river, the ford, and the castle. Being built of stone, the edifice stood in striking contrast to the surrounding houses and churches, which were mostly of wood, and were nearly all burnt down in the conflagration of the year 1174. The occupier of this stone house, with his servants and

The School of Pythagoras.

retainers, could hardly but have been a leading personage in the community, and must have contributed in no slight measure to its importance.

The monastery at Ely, some fourteen miles distant, represented another important influence. It had been refounded and richly endowed by King Edgar, and at the time of the Conquest was one of the wealthiest monastic foundations in England. In the reign of Henry I. Ely became a bishopric, and the control of the monastery was vested in the bishop. As Cambridge lay in the newly created diocese, it is easy to understand that, as a centre of education, it would thus be brought into closer connection with the monastery, while the jurisdiction which the bishops of Ely were now able to assert over the university afterwards developed into an important factor in its history.

<small>Ely and Cambridge.</small>

The reputation of Cambridge as a seat of learning may be further inferred from the fact that, so early as the year 1224, the Franciscans established themselves here; and somewhat less than half a century later the Dominicans also erected a friary on the present site of Emmanuel. The establishment of these two communities in the university cannot but be regarded as of primary importance when we remember that it was the Mendicants who chiefly represented the movement by which the earlier half of the thirteenth century was especially distinguished,—namely, that of religious reform combined with intellectual progress. From their ranks proceeded those distinguished schoolmen whose influence was so largely afterwards to mould both theological and philosophical thought at the universities of

<small>Foundations of the Franciscans and Dominicans.</small>

Europe,—Albertus Magnus and Thomas Aquinas among the Dominicans, Duns Scotus and Alexander Hales among the Franciscans. In the course of the same century, the Carmelites, who had originally occupied an extensive foundation at Newnham, but were driven from thence by the winter inundations, settled near the present site of Queens'; while the Augustinian Friars (the fourth mendicant order) took up their residence near the site of the old Botanic Gardens. It indicates the catholic spirit which then prevailed at the two English universities that the members of the religious orders were admitted to degrees,—a privilege which, until the year 1337, was granted them at no other university excepting Paris.

In the year 1229 there broke out at Paris a feud of more than ordinary gravity between the students and the citizens. Large numbers of the former migrated to the English shores; and Cambridge, from its proximity to the eastern coast, and as the centre where Prince Louis, but a few years before, had raised the royal standard, seems to have attracted the great majority. Two years later, a royal writ, issued from Oxford, makes reference to large numbers of students who, both from within the realm and 'from beyond the seas,' had lately repaired to Cambridge. To this increase in numbers we may partly attribute the fact that about this time it became necessary to take more stringent measures for the maintenance of discipline, and both the bishop of the diocese and the sheriff for the county were instructed to exert their authority for this purpose. It was at the same time decreed that every scholar who had

Migrations to Cambridge.

failed to place himself under the supervision of some master of arts should quit the university within fifteen days. In the year 1240 the university received a further accession to its numbers, owing to another migration from Oxford.

It was not long, however, before Cambridge, in its turn, was visited by intestine commotions. On the Continent the universities were generally divided into 'nations,' the students combining together for mutual protection, according to their nationality. At the English universities this feature was represented by a twofold division according to counties, distinguished as North and South. In the year 1261 an encounter at Cambridge between two students, representatives of the opposing parties, gave rise to a general fray. The townsmen took part with either side, and a sanguinary and brutal struggle ensued. Outrage of every kind was committed; the houses were plundered; the records of the university were burnt. It was in consequence of these disturbances that a body of students betook themselves to Northampton, whither a like migration, induced by similar causes, had already taken place from Oxford. The royal licence was even obtained for the establishment of another *studium generale*; but, to quote the expression of Fuller, the new foundation 'never attained full bachelor,' for in the year 1264 the emigrants were ordered by special mandate to return to the scenes they had quitted. Within three-quarters of a century from this event a like migration took place from Oxford to Stamford, a scheme which was persevered in for a

Migrations from the university to Northampton and to Stamford.

longer period. The conservatism which characterises the English temperament protected, however, both the universities. Every inceptor in any faculty at either university was required, after this time, to bind himself by oath not to resort to any English university except Oxford or Cambridge. And while Paris and Bologna, and not a few of the other Continental universities, were from time to time seriously weakened, and even their very existence menaced, by like secessions, the two English centres continued for centuries to be the only permanent and recognised schools for the higher instruction of our English youth.

The growing numbers of the university may be inferred from the fact that we now begin to hear also of affrays between the students and the townsmen, and the ancient feud between 'town' and 'gown' first comes into prominence. In these collisions the hostels, which offered but little protection against organised violence, were often broken open by the townsmen, who plundered them of everything which they regarded as of value and wantonly destroyed whatever bespoke a lettered community. In 1261 the records of the university were burnt; the year 1322 was marked by a similar act of Vandalism; while in 1381, during the insurrections then prevalent throughout the country, the populace vented their animosity in destruction on a yet larger scale. At Corpus Christi all the books, charters, and writings belonging to the society were destroyed. At St. Mary's the university chest was broken open, and the documents which it contained met with a similar fate. The masters and scholars, under intimidation,

Town and Gown.

surrendered all their charters, muniments, and ordinances, and a grand conflagration ensued in the market-place, where an ancient beldame was to be seen scattering the ashes in the air, as she exclaimed, 'Thus perish the skill of the clerks!'

The conflagrations resulting from accident were also numerous and destructive, although the university historian, Thomas Fuller, holds it a matter for congratulation that far greater calamity was not wrought by such casualties. 'Whoever,' he says, 'shall consider in both universities the ill-contrivance of many chimneys, hollowness of hearths, shallowness of tunnels, carelessness of coals and candles, catchingness of papers, narrowness of studies, late reading, and long watching of scholars, cannot but conclude that an especial Providence preserveth those places.'

Destructive fires.

The destruction has, however, been sufficiently extensive to increase considerably the difficulties attendant upon the investigation of Cambridge University history. It has been attended also by a positive as well as a negative evil. It is not simply that we are unable to determine many points of interest, owing to the loss of the necessary evidence, but that loss has also afforded scope for the exercise of the inventive faculty to an extent which, to a more critical age, seems almost astounding. And it was easy for antiquarians like Fuller, when the sceptical demanded evidence respecting charters granted by King Arthur and Cadwallader, and rules given by Sergius and Honorius, gravely to assert that such documents had once existed, but had perished in the various conflagrations.

CHAPTER II.

*THE UNIVERSITY IN THE THIRTEENTH AND FOUR-
TEENTH CENTURIES—FOUNDATION OF THE EAR-
LIEST COLLEGES.*

IT will be seen from the foregoing chapter that the university existed long before the first college, and that, as an institution, it had an organisation quite independent of the colleges. It is desirable that we should understand clearly what that organisation was, in order that we may more distinctly perceive how, in after times, the original intent and meaning of various institutions, offices, and ceremonies were disregarded, and their real use and significance was thus to a great extent lost sight of. It must, however, be borne in mind that the organisation we are about to describe was not elaborated in all its details all at once,—its full development, as we find it set forth in the ancient collection of statutes known as the *Statuta Antiqua*, not having been reached until some time in the fifteenth century.

Mediæval organisation of the university.

The university of Cambridge, like that of Oxford, was modelled mainly on the university of Paris. Its constitution was consequently oligarchic rather than democratic, the government

Paris the model.

being entirely in the hands of the teaching body, while the bachelors and undergraduates had no share in the passing of new laws and regulations.

The undergraduate of those days generally entered the university when he was fourteen or fifteen years of age, but not infrequently when he was still younger; and various considerations may be suggested which serve to explain his entry at such tender years. In the first place, it is to be remembered that the ordinary, that is to say, the arts course of study, was designed to extend over seven years, although the student often left without completing his curriculum. The acquirements which he was expected to bring with him, again, were very moderate, —amounting to nothing more than reading and writing and the elements of Latin. The average duration of life, moreover, was much shorter; while the rude and severe discipline to which a lad was then subjected at home served to inure him to some extent to hardships like those which then made up the experience of ordinary undergraduate life. In most cases the little knowledge he brought with him had been acquired at a school attached to some monastery or cathedral, or from the priest of his native parish,—in later times at the parish school. But before the foundation of the colleges his acquaintance with Latin would often be acquired in the university itself, and in this manner *grammatica*, as it was termed, originally represented the first stage of the *trivium* or undergraduate course of study. As, however, schools became established throughout the country and colleges multiplied, this branch of instruction demanded less and less of the

The undergraduate course.

time of the academic instructor, and began to be looked upon as scarcely forming a part of the university curriculum. Those who required such instruction were handed over to a special teacher, who was styled *Magister Glomeriæ;* his pupils were known as 'the glomerels,' and their supervision in matters of discipline was entrusted, not to the chancellor of the university, but to the archdeacon of Ely.

In the majority of cases, therefore, the undergraduate, on coming up, was forthwith plunged into the mysteries of the scholastic logic, and in his second year became a sophister or disputant in the schools.

Logic.

In this capacity, he either himself propounded some affirmative position in a question of theology or philosophy, and defended it against all comers,—in which case he was known as the respondent,—or he challenged the position maintained by some other disputant, and was then known as the opponent,—the former being generally regarded as the more honourable and onerous function. It would be difficult to exaggerate the influence exercised upon the habits of thought of scholars of those times by these disputations, and the extent to which a reputation for skill in such dialectical encounters came to be regarded as the most enviable of all academic distinctions. Although the intellect was undoubtedly stimulated and rendered more acute, there was also generated a baneful tendency to suppose that truth might be evolved mainly by such means, rather than by habits of patient investigation and observation and deliberate weighing of evidence.

To logic succeeded rhetoric, that is to say, the study

of a Latin version of the treatise of Aristotle on that
subject; to which the abler teachers sometimes added the reading of one or two of
such Latin poets and orators as were known to the
learned world of Western Europe before the days of
the Renaissance. Ever since the great schism between
the Eastern and the Western Churches in the eighth
century, the ecclesiastical use of the Greek language
had been abandoned in Latin Christendom, and the
Greek patristic literature had come to be regarded as
savouring of heresy. In the universities, accordingly,
at this period, Greek was but rarely studied and never
taught.

Rhetoric.

The reputation gained by a skilful dialectician
greatly surpassed in the general estimation any corresponding reputation acquired as a Latin scholar, and
students consequently concentrated their attention more
and more upon logic, and gave less and less attention to rhetoric. Logic thus became the central study
with the younger students; while every teacher who
sought to distinguish himself in his vocation taxed
his ingenuity to the utmost to produce some new
dialectical refinement upon the refinements of his
predecessors.

When the three years' course of study represented
by the *trivium* had been completed, and the sophister's
exercises in the schools had been duly performed, he entered upon his fourth academic
year, and became an 'incepting' or 'commencing'
bachelor. The commencing bachelor is often also styled,
in the ancient statutes, a 'determiner,' because, during
the Lent term preceding his admission as full bachelor,

The commencing bachelor.

he was called upon to preside at certain disputations in the schools, and to sum up, or 'determine,' the logical value of the arguments adduced by respondent or opponent. In later times, this period of his academic course was marked by his admission to a degree,—that of bachelor of arts. But originally it is probable that entrance upon the stage of bachelordom meant nothing more than the student's *apprenticeship* to a master, under whom he was to serve for four years as he passed through the successive studies of the *quad-rivium;* viz., (1) arithmetic, or the science of numbers; (2) geometry (which included geography) as taught in Pliny and Boethius; (3) music, by which we must understand the science of harmony and an acquaintance with the system of musical notation; (4) astronomy, as conceived, of course, in harmony with the Ptolemaic system. Instruction in these four branches extended over the next four years. At the end of that time he was formally discharged from his state of apprenticeship, and by virtue of a licence granted by his preceptor, was admitted to the degree of master of arts, being himself thereby received into the brotherhood of teachers, and authorised to lecture. At a later period in academic teaching this licence was conferred by the chancellor, and each master of arts was not only permitted but called upon to exercise the function; that is to say, he was called upon to act for two years as a regent or teacher in the schools, and become an instructor in some one or other part of that course of study which he had himself just completed.

If he now proposed to enter upon a further course

of theological study, and to proceed as bachelor and doctor of divinity, he was still required to comply with the above obligation to teach, while his own career involved another ten years' attendance upon lectures in the university. He was required to attend lectures on the Bible for two years; he must himself have lectured 'cursorily'[1] on some book of the canonical Scriptures for at least ten days in each term of the academical year, and have also lectured on the whole of the *Sentences;* he must have preached publicly *ad clerum*, and have responded and opposed in all the schools of his faculty.

Course requisite for the theologian.

The courses for the doctorial degree in civil and canon law were equally laborious. In the former it was not imperative that the candidate should have been a regent in arts, but, failing this qualification, he was required to have heard lectures on the civil law for ten instead of eight years; he must have heard the *Digestum Vetus* twice, the *Digestum Novum* and the *Infortiatum* once. He must also have lectured on the *Infortiatum* and the Institutes, must himself be the possessor of the two Digests, and be able to show that he had at his command (either as borrowed volumes or his own property) all the other text-books of the course. In the course for the canon law the candidate was required to have heard lectures on the civil law for three years, and on the Decretals for another three years; he must have attended cursory lectures on the Bible for at least two years, and must himself have lectured 'cursorily' on one of four treatises, and on some one book of the Decretals.

Course requisite for the civilian or canonist.

[1] See p. 28.

With the fourteenth century, the labours of the canonists had become seriously augmented by the appearance of the sixth book of the Decretals under the auspices of Boniface VIII., and by that of the Clementines; Lollard writers are, indeed, to be found asserting that the demands thus made upon the time of the canonist (demands which he could not disregard, inasmuch as the papal anathema hung over all those who should venture to ignore these additions to the code) was one of the chief causes of that neglect of the Scriptures which becomes more and more observable with the advance of the fifteenth century.

A similarly protracted and laborious course of study awaited the candidate for the degree of doctor of medicine. It was required that he should have lectured as a regent in arts, and have, in turn, attended lectures on medicine either in Cambridge or in some other university; that he should have heard read a series of prescribed authors on specific subjects; and that he should have lectured cursorily on some treatise on the theory, and on another on the practice, of medicine; it was also imperative that he should have been engaged for two years in the actual practice of the art.

<small>Course requisite for the doctor of medicine.</small>

It is obvious, however, that such protracted courses of study, extending over a period varying from fifteen to seventeen years, must have been beyond the reach of the great majority; and so far as regards the teaching element in the university, we must look upon this as composed mainly of masters of arts, a body which varied in number from one to two hundred, according to the numerical strength of the university. The regents and other lecturers gave their

<small>The regents or teachers.</small>

lectures in the public schools. But the earliest portion of these buildings, the north side, was not commenced until the year 1347, and not completed until the year 1400. The entire quadrangle, as it stood, with some slight modifications, down to the reign of George I., was completed in the course of the fifteenth century. Before the year 1400, therefore, the students must have assembled for their lectures in some other buildings; often, probably, in the precincts of the houses of the Franciscans or the Dominicans; while the larger gatherings of the university were generally held in Great St. Mary's. The fact that each master of arts, in turn, was called upon to take part in the work of instruction is one of the most notable features in the mediæval universities. His remuneration was limited to the fees paid by the scholars who formed his auditory to the bedells, and was often consequently extremely small. When once, however, he had discharged this function he became competent to lecture in any faculty to which he might turn his attention, and (as we have seen above) when studying either the civil or the canon law, theology, or medicine, might be a lecturer on subjects included in his own *course*.

Lecturing ordinarie and cursorie.

He was then said to lecture 'cursorily' (*cursorie*), and his subject was generally assigned him by his superior, the lecturer in ordinary. His lectures, however, involved a much smaller amount of preparation and exposition than that which found place in connection with the ordinary lectures. The technical term *legere* would, indeed, suggest that the original lecture involved nothing more than the reading aloud of some accepted text-book of instruction, while the learner, who was rarely himself in possession of such a text-book, copied down what was dictated. As the cursory readers often limited themselves to this amount of instruction (if such it can be termed), the expression *cursorie* seems gradually to have acquired a secondary meaning, and to have been employed to denote those who hastened on with the dictation of the text, adding but little by way of interpretation. The 'ordinary' lecturer, on the other hand, accompanied his lecture by more or less of comment; and in proportion as he did this, he was recognised as aiming at distinction, and when his novel interpretation recommended itself to the judgment or the prejudices of his audience his reputation was established.

As regards the obligation imposed on each master of arts of taking his share in the work of instruction, this appears to have been designed not so much with the view of finding out the best talent for teaching, as of securing an adequate supply of instruction to the student. The funds at the disposal of the university being extremely small, while the numbers of the students sometimes rose to nearly 2000,—of whom the great majority were the sons of humble yeomen, of labourers, and of mechanics,—some such method was probably absolutely necessary. The hostel, indeed, provided in some branches the requisite instruction, but here the scale of payment was such as often to exclude all but the sons of comparatively wealthy parents.

Duties imposed upon the regents.

The university, then, in the thirteenth century was but a very slightly and somewhat imperfectly organised community. It possessed only very slender endowments.

It had no systematic code for the government of its members. It was liable, on the occurrence of any severe crisis, such as an exceptionally violent collision with the town, internal strife, or the outbreak of pestilence, to sudden dispersion; and a dispersion of units thus loosely held together might, as the experience of Continental universities not infrequently showed, be followed by the creation of a rival centre and the permanent alienation of a greater or smaller section of the community. Nor can we suppose that either teacher or scholar could have felt himself very strongly attached to the Cambridge of that day; the former found his labours for the most part very poorly remunerated and his livelihood eminently precarious, while the poor scholar found himself exposed to the extortion of the townsmen, and without a settled residence or any of the associations of home. Until the year 1276, indeed, he seems to have often wandered about under no supervision whatever. His name was inscribed in no matriculation book, and he had no tutor until he became a bachelor. The authorities had consequently no cognisance of him. In the above year, however, the university issued a decree that 'no one' (by which we must understand neither instructor nor lodging-house keeper) was to receive a scholar unless such scholar 'had a fixed master within fifteen days after his entry into the university.'

State of the university in the thirteenth century.

This ordinance appears to have been issued with the special sanction of Hugh de Balsham, bishop of Ely from 1257 to 1286, and one of the most discerning benefactors that the university ever knew. It was with the design of providing

Ordinance of Hugh de Balsham.

some remedy for the evils and defects above described that we find him shortly after coming forward as the founder of our earliest Cambridge college.

It is necessary altogether to dismiss the notion that the original college was an institution modelled on the monastery, or that it in any way reflected the monastic spirit. Such a notion might, indeed, seem to be to some extent warranted by the fact that the plan and arrangement of a Cambridge or Oxford college often present a striking resemblance to those of a monastery. But a careful study of the architectural history of our colleges has clearly shown that this resemblance is entirely fortuitous, and was the result of a gradual development, the original design of our earlier colleges having been of the simplest character. Still less did the college reflect the discipline or the theory of education that pervaded the monastic rule. In the case of Peterhouse this may appear somewhat surprising, when we consider that Hugh Balsham was not only bishop of Ely, but was also sub-prior of the monastery in that city. But Hugh Balsham was a Benedictine, and the Benedictines in England at this period were the upholders of a less stringent and ascetic discipline than that advocated by the Mendicant Orders, and were, in fact, endeavouring in every way to counteract their influence. The foundations of these latter communities at the universities gave them a great advantage in proselytising, for the younger members of each Order, or rather those intending to become such, were here maintained in comparative comfort and instructed, while those who were designing to become simply clergymen were left

Architectural development of the early colleges.

to contend with all the hardships and discomforts of the ordinary student life of the time. It seems to have been the aim of Balsham, in the first instance, to bring about a kind of fusion between the old and the new elements, but this, as we have now to see, resulted in failure.

The Hospital of St. John, as we have already noted, was a foundation of the Augustinian Canons, an order especially favoured by the Norman ecclesiastics, and one which had succeeded to a great extent in displacing the secular canons throughout England. They professed a much more stringent rule or discipline than the secular canons, whose mode of life and theory of education more resembled that of the ordinary clergyman. Hugh Balsham, however, who was a man of public spirit and with strong national sympathies, aimed rather at developing the education of the priest than that of the religious orders, and was an advocate of reforms which tended very much towards what, in modern times, we are wont to designate as popular education. With this view, he first of all introduced into the Hospital of St. John a body of secular scholars, providing for their maintenance by an augmentation of the revenues of the foundation. But the elements were too dissimilar to combine. The canons professed an austerer mode of life; the scholars were governed by a different rule and aimed at a more liberal culture. Differences soon arose; feuds and jealousies sprang up; and eventually the good bishop found himself under the necessity of transplanting his scholars to other quarters. 'Much grieved, no doubt,' observes Baker, the historian of St.

The Hospital of St. John. Foundation of Peterhouse, 1284.

THE EARLIEST COLLEGES. 33

John's College, 'but could he have foreseen that this broken and imperfect society was to give birth to two great and lasting foundations . . . he would have had much joy in his disappointment.' The brethren of the Hospital, by way of compromise, agreed to surrender to the scholars the impropriation of St. Peter's Church, with two adjoining hostels; and in the year 1284, with these very slender resources, the long career of Peterhouse began. In the year 1309 its income was augmented with the revenues of a house of the order *de Pœnitentia Jesu*, which had been founded at Cambridge, but which fell with the suppression of the order. A foundation thus endowed with the alienated revenues of one religious house and the forfeited revenues of another must, it is evident, have been conceived in a spirit that marked a point of departure both from the traditions of monasticism and those of the Mendicants.

When the assent of Edward I. was given to the settlement of Hugh Balsham's 'studious scholars' as inmates at the Hospital, it was expressly provided that they should be permitted to live under the same rule as the scholars of Merton at Oxford. The code was not, however, drawn up by Hugh Balsham, but given, about the year 1338, by Simon Montacute, his successor in the see of Ely. It consisted in the adoption, almost in their entirety, of the statutes which Walter de Merton had given in 1264 to his foundation, and it may safely be asserted that no better model could at that time have been found in any university in Europe. 'A master and fourteen perpetual fellows, studiously engaged in the pursuit of literature,' represent the body supported on the foundation; the 'pensioner' of later times, being, of course, at this period, the inmate of the hostel. In case of a vacancy among the fellows, 'the most able bachelor in logic' is designated as the one on whom, *ceteris paribus*, the choice is to fall; the other requirements being that, 'so far as human frailty admit,' he be 'honourable, chaste, peaceable, humble, and modest.' The 'scholars of Ely'—for so they were at first designated—were bound to devote themselves to the 'study of arts, Aristotle, canon law, or theology;' but, as at Merton, the basis of a sound liberal education was to be laid before the study of theology was entered upon; two of the number were to be permitted to study the civil and the canon law; one, to study medicine. When a fellow was about to incept in any faculty, it devolved upon the master, with the rest of the fellows, to inquire in what manner he had conducted himself, and how he performed his acts in the schools; how long he had heard lectures in the faculty in which he desired to incept; and whether he had gone through the forms according to the statutes of the university. The sizar of later times is perhaps to be recognised in the provision that, if the funds of foundation permit, the master and the two deans shall select two or three youths, 'indigent scholars well grounded in Latin,' to be maintained, 'as long as may seem fit,' by the college alms; such poor scholars being bound to attend upon the master and fellows in church, on feast days, and on other ceremonial occasions, and also to wait on the master and fellows at table and in their rooms.

In common with four other of the earlier Cambridge

THE EARLIEST COLLEGES. 35

colleges, Peterhouse was at first a very simple structure, in the plan of which a chapel found no place. Its religious services were held in St. Peter's Church, and its first library was not built until the early part of the fifteenth century, and it was not until 1628 that the construction of its existing chapel was commenced.

Some forty years after the foundation of Peterhouse we find Hervey de Stanton, Chancellor of the Exchequer and canon of Bath and Wells, obtaining from Edward II. permission to found at Cambridge,—where, as the preamble informs us, 'the labours of a university are well known to shine with lustre,'—the college of the 'scholars of St. Michael.' The statutes of this society, which were drawn up at the time of its foundation, represent the earliest Cambridge college code, being anterior to the statutes given to Peterhouse by some sixteen years. MICHAELHOUSE, accordingly, which was afterwards merged in Trinity College, may thus claim to be the earliest embodiment in the university of the college conception; while Trinity College itself may, in a manner, contest with Peterhouse the claim to represent the earliest example of college discipline. The statutes themselves, again, are apparently the independent expression of the founder's theory of such a discipline, for we find no reference to the code of Merton, or to that of any other foundation. It can scarcely, therefore, be a matter for surprise that, as regards both catholicity of spirit and attention to matters of detail, they are inferior to the statutes which the founder of Peterhouse had so wisely borrowed from the sister university.

Foundation of Michaelhouse, 1324.

The two foundations which next claim our attention

that of Pembroke Hall in 1347, and that of Gonville Hall in 1350, afford satisfactory evidence that the college was not necessarily regarded as an institution hostile to the religious orders; the former owed its creation to Marie de St. Paul, a warm friend of the Franciscans; while the latter was founded by Edmund Gonville, an equally warm friend of the Dominicans. Like many a similar foundation in those times, Pembroke College had its origin in individual calamity; and before its walls arose, the untimely loss of her chivalrous husband had already turned the thoughts of Marie de St. Paul (better known as Marie de Valence) to like acts of penitential beneficence,—to the endowment of a nunnery of Minoresses at Waterbeach and the foundation of Deney Abbey.

Foundation of Pembroke Hall, 1347.

It is much to be regretted that the earliest rule given to the new foundation of Pembroke Hall,—the *Aula*[1] *seu Domus de Valencemarie*, as it was termed,— is no longer extant. A revised rule, of the conjectural date of 1366, and another of perhaps not more than ten years later, are the data from whence Dr. Ainslie[2] compiled the following abstract :—

The college was designed for the support of thirty scholars, more or less, according to the state of its revenues. Of these, twenty-four, denominated fellows, were to be greater and permanent; and the remaining six, being students in grammar or arts, to be less, and at the times of election either to be put out altogether or else promoted to the permanent class. If the whole number of fellows was complete, six at least were to be in holy orders; if there were twenty, there were to be at least four; and

---

[1] 'Aula,' or Hall, was the customary designation of the college at this period.

[2] Dr. Gilbert Ainslie, master of the college from 1828 to 1870.

if twelve or upwards, there were to be two for the performance of divine service. These proportions were altered in the next code, thus: if there were ten fellows or upwards, there were to be at least six in orders; and four, if the number was less. The fellows were to apply themselves solely to the faculty of arts or theology, and when any one should have finished his lectures in arts, he was to betake himself to theology. There were to be annually elected two rectors, the one a Friar Minor, the other a secular, who should have taken degrees in the university. They were to admit fellows elect, and to have visitorial jurisdiction, which, after the death of the foundress, they were to exercise even over the statutes with the consent of the college. The later code, however, did not recognise the rectors at all, but appropriated their several duties to the master either alone or in conjunction with two or more of the fellows; saving only the power of control over the statutes, which was vested in no one after the foundress's death. All connection between the Franciscans and the college was consequently now terminated.

To return to the earlier code. In the election of a fellow preference was to be given to the most orderly, the best proficient in his studies, being withal free-born and legitimate; provided he were a bachelor or sophist in arts, or at least had studied three years in that faculty; and he might be of any nation or realm, *that of France especially*, if there should be found any one qualified, as above stated, in either university of Cambridge or Oxford. The fellow elect was required to swear that he had neither by inheritance nor of his own means above forty shillings a year to spend. By the next code this sum was doubled, being made six marks. The election of a fellow was not confirmed by admission till after the lapse of a year, and then the major part of the fellows might withhold such confirmation. Every fellow before admission pledged himself to vacate his fellowship as soon as ever he was promoted to any more lucrative place, unless previously to such promotion he had become master, for the master was allowed to hold any preferment compatible with his office. The next code did away with the year of probation, and directed that the pledge should be to vacate on the expiration of one year after such promotion as would enable the fellow to expend above six marks, unless promoted in the meantime to the mastership. In the choice of scholars those were to be preferred who came duly qualified from the parishes pertaining to the college rectories, but there were not to be more than two of the same consanguinity.

And, as her final *Vale*, the foundress solemnly adjures the fellows to give their best counsel and aid on all occasions to the abbess and sisters of Deney, who had from her a common origin with them; and she admonishes them further to be kind, devoted, and grateful to all religions, *especially to the Friars Minor*.

The above two codes afford undoubtedly the most interesting study that has as yet presented itself in connection with our college history, and the points of contrast they present are deserving of close attention, especially that whereby the participation of the Franciscans in the management of the society, secured to them by the earlier statutes, is abolished on a second revision. The scholar, in the sense in which the term is now used in the university, is also here first to be met with; it being provided that six of the 'scholars' may be *minor scholars*, eligible at elections to major scholarships, *i.e.*, fellowships, or subject to removal.

The founder of the next college that claims our attention was Edmund Gonville, a member of an ancient county family, a clergyman, and at one time vicar-general of the diocese of Ely; his sympathy with the Mendicants is indicated by the fact that through his influence the Earl of Warren and the Earl of Lancaster were induced to create a foundation for the Dominicans at Thetford. In the year 1348, only two years before his death, he obtained from Edward III. permission to found in Luthborne Lane (now known as Freeschool Lane) a college for twenty scholars, dedicated in honour of the Annunciation of the Blessed Virgin.

Foundation of Gonville Hall, 1348.

The statutes given by Edmund Gonville are still extant, but within two years of their compilation they were considerably modified by other hands; they cannot, therefore, be regarded as having long represented the rule of the new foundation. Their chief value, for our present purpose, is in the contrast they offer to the rule of another college, founded at nearly the same time,—that of Trinity Hall,—to the conception of which they were shortly to be assimilated. According to the design of Edmund Gonville, his college was to represent the usual course of study included in the *trivium* or *quadrivium*, as the basis of an almost exclusively theological training. Each of the fellows was required to have studied, read, and lectured in logic, but on the completion of his course in arts, theology was to form the main subject. The unanimous consent of the master and fellows was necessary before he could apply himself to any other faculty, and not more than two at a time could be permitted to deviate from the usual course. It was, however, permitted to every fellow, though in no way obligatory upon him, to devote two years to the study of the canon law.

The foregoing scheme may be regarded as that of an English clergyman of the fourteenth century, whose aim was simply to do something for the encouragement of learning in his profession, and who, from long residence in the diocese or in neighbouring dioceses, may fairly be presumed to have been well acquainted with the special wants and shortcomings of his order. It will be interesting to contrast his benevolent and patriotic design with that of another ecclesiastic, reared in a different school.

Among the students who were the first to profit by the generosity of Edmund Gonville was William Bateman, afterwards bishop of Norwich from 1344 to 1355. He had gained a high reputation in the university by his proficiency in the civil and canon law, attainments which had been recognised by his promotion to high office in connection with the papal court at Avignon; and it was amid the ostentatious splendour and the glaring profligacy which, in the days of Innocent VI., made that court a by-word in Europe that his life came suddenly to a close. By the more enlightened teachers of the universities at this period the studies of the civilian and the canonist were regarded with no friendly eye, owing to the mercenary spirit in which they were generally pursued as the means to the acquirement of wealth and of political influence; and we find Roger Bacon declaring that men hastened to enrol themselves in these professions just as men hied to some newly discovered gold-mine. The great Plague of 1349, that terrible visitation which reduced the population from four to two millions, doubled wages, and raised prices all round nearly one-fifth, had fallen with especial severity on the local clergy, and it was with the professed design of seeking to repair these losses that, in the following year, Bishop Bateman founded Trinity Hall. It can hardly, however, admit of much doubt that his real object was the education of canonists and civilians rather than of parish priests; for, of the twenty fellows whom, together with a master, he proposed to maintain on the new foundation, ten were required to be

Wm. Bateman and the Canon Law.

Foundation of Trinity Hall, 1350.

students of the civil, and seven of the canon, law. They were, however, prohibited from going about to practise; and it seems, accordingly, a legitimate inference that it was his object to establish a school of legal studies in the university, and thus raise the standard of professional acquirement rather than to augment the numbers of actual practitioners. We would gladly conclude that, as a scheme disinterestedly designed to further the cause of higher education, the foundation of Bishop Bateman might take rank side by side with that of Edmund Gonville, but the evidence will hardly admit of such a conclusion. It would rather seem that it was his primary design to further Ultramontane interests. It was the time when, both in Teutonic and Latin Christendom, the disposition to resist the papal exactions was greater than it had ever been before; and it was as an institution calculated to promote the interests of the Church, and to maintain, in defiance of statutes of provisors and præmunire, the claims of Avignon to levy tribute in England, that Trinity Hall arose. If the design of the foundation, taken by itself, permitted any doubt on this point, that doubt would be set at rest when we turn to note the experiences of Gonville Hall.

Shortly before Bishop Bateman's death, a part of his wealth had been devoted to assisting that struggling institution, where the funds left by the founder were found to be so inadequate for the carrying out of his purpose, that the college would probably have become defunct had not the founder of Trinity Hall now come forward to render it the necessary aid. He took the little society under his protection, removed it from the site it originally occupied in Luthborne Lane to that which forms a part of the present site of Caius College, and endowed it with additional revenues. His munificence, however, can hardly be regarded as entirely disinterested, when we observe that he altogether set aside the statutes given by Edmund Gonville, and substituted for them a code but slightly modified from that which he had given to Trinity Hall. It is true that the fellows of Gonville Hall were not absolutely required to be either civilians or canonists, but the civil and the canon law are placed foremost among the studies to which their attention is especially to be given; and such encouragement, when held out in connection with subjects already sufficiently alluring from their association with a professional career, would scarcely fail to determine the choice of those to whom the option was permitted.

To return to Trinity Hall. The sudden death of its founder at Avignon frustrated the completion of his designs in connection with his own foundation; and, for a century after, the society had to contend with difficulties scarcely less serious than those which had threatened the existence of Gonville Hall, its revenues barely sufficing for the maintenance of a master, three fellows, and three scholars. The buildings rose with corresponding tardiness. First, in the last quarter of the fourteenth century, the principal court, or quadrangle, arose on the present site (although with a different boundary to the north); the chapel, about a century later; and the present library, a century later still. No college library in the university has better maintained its original aspect,—the ancient desks,

THE EARLIEST COLLEGES. 43

which are still retained, constituting a singularly characteristic and almost unique feature. In 1852, owing to an accidental fire, the front portion of the quadrangle was burnt down; it was rebuilt in stone, with a slight increase in the height of the structure.

The second college which refers its origin to the great Plague was that of Corpus Christi, founded by the joint efforts of two Cambridge com-munities,—the Guild of Corpus Christi and the Guild of the Blessed Virgin. The super-stition of the age was a largely contributing cause. Prayers for the dead were held, in those days, to be of efficacy in promoting an earlier release of a soul from purgatory. The fearful mortality had conse-quently given rise to the celebration of an immense number of masses for the repose of the souls of the departed. But among no class had the mortality been greater than among the country clergy themselves, on whom the performance of these services devolved. The diminution in their numbers had thus been coin-cident with a greatly increased demand for their ser-vices. The survivors, however, instead of profiting by the solemn lesson involved in the recent visitation, appear to have exhibited an unbecoming spirit of worldliness in charging exorbitant fees for the dis-charge of their duties as celebrants. The commercial mind of Cambridge was deeply and not unjustifiably incensed; and in founding the new college, the guilds-men made it a condition that the scholars should, whenever called upon, celebrate masses for the repose of the souls of departed members of the two guilds.

Such being the circumstances of its foundation, we

Foundation of Corpus Christi College, 1352.

should scarcely expect to find the statutes of the society reflecting any very original or enlightened conception of education. They appear, indeed, to have been largely taken from the statutes of Michaelhouse, some passages being an almost verbatim reprint of the earlier code of that society. The scholars are described as *capellani*, though it is intimated that others may be admitted to the foundation. It is required that they shall 'one and all' be in priest's orders, and shall have lectured in arts or philosophy, or at least be bachelors in either the civil or the canon law, or in arts, intending to devote themselves to the study of theology or of the canon law, the number of those devoting themselves to the last-named faculty being restricted to four.

But although the two guilds evince no breadth of view in their views respecting the education to be imparted on the new foundation, they manifested a commendable promptitude in erecting the buildings. Josselin, the historian of the college, who was secretary to Archbishop Parker, tells us that 'the building of the college, . . . with walls of enclosure, chambers arranged about a quadrangle, hall, kitchen, and master's habitation, was fully finished in the days of Thomas Ellisley, the first Master (1352–1376), and of his successor, Richard Treton' (1376–1377). Its separate chapel owed its erection to the munificence of Sir Nicholas Bacon, and was brought to completion early in the seventeenth century. After this, no alteration or addition of any importance was made for a lengthened period. The entrance to the premises was from Freeschool Lane, a row of private dwelling-houses completely separating them from Trumpington Street. The new buildings were not erected until the present century, and their erection was unfortunately attended with the destruction of much that was most venerable and interesting in the ancient part.

In the year 1359 we find Elizabeth de Burgh, countess of Clare, coming, like Bishop Bateman, to the aid of another struggling society. 'Being desirous,' says the august lady, in the preamble to the statutes of Clare College given the year before her death, 'being desirous, as far as God has enabled us, to promote the advancement of divine worship, the welfare of the state, and the extension of those sciences, which, by reason of the pestilence having swept away a number of men, are now beginning to fail lamentably, and directing our observation to the university of Cambridge in the diocese of Ely, in which there is an assembly of students, and to a hall therein, *hitherto generally called University Hall*, now existing by our foundation, and which we desire to be called Clare Hall, and to bear no other designation: we have caused this to be augmented with resources, out of the property given us by God, and to be placed among the number of places for study.'

<small>Foundation of Clare Hall, 1359.</small>

The code given by the foundress is chiefly noticeable for a tendency to insist less strongly on requirements with respect to the professedly clerical element. The scholars or fellows are to be twenty in number, of whom six are to be in priest's orders at the time of their admission; but comparatively little stress is laid, as at Michaelhouse, on the order or particular character of the religious services, and the proviso is made apparently rather with the design of securing the presence of a sufficient number for the performance of such services than for the purpose of creating a foundation for the church. The remaining fellows are to be selected from bachelors or sophisters in arts, or from ' skilful and well-conducted' civilians and canonists, with the restriction that only two shall be civilians, and only one a canonist. Three of the fellows, being masters of arts, are to lecture; and, on the inception of any other fellow, one of the three has permission to retire from this function, provided he has lectured for a whole year. *This permission does not, however, imply permission to cease from study;* he is bound to apply himself to some other service wherein, considering his bent and aptitude, he may be expected to make the most rapid progress. Provision is made for ten sizars,—to be educated in singing, grammar, and logic; and their term of residence is to extend to the completion of their twentieth year, when, unless elected to fellowships, they are no longer to be maintained on the foundation.

Clare College suffered severely from fires, having, according to tradition, been completely burnt down in the year 1362. In 1521 it suffered a yet more irretrievable disaster, for not only were the master's chambers and the treasury completely destroyed, but the college archives perished with them. In the seventeenth century, shortly before the outbreak of the civil war, the rebuilding of the entire college was commenced; the work, however, was brought to a standstill by the outbreak of hostilities, and the very materials were carried off by the parliamentary party. It was not until 1715, a period of seventy-six years from the commencement, that the present quadrangle was completed,—buildings which the late Professor Willis characterised as 'among the most beautiful, from their situation and general outline, that he could point out in the university.'

A long succession of distinguished men received their education at this college, or were intimately associated with it. The more familiar names include those of Hugh Latimer (a fellow of the society), Nicholas Ferrar, Abraham Wheelock (the Anglo-Saxon scholar), Ralph Cudworth (master of the college), Archbishop Tillotson, Thomas Burnet, Lord Hervey, William Whiston, Cole, the antiquary, and Masères, the mathematician.

So early as 1326, thirty-two scholars, known as the King's scholars, had been maintained at the university by Edward II. It would seem that the young monarch, who was habitually influenced by the advice of foreign civilians, was designing, like Bishop Bateman, to encourage the study of the civil and the canon law, for we find him presenting books on these subjects to Simon de Bury, the warden, who was subsequently deprived of them by the order of Queen Isabella. It had been the king's intention to provide his scholars with a hall of residence, but during his lifetime they resided in hired houses, and the execution of his design devolved upon Edward III. By this monarch a mansion was erected in the vicinity of the Hospital of St. John, 'to the honour of God, the blessed Virgin, and all the saints, and for the souls of Edward II., of Philippa the Queen, and of his children and his ancestors.' Such was the origin of the society, which, amid the sweeping reforms that marked the reign of Henry VIII., was, in con-

Foundation of King's Hall, 1337.

junction with Michaelhouse, subsequently merged in the illustrious foundation of Trinity College.

The statutes of King's Hall were given by Richard II., and have a close resemblance to those of Merton College, a resemblance derived possibly through Peterhouse. It is here that we have the earliest evidence respecting the limitation imposed in the colleges as to age at the time of admission, no student being admissible under fourteen years,—a point on which the master is to be satisfied by the testimony of trustworthy witnesses.

It can scarcely be said that the codes of the seven Cambridge foundations which we have now passed under review present us with any definite advance in the theory of education. Peterhouse, Clare, and King's Hall were content to adopt, without attempt at originality, the main outlines of Walter de Merton's conception. In Trinity Hall and in Gonville Hall (as left by its second founder) we can detect little more than an echo of the traditions of Avignon,—traditions, it need scarcely be said, of which all centres of culture of the higher order have special need to beware. The question whether a university may advantageously concern itself with education of a purely technical character was one which presented itself to the minds of the thirteenth and fourteenth centuries, as well as to those of the nineteenth. At Paris it had been decided in the negative. The civil and the canon law had been excluded from her curriculum, for in the hands of the jurist and the canonist they had become a trade rather than a branch of liberal learning; and it is evident that those who

Theories of education exemplified in the foregoing foundations.

then prescribed the limits of education at Paris, whatever may have been their errors and shortcomings, saw clearly that if once the lower arts, conducive chiefly to worldly success and professional advancement, were admitted within the walls of a university, they would soon overshadow and blight the studies which appealed to a less selfish devotion.

The statutes of the other foundations scarcely call for comment. Those of Pembroke are interesting as an illustration of the persevering endeavours of the religious orders to upset what it is no exaggeration to describe as the fundamental conception of the new institutions,—an endeavour which, as we shall shortly see, was prosecuted at nearly the same time with greater success at Oxford. In Michaelhouse and Corpus Christi we have simply the sentiments of the devout laity, inspired, in all probability, by the priest and the confessor.

CHAPTER III.

*THE UNIVERSITY IN THE FIFTEENTH CENTURY—
CHARACTERISTICS OF UNIVERSITY MEDIÆVAL
LIFE.*

THE fifteenth century, although, in connection with the new foundations, a period of considerable interest, was one of torpor and decline in the history of the university at large. Down to the close of the previous century the mental activity of both Oxford and Cambridge had been quickened by the doctrinal teaching of Wyclif and his followers. That teaching had reference not merely to questions of religious reform and popular rights, but also, to a much greater extent than has generally been supposed, to questions of philosophy, such as were then being hotly contested in the universities of Europe, and especially those between the Nominalists and Realists. Wyclif, who in his day was the most distinguished teacher and schoolman in Oxford, espoused the cause of the reactionary party in philosophy, and was known as a leader of the Realists. But after his death the Lollards preached and sought to put into practice doctrines marked by an extravagance and by revolutionising tendencies to which his sanction would never have been given. And just as, four

<small>Influence of Lollardism at both universities.</small>

THE FIFTEENTH CENTURY. 51

centuries before, Innocent III. had repressed the heresy of the Albigenses, so the English Church, under the guidance of Archbishop Arundel, now put forth the strong arm for the repression of Lollardism.

Its suppression under Archbishop Arundel.

After this time we hear very little of Lollards at Oxford, and still less at Cambridge. Both universities, seeking to win the favour of the superstitious house of Lancaster, became distinguished by their advocacy of ultramontane doctrines. Their deputies filled, indeed, no contemptible place at the great Councils at Pisa and Constance, but we have no evidence that their voice was ever lifted in favour of freedom or reform.

Prevalence of ultramontane doctrines both at Oxford and Cambridge.

A notable event in the history of the university during this period illustrates these tendencies very forcibly. It was the theory maintained by the university itself that, by virtue of certain ancient privileges, it had been set free from the jurisdiction of the bishops of the diocese. Those privileges, however, were derived from somewhat questionable sources, going back for their authentication to the dim days of Pope Honorius, and to supposed documents which it was plausibly alleged had perished in past conflagrations. The bishops of Ely, in fact, altogether refused to believe in them, although they appear from time to time to have abstained from the exercise of those visitatorial rights which they maintained in theory.

Opposition between these doctrines and the claims of the bishops of Ely.

The high-spirited and nobly-born Arundel, who filled the see from 1374 to 1388, had adopted a bolder policy. He cited the chancellor of the university before him to take the canonical oath of obedience; and when the latter denied his jurisdiction, carried the question before the Court of Arches, where it was decided in his favour. But such claims were not in harmony with the policy of ultramontanism, which habitually aimed at curbing the authority of the bishop in order to assert its own immediate jurisdiction. When, accordingly, in 1430, the university appealed to Pope Martin V., and besought him to reconsider the whole question, he willingly responded to their petition. A commission was appointed to inquire into all the evidence. And on the appointed day, the prior of Barnwell, in the chapter-house of the church attached to the priory, having heard the witnesses and weighed the arguments of the university, ultimately gave judgment in its favour, thus completely reversing the decision of the Court of Arches. Such was the celebrated Barnwell Process, whereby the claim of the chancellor of the university to ecclesiastical jurisdiction, *exclusive of any archbishop, bishop, or their officials*, was recognised and confirmed; and so, says Baker, the historian of St. John's College, 'there was an end of ordinary jurisdiction.'

The Barnwell Process.

Of the disfavour with which all tendencies to speculation in matters of doctrine were now regarded, we have a notable instance in the case of Reginald Pecock, an Oxford scholar, who was bishop of Chichester from 1450 to 1459. Pecock sympathised with ultramontane theories of Church government, and was one of those who wrote against Wyclif, but, at the same time, he was an ardent advocate of popular education. His views and arguments would lead us, indeed, to conclude that

Influences unfavourable to free speculation in philosophy.

he would have been a vigorous supporter of the university extension movement of the present day. Such opinions would not in themselves have sufficed to expose him to the censure of the Church, for the influence of Italian scholars and the new learning was already beginning to make itself felt in England. But, unfortunately, in giving expression to his views, Pecock exhibited an originality and independence of thought which led to his being arraigned for heresy. He was deprived of his bishopric and placed in confinement for the rest of his life. The warning was not lost upon the freethinkers whom England possessed in those days; and, after Pecock's time, nothing that savoured of new doctrine was heard of either at Oxford or Cambridge, until, in the sixteenth century, the minds of their ablest scholars were roused to new activity by the powerful influences of the Renaissance.

This inactivity of thought was rather fostered than dispelled by the prosperity which, until the commencement of the Civil War, the country at large enjoyed, and especially by its commercial prosperity, which directed attention more to trade and agriculture. This advance in material wealth, however, was not without its good effects on the universities themselves. The Church shared in the general gain; and not a few bishops, like Balsham and Bateman in the preceding centuries, devoted some of their wealth to founding colleges where youth might be trained in strictly orthodox doctrines. It marks a further development in the whole conception of education, when we find the charitable and wealthy turning away in despair alike from the monastery and the friary, and transferring their sympathies to those two academic centres where, amid much that was narrow, mechanical, and false, a certain amount of genuine and far from useless mental activity was undoubtedly going on. Such were the feelings, such were the sympathies, which had already actuated William of Wykeham when, in 1380, he founded New College, Oxford,—a foundation which, in its organisation and prescribed discipline, resembled a monastery more than any preceding college, but which was itself endowed with lands which the founder had purchased from various monastic societies.

The foundation of Eton College and King's College, Cambridge, marks another stage in this notable change in public feeling; for both societies were endowed with the estates of the alien priories, certain 'cells,' that is to say, of different religious orders in England which represented dependencies of foreign monasteries. Henry V. had already appropriated their revenues in the time of war; and his son, Henry VI., next proceeded to confiscate them permanently as an endowment for Eton and King's College. The amply endowed society, the buildings of which now rose on the original site, to the north of the chapel and to the west of the Schools, was superior in wealth and prestige to any preceding Cambridge foundation. Its code was in most respects a simple adaptation of that of New College. Theology, the arts, and philosophy were to form the ordinary course of study. It is, however, a significant fact that the commissioners who originally received the royal command to prepare the

<small>Foundation of Eton College and King's College.</small>

statutes evaded their task by voluntary resignation, and that William Millington, the first provost (as the head of the new foundation was termed), was ejected from his office owing to his unconcealed disapproval of certain provisions of the code. There can be little doubt that the cause of these circumstances lay in the exclusive privileges with which it was proposed to invest the new foundation—provisions which the provost and the commissioners alike regarded as so objectionable that they could not but withhold their concurrence. It was the aim of the royal founder to make the college independent not only of the bishop of the diocese, but also of the university authorities, and for this purpose he applied to Rome. The necessary bulls were granted; and on 31st January 1448-9, the university itself, by an instrument under its common seal, granted that 'the provost, fellows, and scholars, their servants and ministers, should be exempt from the power, dominion, and jurisdiction of the chancellor, vice-chancellor, proctors, and ministers of the university; but in all matters relating to the various scholastic acts, exercises, lectures, and disputations necessary for degrees, and the sermons, masses, general processions, congregations, convocations, elections of chancellor, proctors, and other officers (not being repugnant to their peculiar privileges), they were, as true gremials and scholars of the university, to be obedient to the chancellor, vice-chancellor, and proctors, as other scholars were.' In other words, in the highly important relation of discipline, as distinguished from instruction, the college was made altogether independent of the university. Another grave objection, as it appeared at least to Millington, was the limitation of a foundation designed on so princely a scale to scholars coming from Eton, a provision which stands in striking contrast to the catholicity of the designs of some preceding founders. In this manner an exclusive class endowed with exclusive privileges was founded in the university; nor was it until more than four centuries had elapsed that King's College was eventually liberated from the incubus which had so long rested upon it. It is true that during that lengthened period the society could point to not a few distinguished scholars and men otherwise eminent who had been educated within its walls. But the real efficiency of such institutions is to be estimated rather by the average character than the exceptional celebrity of its members; and the reputation of the society during this time was too generally that of one where the primary designs of academic life were systematically ignored, where elegant amusement took the place of severer studies, and the active duties of the parish priest were evaded for the easy leisure of the college fellowship.

It was at the petition of Margaret of Anjou, then scarcely twenty years of age, but 'restless,' to use the expression of Fuller, 'with holy emulation of her husband's bounty in building King's College,' that the 'Queen's College of St. Margaret and St. Bernard in the university of Cambridge,' was founded. The charter bears the date 15th April 1448, but no statutes were given for more than a quarter of a century after,—the outbreak of the Civil War having probably called away the attention of

Foundation of Queen's College, 1448.

royalty to more urgent matters. And when a code was eventually given, in 1475, it was by Elizabeth Woodville, the consort of Edward IV. Elizabeth had once sympathised strongly with the Lancastrian party: she had been one of the ladies-in-waiting attached to the person of Margaret of Anjou, and her husband had fallen fighting for the Lancastrian cause. It is not improbable, therefore, that sympathy with her former mistress, then passing her days in retirement in Anjou, may have prompted her to accede to the prayer of Andrew Doket, the first president of the society, and to take the new foundation, the name of which is henceforth to be written Queens' College,[1] under her protection. By the original statutes, the new foundation was designed for the support of a president and twelve fellows—all of whom were to take priest's orders. A fellow, at the time of his election, might be of no higher status than that of a questionist in arts; or, if already studying theology, might be chosen from scholars on the foundation. On taking his master of arts degree, he was required either to devote himself to teaching, or further to prosecute his studies in the natural or metaphysical philosophy of Aristotle. Andrew Doket ruled the society of Queens' College for many years, from 1448 to 1484; but there are no signs that he was in any way a promoter of that new learning which, before his death, was beginning to be heard of at Cambridge.

A society of humbler origin was the next to rise after the two royal foundations. Among the first scholars of

[1] As distinguishable from Queen's College, Oxford, founded by Queen Philippa, where the *s* and the possessive are transposed.

King's College was Robert Woodlark, afterwards founder and master of St. Catherine's Hall. In 1452, John Chadworth, the second provost, was elected to the bishopric of Lincoln, and Woodlark was appointed his successor; and it was under his guidance that King's College extorted from the university those exceptional privileges to which we have above referred. That he was an able administrator may be inferred from the prominent part assigned to him on different occasions; 'but herein,' says Fuller, 'he stands alone, without any to accompany him, being the first and last, who was master of one college and at the same time founder of another.' St. Catherine's Hall[1] was founded in 1475. There is little in the statutes given by Woodlark that calls for comment, beyond the fact that both the canon and the civil law are rigorously excluded from the course of study, and that it appears to have been the founder's design that the new college should be subservient solely to the wants of the secular clergy.

Foundation of St. Catherine's Hall, 1475.

The nunnery of St. Rhadegund, whose foundation we have already noted, affords a further illustration of that gradual revolution in the religious sympathies of the community at large which had paved the way for the Reformation long before Luther appeared upon the scene. St. Rhadegund was another of those religious houses which were at this time filling the hearts of pious reformers like William of Wykeham with despair.

Foundation of Jesus College, 1497.

---

[1] No distinction appears to have been involved by the use of the term *aula* instead of *collegium*: Woodlark's statutes say, 'Hujus collegii sive aulæ.'

In the reign of Henry VII. it was, in fact, on the verge of a natural dissolution. Its revenues had been squandered and dissipated; only two nuns remained on the foundation; so that, to quote the language of the charter of Jesus College, 'divine service, hospitality, or other works of mercy and piety, according to the primary foundation and ordinance of their founders there used, could not be discharged.' In the year 1497, through the exertions of John Alcock, bishop of Ely, the nunnery was suppressed by royal patent. Alcock was a munificent encourager of the arts, and to his liberality and taste the church of Great St. Mary and his own chapel in the cathedral at Ely are still eloquent though silent witnesses. The historian of the college, a fellow on the foundation in the seventeenth century, observes that it appears to have been designed that, in form at least, the new erection should suggest the monastic life; and to this resemblance the retired and tranquil character of the site, which afterwards gained for it from King James I. the designation of the 'Muses' haunt,' still further contributed. The first statutes of the college were not given until early in the sixteenth century. Their author was Stanley, the successor, one removed, to Alcock, in the see of Ely, and son-in-law of Margaret, countess of Richmond; they were also considerably modified by Stanley's illustrious successor in the same see, Nicholas West, fellow of King's, and the friend of Bishop Fisher and Sir Thomas More. The most noteworthy feature in these statutes, for our present purpose, is the fact that, although both Alcock and West were distinguished by their acquirements in the canon law, not one of the twelve fellows to be maintained on the foundation was permitted to become a canonist, and only one a civilian. In this proviso we have probably another indication that sympathy with the principles of ultramontanism was on the decline; and although Luther had not yet nailed his theses to the door of the church at Wittenberg, the wiser minds of England were already disposed to think less about Rome and the Roman pretensions, and to direct their efforts towards the promotion of a learning more likely to serve the true interests of the Church and the laity throughout the realm. It is difficult, however, to suppose that these efforts would have effected much had they not been aided by those other influences which will shortly demand our attention. How little there was in the teaching of the Cambridge of this period, or in that of any other university north of the Alps, to stimulate a genuine spirit of inquiry will be evident if we simply bear in mind the fact that the function of the lecturer was generally supposed to be limited to the interpretation of the *dicta* of recognised authorities. The doctrines of Aristotle, whether those which he really taught or those attributed to him by others, the commentaries of Aquinas and Duns Scotus, and those on 'the Master of the *Sentences*,' such were mainly the sum of the theology and the philosophy which the university lecturer was called upon to make known and to interpret to his audience. Owing to the extreme scarcity of text-books, whether in manuscript or printed, the student's first acquaintance with an author was generally made in the class-room. The method employed by the lecturer was of two kinds,—the analytical and

Character of the university instruction at this period.

the dialectical. Of the former, the commentary by Aquinas on the *Ethics* of Aristotle,—of the latter, the *Quæstiones* of Buridanus (an eminent schoolman of the fourteenth century), may serve as examples.

The analytical method.

In the employment of the analytical method, the plan pursued was purely traditional, and never varied. The lecturer commenced by discussing a few general questions having reference to the treatise which he was called upon to explain, and in the customary Aristotelian fashion treated of its material, formal, final, and efficient cause. He pointed out the principal divisions; took the first division and subdivided it; divided again the subdivision, and repeated the process until he had subdivided down to the first chapter. He then again divided until he had reached a subdivision which included only a simple sentence or complete idea. He finally took this sentence and expressed it in terms, somewhat varied, so as to make the conception more clear. He never passed from one part of the work to another, from one chapter to another, or even from one sentence to another, without a minute analysis of the reasons for which each division, chapter, or sentence was placed after that by which it was immediately preceded; while, at the conclusion of this painful toil, he would sometimes be found hanging painfully over a single letter or mark of punctuation.

The dialectical method.

The second method, and probably by far the more popular one, was designed to assist the student in the practice of casting the thought of an author into a form that might serve as subject-matter for the all-prevailing logic. Whenever a passage presented itself that admitted of a twofold interpretation, the one or other interpretation was thrown into the form of a *quæstio*, and then discussed *pro* and *con*, the arguments on either side being drawn up in the usual array. It is probable that it was at lectures of this kind that the instruction often assumed a catechetical form,—one of the statutes expressly requiring that students should be ready with their answers to any questions that might be put, 'according to the method of questioning used by the masters, if the mode of lecturing used in that faculty required questions and answers.' Finally, the lecturer brought forward his own interpretation, and defended it against every objection to which it might appear liable; each solution being formulated in the ordinary syllogistic fashion, and the student being thus furnished with a stock of *quæstiones* and arguments requisite for enabling him to take his part as a disputant in the schools. Hence the second stage of the *trivium* not only absorbed an excessive amount of attention, but it overwhelmed and moulded the whole course of study. Even the study of grammar was subjected to the same process. Priscian and Donatus were cast into the form of *quæstiones*, wherein the grammar student was required to exhibit something of dialectical skill. It was undoubtedly from the prevalence of this method of treatment that disputation became that besetting vice of the age which the opponents of the scholastic culture so severely satirised. 'They dispute,' said Vives, in his celebrated treatise, 'before dinner, at dinner, and after dinner; in public and in private; in all places and at all times.'

MEDIÆVAL STUDENT LIFE. 63

When the student in arts had incepted and delivered his lectures as regent his duties were at an end. He had become recognised as one of the great guild of teachers, and was qualified to give instruction on any of the subjects of the *trivium* and *quadrivium* in any university in Europe. He had also discharged his obligations to the university in which he had been educated; and was henceforth known, if he continued to reside, as a non-regent. If he left the academic precincts and went forth into the world, he was certain to be regarded as a marvel in learning, and he might probably rely on obtaining employment as a teacher, and earning a modest though somewhat precarious income. But, as in every age with the majority of students, learning was seldom valued in those days as an ultimate good, but for its reproductive capacity, and, viewed in this light, the degree of master of arts had but a moderate value. The ambitious scholar, intent upon worldly and professional success, directed his efforts to theology or to the civil or canon law. And here we must carefully guard against the notion that any member of the university, in those days, could look forward to the degree of LL.D., D.C.L., D.D., or B.D. as obtainable by the simple process of retaining his name on the university register and performing one or two exercises. The conditions obligatory upon the theologian, the civilian, or the canonist who aimed at such academic honours involved further residence at the university for another eight or ten years, during which time he must have attended various courses of lectures,

Subsequent career of the master of arts.

have given proof of his own acquirements by lecturing on the same subjects to others, and have kept numerous oppositions and responsions. It is necessary also to bear in mind that the appearance from time to time of new commentaries, whether on the Scriptures or on Aristotle, the result generally of great labour, and sometimes of considerable acumen, often imposed no little additional toil on the university lecturer. The logician was oppressed by the ever-multiplying commentaries on the *Organon;* the expositions of De Lyra, which appeared in the fourteenth century, alone demanded no slight labour on the part of the professed theologian; the new decretals promulgated by Boniface VIII. and Clement V. added no less to the toil of the canonist. It was a frequent assertion on the part of Lollard writers, that the demands thus made on his time (demands which he dared not disregard, for the papal anathema hung over all who should neglect the study of these additions to the code of Rome) were one of the chief causes of that neglect of the Scriptures which now began to characterise the labours of the academic divine.

But in proportion to the efforts expended in mastering the lore thus handed down through a succession of preceding teachers was the value attached to the labour; and in justice to the university teacher of this period, whose conception of learning and its aims was conceived solely on the traditional lines, it must be remembered what an amount of self-abnegation was demanded of him when he was called upon to lay aside, as well nigh valueless, the acquirements to which the best part of his life had been given,—to admit that much of his theology was baseless ; that his philosophy was for the most part but ingenious cobweb-spinning ; and that his canon law was a system of which both foundation and superstructure required to be almost entirely swept away!

CHAPTER IV.

THE UNIVERSITY AND THE RENAISSANCE.

THE remarkable movement known as the Renaissance, which brought back to the knowledge of the scholars of Western Europe the masterpieces of classical antiquity, and eventually made them a leading study in the universities, did not reach Cambridge until quite the close of the fifteenth century. It was apprehended in its true significance much earlier by the scholars of Oxford, and the names of William Selling, Linacre, Grocyn, Colet, and Sir Thomas More represent a tradition to which, at the same period, Cambridge can offer no parallel. Even William Gray, who was bishop of Ely from 1454 to 1478, and who had studied under Guarino at Ferrara, seems to have done nothing towards promoting a like activity at Cambridge, and his valuable collection of classical manuscripts was bequeathed to Balliol College. With the advance of the sixteenth century, however, this inferiority began rapidly to disappear, and for the remainder of that period it hardly admits of question that Cambridge, when compared with Oxford, exerted the more potent influence over the nation at large and commanded the larger share of the national regard. The remarkable progress

THE RENAISSANCE. 67

which the university now began to make in classical learning must be attributed, in the first instance, to the example and teaching of Erasmus; while its more general growth in culture, numbers, and endowments must be held to date from the commencement of the untiring exertions of Bishop Fisher. It was in the year 1497 that Fisher succeeded to the mastership of Michaelhouse, and it was probably about the same time that he was appointed confessor to the Lady Margaret, countess of Richmond, mother of Henry VII. This illustrious lady, distinguished no less by her piety and benevolence than by her august descent, seems very soon to have discerned the eminent virtues and abilities of her spiritual adviser; and when, in 1503, she founded at Cambridge that professorship of divinity which bears her name, she appointed Fisher the first professor. He had already, in 1501, been elected to the office of vice-chancellor, and from 1505 to 1508 he presided over the society of Queens' College; he was thus well qualified to estimate the condition of the academic discipline, as well as the merits and defects of the theological training, of his time. His individual convictions are clearly to be discerned in the salutary measures which he advised and carried into effect: in his inciting Erasmus to indite a treatise, *De Ratione Concionandi* (*i.e.*, on the composition of sermons), with a view towards bringing about a less disputatious and more practical kind of preaching than that which then prevailed, in the institution of the Lady Margaret preachership, which his patroness founded mainly by his advice, its object being to provide for the systematic religious

Bishop Fisher.

The Lady Margaret.

instruction of the laity in *English*, by divines of the university; and, finally, in the foundation of the two societies of Christ's College and St. John's College, and in the codes given for their observance.

Christ's College, founded in 1505, rose on a yet earlier foundation, an ancient school for instruction in grammar, known as God's House. The new society was munificently endowed by the Lady Margaret; and in the following year, along with her royal son, she honoured Cambridge with a visit,—a visit attended with memorable results. King's College Chapel, then but half completed, the work standing still owing to insufficient funds, arrested the monarch's attention, and within three years after, shortly before his death, he left those princely bequests which converted a spectacle of apparent failure into one of splendid completion. It has been supposed that Erasmus was in the royal train on this occasion. It is certain that he was already well known to Fisher, whose guest he afterwards became at Queens' College; and it is in every way probable that in the code of Christ's College, which presents us with the first endeavour to introduce a new element of culture in the studies of the university, his influence is to be traced. The new foundation was designed exclusively as a seminary of theology, the studies of the canon and the civil law and that of medicine being alike unrecognised. Another feature which must not be passed by, as having probably exercised material influence on its subsequent history, is a certain preference shown in the election of fellows to those who should be natives of certain northern counties. Of the twelve fellowships,

Foundation of Christ's College, 1505.

nine might be from the counties of Northumberland, Durham, Westmoreland, Cumberland, York, Richmond, Lancashire, Derby, and Nottingham; while the remaining three were to be taken from any three of the remaining counties of the realm. It was not obligatory that more than six should be taken from the northern counties, but the permission to extend the number to nine was, in practice, generally construed into a precept. No one county, however, was at any time to be represented by more than one fellow. The pensioner, —that is to say, the undergraduate who paid *rent* for a chamber or a share of a chamber within college precincts,—existed as early as the fourteenth century. In the present code, however, he first appears under the somewhat more comprehensive designation of *conviva*, —the *convivæ* being students admitted as members of the college on condition of defraying their own expenses,—*i.e.*, both board and lodging. They are required to be of unexceptionable character, and to bind themselves by oath to a strict compliance with the prescribed order of discipline and instruction. But the most significant of all the innovations is undoubtedly that whereby provision is made for the regular delivery of lectures on the *works of the poets and orators*, an unmistakable proof of the extending influence of the Renaissance, if not of the personal influence of Erasmus himself.

Before King Henry and his noble mother died, they had been induced by Fisher's representations, the one to sanction, the other liberally to endow, a second college,—that of St. John the Evangelist. Christ's College had been partly founded by the incorporation of an older society; St. John's was formed by the extinction of the ancient Hospital. Ever since the failure of Hugh Balsham's well-meant endeavour to amalgamate that society with a more progressive element, the brethren of the Hospital of St. John had been steadily advancing on the downward path of misrule, licence, and profuse expenditure. Like the nunnery of St. Rhadegund, the Hospital had become a scandal; but few of its members remained on the foundation, and, to quote the description of Baker, 'hospitality and the service of God, the two great ends of their institution, were equally neglected.' It was now proposed by Fisher altogether to suppress the society, and to found a college in its place. Not a few difficulties, however, obstructed his design. Stanley, the young and licentious bishop of Ely, opposed the dissolution of the Hospital, and it was only after a peremptory mandate from Pope Julius at Rome that his resistance was overcome. The endowment bequeathed by Margaret Richmond would have furnished revenues for the new foundation second only to those of King's, but exceptions were taken, after her death, to the technical validity of her bequest; Wolsey's all-potent influence (from causes which could only be surmised) was thrown into the adverse scale; and ultimately it was found necessary to surrender the whole of the noble benefaction. It was only through Fisher's strenuous efforts that, as some compensation, other estates, representing a revenue less than one-fifth of the original endowment, were ultimately granted for the new society. By the exercise

Foundation of St. John's College, 1511.

of a rigid economy they were, however, made to suffice for the maintenance of thirty-one fellows; and under the long and able rule of Nicholas Metcalfe, who succeeded to the mastership in 1518, the college grew rapidly in numbers and reputation. The statutes given by Fisher in 1516 were identical in their tenor with those of Christ's College; but in 1524 he substituted for these another code, and in 1530 a third. The code of 1530 may accordingly be fairly regarded as the final embodiment of his views and aims with respect to college education. It is not difficult to recognise in the different provisions at once the strength and the weakness of his character. His life presents us with more than one significant proof how little mere moral rectitude of purpose avails to preserve men from pitiable superstition and fatal mistakes. As his faith in the past amounted to a foolish credulity, so his distrust of the future became an unreasoning dread. In the 130 closely printed pages which these statutes fill, we recognise the vitiating defect of mediæval discipline,—the incapacity for recognising both the necessity of progress and the wisdom of conceding that liberty of action on which progress depends. And accordingly, amid many provisions, characterised by much prudent forethought, and statutes which really pointed to something like a revolution in academic studies, we cannot but be conscious that it was Fisher's aim to stereotype, as far as possible, the entire constitution of the society, so as to preclude all possibility of further innovation on a code which itself represented no slight modi-

[margin: Bishop Fisher's different statutes for the College.]

fication of that which he had himself given only fourteen years before.

How little his purpose, if successful, would have redounded to the advantage of those for whom he legislated may be inferred from provisions such as those which directed that questions from Duns Scotus should always continue to be introduced at every logical discussion,—that undergraduates under twenty, guilty of breaches of discipline, should be whipped for their offences,—that the permission of the dean should always be necessary before any of their number could pass the college gates,—that recreation in the fields should be permissible only when there were at least three together,—and that no scholar should be allowed to be absent from college more then forty days in the year. It indicates, on the other hand, the change that was coming over the classical studies of the university, that both Hebrew and Greek are indicated as fitting subjects of study for a certain proportion of the fellows and scholars. It may even be regarded as a provision contrasting favourably with the method of much later times, that only those fellows and scholars are to devote themselves to these studies, who, in the opinion of the masters and seniors, evince an aptitude for them. Not less commendable is the obligation imposed upon a fourth part of the fellows to occupy themselves with preaching to the people in English.

It was during the interval between the foundation of Fisher's two colleges, about the year 1510, that Erasmus, after residing for some time at Louvain, and subsequently at

Residence of Erasmus in Cambridge.

Oxford, came to seek a new field of labour in Cambridge. Under Fisher's protection, he took up his residence in Queens' College, in the turret which rises at the south-east angle of Pump Court. From 1511 to 1515 he filled the chair of the Lady Margaret professorship; and with the chancellor's encouragement, and aided by the influence of other scholars, he commenced the somewhat perilous experiment of forming a class in Greek. His manual of instruction was the little Grammar which Emmanuel Chrysoloras had compiled for the use of the young Italian students who sought his instruction in Florence; but his experience was a less fortunate one than that which waited on the corresponding efforts of Guarino and Politian. His pupils were few, and paid him little or nothing. By the great majority of the seniors of the university, violently opposed to the new learning, he was regarded with suspicion and dislike. He was the object of malicious annoyance on the part of the townsmen, full of brutal contempt for the foreign scholar who was unable to converse with them in their vernacular. His class proved a failure; and, disappointed in the class-room, he took refuge in his study; and to his labours there, the men of his generation were indebted for his two most notable achievements,—the *Novum Instrumentum* and his edition of Jerome. By the one he directly paved the way for the Reformation; by the other he guided the student of his age to that juster estimate of the value and authority of mediæval theologians, which so largely, though less immediately, conduced to the same great revolution. In brief, we cannot, perhaps, better express the importance and significance of his work than when we say that the new Margaret professor,—whom, during the greater part of his residence at Cambridge, we may picture to ourselves as thus toiling away in his lonely college tower,—was mostly engaged in investigations the result of which was to be the eventual consignment to neglect and oblivion of nearly nine-tenths of the literature on which the theologians in the university around him looked with most reverence and regard.

It was in the winter of 1513–14 that Erasmus left Cambridge,—his departure hastened, if not occasioned, by the outbreak of the plague. His experiences during his sojourn had not been of a character that he could afterwards recall with satisfaction, but he did not refuse to do justice to the ability and worth of the leading minds of the university, and readily admitted that it could already compare not unfavourably with some of the most distinguished centres on the Continent. To the three colleges which enjoyed the advantage of being under Fisher's direct influence and guidance,—Queens', Christ's, and St. John's,—he refers with special satisfaction, as schools where a sounder learning was being fostered and a more truly evangelic spirit diffused among their alumni. It is to these colleges, without doubt, that we must turn, if we would follow the main current of the new movement in the university.

His experiences, and estimate of the work going on in the university.

The light which Erasmus had kindled was not extinguished. Among the young scholars whom he taught and befriended at Cambridge was Richard Croke of King's College. Croke subsequently went abroad, and appeared as a lecturer on Greek at Cologne, Louvain, Leipzig, and other centres. In this capacity he achieved a considerable reputation, and when, about the year 1519, he returned to the university, he was forthwith appointed public orator for life. On entering upon office, he delivered an inaugural address, which was shortly followed by a second, and the two may be regarded as among the most noteworthy compositions in the literary history of the time, and especially valuable as showing how closely the new studies for which he pleaded were associated with that revived and more intelligent study of the Scriptures on which it was felt that the education of a more learned and efficient clergy mainly depended. Although it is difficult to suppose that Croke's estimate was quite impartial, it is deserving of note that he addresses his Cambridge audience as composed of those who had hitherto outstripped the Oxford men in every department of knowledge.

Such was the character and such were the tendencies of learning at Cambridge, when they suddenly became, for a time, almost lost to view amid the revolutionary changes and the ferment of thought which ushered in the English Reformation. During the years which immediately preceded the movement, a less benign presence than that of Bishop Fisher, the dread Cardinal himself, by turns excited the hopes and the apprehensions of the university. It was well understood at

Visit of Wolsey to the university.

Cambridge that Wolsey bore their chancellor[1] no goodwill, and it was believed that this unfriendly feeling extended, in some measure, to the whole community, and had already entailed upon them one serious loss. His munificent endowment of his new college at Ipswich, designed as it was as a nursery for his splendid foundation at Oxford, might well seem likely to divert from Cambridge not a few promising scholars from the eastern counties. The authorities now hastened, accordingly, to turn aside his displeasure by complete and unqualified submission. When Wolsey visited Cambridge in 1520, the language with which they approached him might compare for adulation and self-abasement with that customary in addressing an Oriental despot. And in 1524, following an example already set by Oxford, the university proceeded to make a complete surrender of its statutes and privileges into the Cardinal's hands, to be altered and remodelled at his pleasure, and beseeching him to continue to exercise these autocratic powers for the remainder of his lifetime.

The printing-press, which proved elsewhere such a powerful ally of the Reformation movement, took its rise in Cambridge soon after Erasmus' sojourn. In a letter written to Dr. Robert Aldrich of King's College, on Christmas Day 1525, we find the great scholar sending greetings to old acquaintances in the university, and among them to one John Siberch. Siberch was both a bookseller and a printer, and in the years 1521 and 1522 he printed

The early Cambridge press.

---

[1] In 1504 Fisher had been elected chancellor, and after having been re-elected annually for ten years, was re-elected for life.

eight different volumes, among them a well-known treatise by Erasmus himself, entitled *De Conscribendis Epistolis*. In some of these Greek type is used, and the Cambridge press would accordingly appear entitled to the distinction of having been the first in England where this feature in typography was introduced. Siberch, in fact, speaks of himself, in one of the prefaces, as 'primus utriusque linguæ in Anglia impressor,'—that is, the first printer in England to print both in Greek and in Latin. There were other booksellers and printers at that time in Cambridge, and one of them, Sygar Nicholson, who had been educated at Gonville Hall, was charged in 1529 with holding Lutheran opinions, and having Lutheran books in his possession. In the same year the opponents of the Reformation movement in the university petitioned Wolsey that only three booksellers might be permitted to ply their trade at Cambridge, who should be men of reputation and 'gravity,' and foreigners, with full authority to purchase books of foreign merchants. The petition appears to have received no immediate response; but in the year 1534 a royal licence was issued to the chancellor, masters, and scholars of the university to appoint, from time to time, three stationers and printers, or sellers of books, residing within the university, who might be either aliens or natives. Those thus appointed were empowered both to print and to vend any books licensed by the academic authorities. In pursuance of this licence three stationers and printers were appointed, one of the three being Sygar Nicholson, whom it may possibly have been designed

After-effects of his labours.

to compensate for the persecution and imprisonment to which he had been subjected. It indicates, however, the extent to which the printer's enterprise was at that time associated rather with liberty of thought than university traditions, that the licensed press proved altogether sterile; and for more than half a century, from the year 1522 to 1584, it would appear that not a single book was printed at Cambridge.

CHAPTER V.

THE UNIVERSITY DURING THE REFORMATION.

WE have already seen how the two great contributing causes to the success of the Reformation,—the degeneracy of the religious orders and of ecclesiastical institutions, and the more critical and at the same time more liberal spirit generated by the Renaissance,—are clearly to be discerned as operating with considerable effect at Cambridge. We have now to note how the more direct influence of Luther's writings, combining with these causes, resulted in the formation of a theological school in the university which rendered it for a considerable period the chief centre of Protestant thought in England. It had been the boast of Lydgate in the fifteenth century, that 'of heresie Cambridge bare never blame'; in the sixteenth century, however, Cambridge was to become a noted haunt of what, in the eyes of Rome, was regarded as heresy of the blackest dye.

The commercial intercourse between Northern Germany and the eastern English coast, and especially with the towns of King's Lynn, Norwich, Yarmouth, and Ipswich, was in those days considerable; Luther's writings frequently found their way across the sea concealed in ships' cargoes; and in this manner the inhabitants of these districts became the first to embrace the doctrines of the Reformation.

Pre-Lutheran Reformation movement in Cambridge.

Those of them, again, who designed to pass through a university career naturally resorted to Cambridge, which thus very early became a centre of Lutheran, or at least of Reformation, teaching. But before Luther's name had even been heard at Cambridge, views such as the great Reformer advocated were not unfamiliar to the university. So early as the year 1517, a young Norman student, Peter de Valence by name, had ventured to impugn the glaring abuse of indulgences in a few words of bold denunciation written over a proclamation of Leo X. which Fisher himself had affixed to the doors of the schools. His daring deed drew down upon him a sentence of excommunication from the chancellor, and resulted in his flight from the university. By this time, moreover, the labours of Erasmus were beginning to bear fruit, and Thomas Bilney, a native of Norwich and a member of Trinity Hall, who must be regarded as the first leader of the Reformation in the university, always referred back the commencement of his spiritual enlightenment to 'even then when the New Testament was first set forth by Erasmus.' An indefatigable student, whose high attainments and winning disposition averted the ridicule which some harmless eccentricities and a remarkably diminutive stature might otherwise have evoked, Bilney now became an active proselytiser to the Reformation doctrines, and attracted not a few followers. Among the number

Its chief leaders.

was Thomas Arthur, master of St. Mary's Hostel, William Paget (afterwards lord high steward of the university), John Lambert, fellow of Queens', Shaxton (afterwards bishop of Sarum), Thomas Forman (afterwards president of Queens'),—all mostly Norfolk men. The house of the Augustinian friars was at this time under the presidency of Robert Barnes, also a Norfolk man, who had studied at Louvain; in conjunction with William Paynell, who had been a fellow-student with him at that famous school, he also began to venture upon some daring innovations,—to lecture on Latin authors like Terence, Plautus, and Cicero; and, in the language of Foxe, 'putting aside Duns and Dorbel' (that is to say, the schoolmen and the Byzantine logic), to comment on the Pauline Epistles. Latimer long after described him as one who in power of lucid and effective exposition had no equal in the university. So again at Pembroke, always a home of the best traditions of the university, George Stafford, a fellow of the college, attracted, about the years 1525 and 1526, enthusiastic audiences by his lectures on the Gospels and Epistles.

The next stage is marked by the introduction of the Lutheran writings. At the very time that King Henry and Bishop Fisher were wielding their pens in unsparing condemnation of the great Reformer, whose works were publicly committed to the flames on Market Hill, a little band of Cambridge scholars were assembling periodically together for the purpose of studying and discussing his earlier treatises; among their number was William Tyndale, who was resident in the university from 1514 to 1521. The White Horse Inn,

William Tyndale, Barnes, and Latimer.

which occupied at that time very nearly the present site of 'The Bull,' was their place of meeting. Stealing in by the back entrance from Milne Street, they gradually began to assemble in such numbers that the inn itself was known as 'Germany,' and its devout frequenters as 'the Germans.' It was the taunt of their adversaries that they were mostly young men; but it is certain that they were among the most able and diligent of the student class in the university, and their influence made numerous converts. For a time they appear to have been left unmolested. But in 1526 Barnes, in a sermon at St. Edward's Church, having ventured, with singular imprudence, upon the utterance of words which were understood to glance at Wolsey himself, was called to account by the authorities, and the demonstration which then took place plainly revealed the extent to which the movement had spread. The prior was eventually arrested and brought to London, where, under the fear of martyrdom, he was induced to sign a recantation. The loss thus sustained by his party at Cambridge was, however, more than made good by the accession to its ranks of the celebrated Hugh Latimer. The appearance of Tyndale's version of the New Testament, a production which, on account of its new renderings, was stigmatised by Sir Thomas More as 'the father of all the heresies,' only added strength to the convictions of the Reformers. Of the extent to which the best scholarship of the university was represented among their number, we need seek no more decisive proof than the fact that when Wolsey, in 1525, was founding Cardinal College at Oxford, and was selecting from Cambridge the most efficient teachers and lecturers whom he could find to give prestige to the new society, out of the eight thus chosen no less than six were notably supporters of the Reformation doctrines. When those doctrines began, in turn, to make their appearance at the sister university, Archbishop Warham, in a letter deploring the growth of the heresy, declared that Cambridge was generally held to be 'the original occasion and cause of the fall in Oxford.' Latimer was now the leading figure in the movement at Cambridge, and was consequently marked out for the fiercest attacks. By Buckenham, the prior of the Dominican foundation, he was assailed with especial vehemence, while Fisher's whole influence was also thrown into the opposing scale. The whole university was divided into two bitterly hostile parties, and signs were not wanting that before long the fires of persecution might be lighted to decide the struggle. In January 1531–2, Thomas Benet, a master of arts of the university, was burnt as a Protestant at Exeter. And the fate of the movement throughout England might have been prematurely sealed had not the question of the royal divorce suddenly introduced a new element which served effectually to reverse the relative strength of the two parties. For the final solution arrived at in connection with that memorable question Cambridge would seem to have been in no small measure responsible. Thomas Cranmer, a fellow of Jesus College, was at that time living in the house of a Mr. Cressy at Waltham; and it was there that, in conference with two other

Influence of Cambridge on Oxford.

The university and the Royal Divorce.

Cambridge divines,—Stephen Gardiner, who in 1525 had succeeded to the mastership of Trinity Hall, and Edward Fox, who in 1528 had been elected provost of King's,—he suggested the expedient of referring the question of the legality of Henry's marriage to the universities of Christendom and holding a special court in England. As Cranmer was, at that very time, acting as tutor to Anne Boleyn, it is impossible to regard his position in relation to the question as an impartial one. In the university itself the suffrages were strangely divided. The academic authorities, actuated mainly by considerations of expediency, sought to win the royal favour by an ignoble servility. Croke was especially distinguished by the compliant readiness with which he lent himself to Henry's designs, visiting in turn the chief universities on the Continent, with the ostensible object of obtaining the opinions of the most eminent canonists as to the legality of the royal marriage with Catherine, but in reality for the purpose of bribing those whom he professed to consult into giving their subscriptions in favour of the divorce. The younger members of the university, on the other hand, less exposed to temptations like those which swayed the sentiments of their seniors, and partly, perhaps, under the influence of their broader culture and its more generous spirit, displayed a feeling of sympathy with the injured queen which it required energetic measures to repress. A decision (9th March 1529–30) favourable to Henry's design was indeed eventually wrung from the university, but it had been obtained only by the appointment of a Commission which in its composition was little better than a packed jury. The appointment itself had encountered strenuous opposition. The first time it was proposed to the senate it was non-placeted; when again brought forward the votes were equal; and it was eventually carried only by the device of inducing those hostile to the measure to abstain from voting. Even when thus appointed, the members of the Commission found it necessary, in order to arrive at the foregone conclusion, to persuade at least one of their number to absent himself. And, finally, their decision, when arrived at, was qualified by an important reservation, which, if Queen Catherine herself was to be believed, involved a conclusion unfavourable to the divorce.

After Wolsey's death (November 1530), the precedent which he had set in the foundation of Cardinal College, of confiscating monastic property, was readily acted upon by those who, while they shared his greed of wealth, had none of his regard for learning. The work of spoliation went on apace; and when, on 22d June 1535, Bishop Fisher heroically met his death on Tower Hill, the university felt that the last defence which intervened between itself and a like fate to that of the monasteries had fallen. The election of Thomas Cromwell, the foremost contriver of Fisher's death, to be his successor in the chancellorship must be regarded as an almost despairing effort dictated solely by the instinct of self-preservation. The payment of first-fruits and tenths imposed on the university in 1534 was soon found to be a serious burden; in some colleges it had made it necessary to diminish the

Election of Thomas Cromwell as chancellor.

number of the fellowships. And it hardly admits of doubt that many of the endowments would now have been snatched away, had not Henry and his minister been able to discriminate between the monastic revenues wasted by neglect and maladministration, and those of the colleges which from the first had but inadequately subserved the ennobling uses of honest learning. It was in the same year that he himself decreed the despoiling and destruction of Becket's shrine at Canterbury, that Henry uttered his well-known refusal to his courtiers to sanction the plundering of the universities, declaring that he judged no land in England better bestowed than that which had been devoted to such uses.

Towards the traditional learning and the ancient text-books the hostility of the new chancellor was, however, shown in an unmistakable manner. In 1535 the apprehensions and the hopes of the two contending parties in the university were alike set at rest by the promulgation of those famous Royal Injunctions which constitute the great boundary-line, in the history of Cambridge learning, between the mediæval and the more modern culture. These Injunctions required, in the first place, an unqualified acceptance of the royal supremacy, to which, as a necessary corollary, was attached the discontinuance of lectures on the canon law and the conferring of degrees in that faculty. They next enjoined that in each of the colleges there should be 'founded and continued for ever' '*two daily public lectures, one of Greek, the other of Latin.*' They abolished the *Sentences* as a text-book, substituting the

<small>The Royal Injunctions of 1535.</small>

Old and New Testaments, and directing that the exposition on these should be in harmony with the new exegesis. At the same time, it was ordered that students in arts should be instructed in the elements of logic, rhetoric, arithmetic, geography, music, and should study Aristotle and logic by the aid of the Humanists, putting aside 'the frivolous questions and obscure glosses' of the Schoolmen.

The college discipline was also found not incapable of amendment. Although, in his anxiety to regulate every detail, Bishop Fisher had carefully excluded 'fierce birds,'—a statute which was subsequently interpreted to include the most harmless of the feathered races, the thrush, the linnet, and the blackbird,—he had altogether failed to guard against the intrusion of a much more dangerous element,—the unqualified pensioner. The statute relating to pensioners had required that they should have furnished satisfactory evidence with respect to character, but it had not been deemed necessary to insert a similar requirement with respect to *attainments*, and an inlet was thus afforded at both colleges to a class whose ignorance was only equalled by their disinclination to study, and who, as it was soon found, were a scarcely less formidable element of demoralisation than the riotous and the dissolute. In less than twelve years after Fisher's death we accordingly find Ascham, in a letter to Cranmer, observing that, among the evils 'which proved great hindrances to the flourishing estate of the university,' none was more serious than the admission of those 'who were, for the most part, only the sons of rich men, and such

<small>Further reforms in college discipline.</small>

as never intended to pursue their studies to that degree as to arrive at any eminent proficiency and perfection in learning, but only the better to qualify themselves for some places in the State by a slighter and more superficial knowledge.' Of the general concurrence of the college authorities in Ascham's view, we have satisfactory proof in the fact that in the statutes given by King Henry to St. John's in the year 1545 an endeavour is made to remedy the above evil (so far, at least, as the college was concerned), by the insertion of a clause requiring that no pensioner should be admitted who did not already possess such a knowledge of Latin as would enable him to profit by the regular course of instruction, and prevent his proving an impediment to the progress of others.

These changes, necessary and inevitable although they were, did not fail to encounter a large amount of resistance. In the same year that the Royal Injunctions were promulgated, Alexander Alane, the nominee of Cromwell, appeared in Cambridge as duly elected 'King's scholar,' and expressly charged with the office of lecturing in the university on the Scriptures, and thus instructing his hearers in the theology of the German Reformers. His arguments, however, were at once called in question, and he was challenged to defend them in the schools. The salary which Cromwell had promised never reached him, while the hostility which confronted him in every direction was so marked that he deemed it prudent to quit the university. In the following year he appeared before Convocation and defended the doctrines of the Reformers; and it was

Alexander Alane appointed King's scholar.

on that occasion that Edward Fox, bishop of Hereford, when seeking to exculpate Alane, made his memorable admission that the laity were already more familiar with the Scriptures than the majority of the professed divines whom he addressed. In other words, the middle lay class now knew their Bible better than most men of university training and education. It is evident, however, that it was to theologians who had been educated at Cambridge that the nation now looked for authoritative guidance in matters of religious belief, when we note how largely the university was represented on the board of forty-six divines to whom was entrusted the compilation of the famous manual of theological doctrine of that time,—*The Institution of a Christian Man.*

So far as regarded the studies and discipline of the universities, the final dissolution of the monasteries and friaries was attended with but unimportant results. The latter were institutions, for the most part, out of all sympathy both with the new learning and the new belief, and they fell lamented only by the indigent and the superstitious. At Cambridge, however, the outward and visible traces of their overthrow were visible long afterwards. The map executed under the direction of Archbishop Parker in the year 1574 shows the sites and surrounding orchards of three out of the four foundations of the Mendicant Orders still unoccupied,—the house of the Augustinian Friars near the old Botanic Gardens, looking on to what is now Pembroke Street,—that of the Dominicans standing where Emmanuel College, with its gardens, was

Effects of the dissolution of the monasteries.

shortly to appear,—while a solitary small tenement in one corner of a broad expanse of orchard ground, traversed by the King's Brook, alone represents the once splendid buildings of the Franciscans.

The apprehension of being involved in a somewhat similar fate now gradually gave place at the universities to feelings of lively expectation.

<small>Gains of the colleges.</small>

Just as the most influential among the nobility and gentry had been bribed into acquiescence by the promise or the actual bestowal of the richest abbey lands, so the scholar and the Churchman were now induced to keep silence by the hope of seeing new and splendid homes of learning endowed from the monastic spoils. And as the confiscation of the estates of the alien priories under Henry V. had given birth to Eton and King's College,—while that of the lands of the smaller monasteries under Wolsey had resulted in the foundation of Cardinal College and of the grammar-school at Ipswich,—so, it was imagined, the final abolition of the monasteries would prove to the universities a yet more splendid gain. Nor were these hopes destined to be altogether disappointed. Queens' College, under the able rule of Dr. Mey, acquired for a small payment the site and somewhat ruinous premises of the Carmelites. Magdalene College was endowed partly from the property which Sir Thomas Audley had acquired by the confiscation of monastic lands, and partly from those which Hugh Dennis had designed for monastic use; while the very fabric of Trinity College was largely constructed out of the materials obtained by the demolition of the stately church and cloisters of the

Franciscans. That there was much to be deprecated in the aims whereby these momentous changes were brought about, and in the manner in which they were carried out, seems scarcely to admit of denial. But, on the whole, it seems no less undeniable that their preponderating result was for good rather than for evil, and a consideration of some of the chief characters who were largely formed under the influence of these changes can hardly fail to confirm us in such a conclusion. At St. John's, the names of John Madew, master of Clare Hall,—of John Redman of King's Hall, for a short time public orator, and the first master of Trinity,—of Robert Pember, the tutor of Ascham,—and of William Bill, who succeeded Redman in the mastership of Trinity, would alone have sufficed to establish the reputation of the society for scholarship and enlightened faith. But the two brightest ornaments of the college at this time were undoubtedly Roger Ascham and John Cheke. Of these, the former, renowned in his own day for his classical learning, still survives in the pages of his *Scholemaster* as one of our most sagacious and original thinkers on the subject of education; while the latter, who succeeded Alane as King's scholar, rendered a yet more direct service to the university by the energy and ability with which he revived the study of Greek,—the interest in which, since the time of Erasmus, seems at one time almost to have expired. Among those who shared his enthusiasm was William Cecil, afterwards Lord Burghley, for a short time college lecturer on Greek. With such ardour, indeed, did these three pursue

Leading characters in the university at this period.

the study of the masterpieces of Athenian eloquence, that, as we are told, they often lit their lamps before four o'clock, unable to await the break of day. Estimated by its services to learning, Queens' College might claim at this period a place second only to St. John's. Its most distinguished member was Sir Thomas Smith, whose services as a scholar to Greek learning and to constitutional history might seem as of but minor importance when compared with those which he subsequently rendered as a financier to the colleges at large. Like Cheke, he obtained the distinction of being appointed King's scholar, and a friendship was gradually formed between the two young scholars, which Smith himself on one occasion thus described to Gardiner:—'We are of the same age, and of like condition in life; our studies have been the same, and we are recipients of the same royal bounty; we have been engaged in a continual emulation with each other in the arena of intellectual achievement, but this rivalry, which is wont to kindle envy and strife between others, has hitherto only bound us more closely together in fraternal affection.' Among Smith's pupils were two who afterwards attained to high distinction, —these were John Ponet of Queens' and Walter Haddon of King's. Among members of other societies who afterwards rose to eminence, two names seem especially to call for note. The one was Nicholas Ridley, the newly elected master of Pembroke, often at that time to be seen pacing the orchard walk of his college, and sedulously committing to heart passages from a volume of the Pauline Epistles. The

Thomas Smith and John Cheke.

other was Matthew Parker, fellow of Corpus, who as a preacher had already gained a reputation second only to that of Latimer, but was now temporarily withdrawn from Cambridge, and filling the office of dean at the College of Stoke-by-Clare,—a foundation (long since extinct) for the education of the secular clergy.

But although the standard of scholarship was rising, and the promise of not a few of the younger students was singularly hopeful, the recent changes were telling with serious effect on the general prosperity of both universities.

Less favourable aspects of the period.

At Cambridge the embarrassment resulting from the decline in numbers was so serious that, in February 1538, a statute was promulgated whereby the students were required to discharge their functions in the schools for two years instead of one,—a measure rendered necessary by the fewness of those who were both of the requisite standing and in other respects qualified for the performance of these duties. Other measures plainly indicate the pressure resulting from an impoverished exchequer. The office of taxor to the university was abolished, his functions being superadded to those of the proctors. The 'useless books' in the library were sold. The amount contained in the 'common chest' of the university was found, on one occasion, to be less than £20, and it was necessary to borrow from other sources. The Hebrew and Greek lecturers in the university were, on two occasions, paid only by the expedient of suspending the mathematical lecturer for the current year, and appropriating his salary. It marked the turning-point in this depressing experience, when, in 1540, the five

Regius professorships were founded, representing the several subjects of Divinity, Civil Law, Physic, Hebrew, and Greek, and each endowed with a salary of £40. Ascham, writing to a friend only a few years after, gives an enthusiastic description of the change brought about by the creation of these august chairs. 'Cambridge,' he says, 'is quite another place, so substantially and splendidly has it been endowed by the royal munificence.' Aristotle and Plato are being read even by 'the boys,' although this, indeed, had already been the case at St. John's for some five years. 'Sophocles and Euripides,' he goes on to say, 'are more familiar authors than Plautus was in your time. Herodotus, Thucydides, and Xenophon are more conned and discussed than Livy was then. Demosthenes is as familiar an author as Cicero used to be; and there are more copies of Isocrates in use than there formerly were of Terence. Nor do we disregard the Latin authors, but study with the greatest zeal the choicest writers of the best period.' The first Regius professor of Greek was Cheke, and in conjunction with Smith he now proceeded on a somewhat bold innovation, namely, that of endeavouring to introduce a new method of pronouncing the language,—an idea for which Erasmus had already published suggestions. The method at that time in vogue was singularly monotonous and unpleasing, resulting, according to Ascham, either in 'a feeble piping like that of sparrows, or an unpleasant hissing like that of snakes.'[1] The new method was undoubt-

Foundation of the Regius Professorships.

Proposed changes in the pronunciation of Greek.

---

[1] On the method then in use, see author's *History of the University of Cambridge*, vol. ii. p. 54.

edly a great improvement. It was warmly sanctioned by the best scholars, and was already just making its way in the university, when Gardiner, who had succeeded to the office of chancellor, suddenly issued a decree, in May 1542, imperatively enjoining a return to the ancient practice. An animated pamphlet controversy, between Gardiner on the one hand, and Ascham and Smith on the other, now ensued. For a time, however, the chancellor's mandate prevailed, although not infrequently disregarded in actual practice. But, after his death, the voice of reason carried the day, and the Erasmian mode of pronunciation became generally adopted. In England, in the course of the seventeenth century, this method was, in turn, abandoned for the method now in use, which differs alike from that of Erasmus and that by which it was preceded.

During the academic year 1543–4, the office of vice-chancellor was filled by Smith, and to his practical good sense we may probably refer the passing in that year of a statute for the due matriculation and registration of students. Prior to that time the only formality observed had been that of an oath administered to all students above the age of fourteen by the head of the college or hall to which they belonged, whereby they pledged themselves to obey the authorities, preserve the peace, and defend the interests of the university. By the statute of 1544 the student was required to go before the registrary and give in his name, together with that of his tutor and that of his college, to pay the matriculation fees, and then, if of the required age, to take an oath binding him

Statute for matriculation of students.

to the observance of the laws, statutes, and privileges of the university, and to the maintenance of its honour and dignity.

On the present site of Magdalene College there formerly stood an ancient house, known as Buckingham College, which itself stood in the place of a yet older foundation designed by the Benedictines for the reception of members of their Order studying in the university. In the year 1542 Buckingham College was converted by Sir Thomas Audley into Magdalene College. Few courtiers or politicians had profited more largely by the plunder of the monasteries, and the original endowment was ample; but, from various causes, the revenues for some time proved insufficient for the maintenance of a master and eight fellows, as contemplated by the founder, and it was only by successive subsequent bequests that, in the course of the seventeenth century, the number of fellowships was raised to sixteen, and that of the scholarships to thirty-one. The original statutes of the college were first sanctioned by Philip and Mary in the year 1554, and, as may be easily conjectured, reflect none of that regard for the new learning which we find in the statutes of Christ's College and St. John's. Their most noteworthy feature is the powers and the large discretion which they assign to the master, and the almost entire freedom which he thereby acquires from responsibility to the governing body, it being apparently the design of the founder to place the college practically under the control of the successive owners of Audley End.

Foundation of Magdalene College, 1542.

The return of Parker to Cambridge, to succeed to the mastership of Corpus, and his election to the vice-chancellorship in the following year, were events of no ordinary importance in the history of the university. To his tact and good sense, in conjunction with the judicious advocacy of Smith and Cheke at Court (where the latter was now acting as tutor to Prince Edward), we must mainly attribute the fact that the ominous 'Act for the Dissolution of Colleges' passed so harmlessly over the Cambridge foundations. Fortunately the university managed to secure the appointment of not only Parker, but also of the wise and able Redman and good John Mey upon the Commission, both of whom proved no unskilful advocates. It was, however, a critical day for Cambridge when their whole number were summoned to Hampton Court to hear the royal decision. Along with the courtiers, some of whom Parker, in his description of the event, does not hesitate to characterise as 'ravening wolves,' they took their stand round the royal chair. King Henry, who, when not blinded by passion or prejudiced by personal dislike, could approve himself a capable and impartial judge, had already looked through the financial statement of each foundation with care. The indisputable evidence exhibited only a series of struggling societies, for the most part very inadequately endowed, where unobtrusive merit and genuine desire for learning were already too often robbed of a modest reward by the partialities of some too potent courtier or ecclesiastic. Henry himself was fain to confess that 'he thought he had not

Designs of the courtiers on the colleges defeated.

in his realme so many persons so honestly mayntayned in lyvyng bi so little lond and rent.' Something, indeed, he let drop about the necessity he found himself under of rewarding the servants of the State. But he added, says Parker, that 'he wold put us to our choyce wether we shulde gratifie them or no, and bad us hold our owne. With which wordes we were wel armyd and so departed.'

Although Trinity College claims King Henry as its founder, it probably lies under a far greater debt of obligation to Katherine Parr; and as the Lady Margaret had been moved by the representations and pleadings of John Fisher, so the employment of like means by Thomas Smith aroused the sympathies of Queen Katherine. In the year 1546 it became known that the master and fellows of the ancient foundation of Michaelhouse, and the master and scholars of the aristocratic society of King's Hall, had alike been summoned to deliver up their respective houses into the royal hands. And on the 19th of December 1546, the royal letters were granted for the foundation of a college of literature, the sciences, philosophy, good arts, and sacred theology; consisting of one master and sixty fellows and scholars, to be called 'TRYNITIE COLLEGE, within the towne and universitie of Cambrydge, of Kynge Henry the Eights foundacion.' No academic institution in Europe furnishes a more striking example of the change from the mediæval to the modern, from the Catholic to the Protestant, conception of education and learning. But not even in this instance could the courtier's greed be altogether evaded; and we

Foundation of Trinity College, 1546.

learn from a sermon by Thomas Lever that a considerable sum designed by the royal bounty for the college was, in this manner, diverted from its original purpose. Unlike Wolsey's great foundation at Oxford, Trinity could claim that its original society was composed exclusively of members of its own university. The mastership was bestowed on John Redman, who for the preceding four years had held the mastership of King's Hall; while several of the most distinguished fellows, and especially those best known as Greek scholars, came from St. John's. The first statutes, which were given in 1552, much resemble Bishop Fisher's later codes in their attention to points of detail; and in addition to this minuteness with respect to college discipline, and many unnecessary and irksome restrictions on the daily conduct of the students, there is also to be noted the large amount of attention given towards defining more accurately the duties of the numerous college officers. In one respect the code contrasts favourably with most other sixteenth century college statutes, in that the restriction whereby it was usually sought to maintain the balance between 'north' and 'south' does not appear, the only limitation of this character being of that more common kind requiring that not more than three fellows at any one time shall be natives of the same county. In the requirements with respect to the admission of scholars, a regulation, similar to that contained in the Johnian statutes of 1545 with reference to the admission of pensioners, is laid down; and the two provisions may probably be regarded as the earliest

Noteworthy features in its first statutes.

traces of the existence of an entrance examination. Candidates must possess such a knowledge of Latin and polite learning as will enable them to stand the test of the examinations in the hall, and to take part in the college disputations. The general scheme of study corresponds in the main with that laid down in the Edwardian statutes for the university.

CHAPTER VI.

FROM THE FOUNDATION OF TRINITY COLLEGE TO THE ACCESSION OF ELIZABETH.

THE diminution of numbers which followed upon the expulsion of the religious orders from the universities was in a great measure repaired by the increase in another class, which at first seemed likely materially to affect the general standard of attainment. The monk and the friar gave place to the schoolboy. Parents belonging to the more opulent classes began to send their sons as pensioners, feeling confident that they would now no longer be exposed to the proselytising activity of either Franciscan or Benedictine; knowing also that they would be watched over and cared for in the colleges; and, reassured on these points, not especially solicitous that their lads should become either accomplished scholars or profound theologians. 'There be none now,' said Latimer in 1549, 'but great men's sons in college, and their fathers look not to have them preachers.' Patronage now began also to exert its most pernicious influences. The acquirement of wealth had become more than ever a passion with the aristocracy; while with the mar-

marginal note: Abuses in the admission of students into the colleges.

ried bishop it was too frequently his first thought how to provide for his own descendants. Ascham, in a letter written two years before the delivery of Latimer's sermon, declared that 'talent, learning, poverty, and discretion all went for nothing in the college, when interest, favour, and letters from the great exerted their pressure from without.' While Thomas Lever, preaching at Paul's Cross in 1551, declared that one courtier was worse than 'fifty tun-bellied monks,' and that those who possessed influential connections were now not ashamed to usurp the college endowments and 'to put poore men from bare lyvynges.' It was only natural, accordingly, that men of mature years and ripe attainments should have begun to seek other spheres of labour; weary of a field where merit was becoming rare and rarer, chiefly owing to the fact that when it made its appearance it met with no reward. So, indeed, matters appear to have remained throughout the troublous times which preceded the accession of Elizabeth. Down to that date, says Huber in his well-known work on the English universities, the Reformation had inflicted on both Oxford and Cambridge 'only injury, both outward and inward.' More than one thoughtful contemporary observer would seem, in fact, to have been much of the same opinion. When, in the year of Elizabeth's accession, after a lengthened absence from Cambridge, Dr. Caius revisited the university, his surprise at the changes that had taken place, and his sense of the evils which had accompanied them, induced him to give them formal record in his history.

State of the university as described by Dr. Caius.

He missed, he tells us, the dignified elders of former times, proceeding with sedate countenance and stately mien to the disputations in the schools, attended by the chief members of their respective colleges, each in his distinctive academic dress, and preceded both going and coming by heralds. The undergraduates no longer respectfully saluted their seniors from afar and made way for them in the streets; many seemed to have altogether discarded the long gown and the cap. Their pocket-money, he learned, was no longer spent on books, their minds were no longer given to study, but both were alike devoted to dress and the adornment of their persons. They wandered about the town frequenting taverns and wine-shops; their nether garments were of gaudy colours; they gambled and ran into debt. Expulsions were not infrequent. Students, he was told, complained loudly that the generous patrons of learning of former times no longer existed; but he takes occasion to observe that it is first of all necessary that the requisite merit should make itself apparent, whereas many students only bring discredit on the university and load their patrons with shame.

Although Dr. Caius' description is characterised by something of exaggeration, it evidently points to a condition of things which no well-wisher to the university could regard with satisfaction. Nor can we doubt that this demoralisation was largely due to the circumstance which Ascham and Lever agreed in deploring, — namely, that the enthusiastic little band of scholars of which Cheke and Smith had been

Loss of the university's chief leaders.

the leaders was broken up, and that no worthy successors were now forthcoming who by their attainments and example might stimulate others to honourable exertion. In no sphere of labour, indeed, as academic history again and again shows us, is personal influence more potent for good or for evil than in universities.

The enactment of the statutes of 1549 effected some material changes in the constitution of the university, but they also deserve the praise bestowed upon them by Dean Peacock of being 'brief, distinct, and reasonable.' They were the result of the labours of men well acquainted with the state and needs of the whole community, among whom were Bishop Ridley, Sir Thomas Smith, Sir John Cheke, and Dr. Mey. To these statutes were added certain 'Injunctions,' or additions made by the commissioners in concert with the academic authorities. They are mainly devoted to defining with greater precision the duties of the university lecturers and the text-books to be used. The ancient *trivium* was completely recast, while grammar was altogether discarded,—Jesus College being the only foundation where it was still permissible to give instruction in the subject. In its place 'mathematics' appear as the initiatory study for the youth fresh from school; they were to be succeeded by dialectic, and this again by philosophy. Further instruction in philosophy, perspective, astronomy, and Greek took the place of the subjects of the old *quadrivium* or bachelor's course of study; while the master of arts, after the time of his regency had elapsed, was re-

The statutes of 1549.

quired, unless intending the study of law or medicine, to devote his attention solely to theology and Hebrew. Bachelors of divinity were required to hear a theological lecture daily; to respond once and dispute twice in theological questions; and to preach twice in Latin and once in English in St. Mary's Church. It was not until the student had attained to the full-blown dignity of doctor that the decision as to whether he should or should not continue to add to the stores of his already acquired knowledge was confided to his own discretion. A large number appear to have generally decided this question in the negative, but their conduct, as we shall shortly see, was regarded with much concern, if not actual disapproval, by the mentors of the university.

The low state of learning, and especially of theological learning, was regarded with much concern by Cranmer, and with a view to bringing about some improvement, he had recourse to the expedient of inviting over learned foreigners, especially those of the Zwinglian persuasion. Among their number was Paul Fagius, a divine of considerable eminence, who, through Cranmer's influence, was appointed reader in Hebrew to the university. He was carried off by death, in November 1549, a few days after his arrival in Cambridge. A somewhat longer tenure of office awaited Martin Bucer, who at the same time was appointed Regius professor of divinity, and whose incidental criticisms of what he observed in the university are valuable as those of a candid and judicious foreigner of unquestionable honesty of purpose. Bucer him-

Fagius and Bucer appointed professors.

self was in some measure an eclectic, and he had been untiring in his efforts to reconcile the two contending parties of Protestantism abroad. From the tone of his observations while in Cambridge, it is evident that he looked upon learning in the university as at a low ebb, and that he regarded the indolent fellows who were growing old on the different foundations as an incubus from which it would be well if the colleges could be relieved. His brief labours as a professor gave proof of no ordinary learning, and were characterised by a genuine modesty; but they were not suffered to pass unchallenged by theologians of the opposite school, and involved him in more than one painful controversy. It was perhaps well for his fame that he was carried off by sudden death within little more than twelve months after his arrival, and while a sense of his worth and learning was still the prevailing conviction of the university and the Church at large. 'The master workman,' exclaimed Parker, 'has fallen.'

The reappearance of Smith in Cambridge as Regius professor of the civil law was hailed with no little expectation by the students in that faculty, conscious as they probably were that the study was already on the wane, not merely in the university, but as the means to a professional career in the wider world without. The two orations which he delivered upon entering upon office, although characterised by his usual ability, could not impart new life to a branch of learning which was already, in a great measure, doomed. The students of the civil law continued to be but few, and those

State of the study of the civil law.

who embraced the profession of a civilian yet fewer. From the year 1544 to 1551 only one graduate proceeded to the degree of LL.D., and only eight to that of bachelor of laws. An endeavour was, indeed, made to give further encouragement to the study by the formation of a new legal college, which it was proposed to found by an amalgamation of Trinity Hall and Clare; but the scheme was strenuously and successfully opposed by the members of the latter society and ultimately abandoned.

Both the Protector Somerset and his rival, Northumberland, filled in succession the office of chancellor, but under neither did learning flourish.

<small>Chief incidents which followed upon the accession of Mary.</small> A scheme, it is true, was projected during the brief supremacy of the latter for the foundation of a college to be designated 'Edward's College,' and to be munificently endowed, but it never came to accomplishment. In the political commotion which followed upon Northumberland's endeavour to divert the crown from the rightful succession, Cambridge had its full share. It was in King's College that he was arrested, and it was from Cambridge that, along with Dr. Sandys, the master of St. Catherine's and vice-chancellor, who had imprudently advocated the cause of the usurper from the university pulpit, he was conducted in ignominy to the Tower. Thither, too, were conveyed John Bradford and Ridley; while Norfolk and Gardiner, liberated at the same time from their captivity within the same walls, resumed together with their liberty the offices they had formerly filled in connection with the university, the one as high-steward, the latter as

chancellor. The repeal of the Edwardian statutes followed almost immediately; and before another six months had passed, all the colleges, with the exception of Gonville Hall, Jesus, and Magdalene, had seen a change of heads. Parker, at Corpus, anticipated expulsion by resignation, and throughout Queen Mary's reign remained hid from the pursuit of his enemies in obscure retirement,—a leisure which he devoted to congenial studies, which afterwards bore good fruit for the Church. If, indeed, we were prepared to give unqualified acceptance to the assertions of Protestant writers, the 'Marian quinquennium' would appear to have been a period of almost unmitigated disaster for learning, and scarcely less detrimental to the material interests of the university. 'The two faire groves of learning in England,' wrote Ascham long after, 'were eyther cut up by the roote or troden downe to the ground and wholelie went to wracke'; while, with respect to his own college, he affirms that 'mo perfite scholars' were dispersed from St. John's 'in one moneth, than many yeares could reare up againe.' It is impossible, however, to conclude that these, and similar statements with which we meet in other writers, are not exaggerations, when we find that, according to the statistics of the *Grace Book*, there was at Cambridge a considerable increase in the number of those proceeding to the degrees of master and bachelor of arts. During the last five years of Edward's reign the aggregate number had been only 90 and 167 respectively; during the five years from 1553 to 1558 the corresponding numbers were 125 and 195. On the other hand, it cannot be denied that the changes introduced were retrograde in character and unfavourable to a real advance in knowledge. The old pronunciation of Greek was again prescribed, and probably for a time more successfully enforced. In the place of the Forty-two Articles, a syndicate, appointed by the senate, proceeded to draw up a series of fifteen articles embodying the distinctive tenets of Catholicism and the recognition of the papal supremacy, and condemning as 'pestiferous heresies' the dogmas of Luther, Œcolampadius, Zwinglius, and Bucer. The new articles were forthwith subscribed by the great majority of the resident electors in the university, and during the reign of Mary a like subscription was an indispensable condition of admission to degrees. Gardiner had scarcely carried these changes into effect, when he was carried off by death, 12th November 1555. He was succeeded in his office as chancellor by Cardinal Pole, who in the following year was also elected to the chancellorship of the university of Oxford. It does not appear that Pole ever visited Cambridge, and his interest was naturally more active in Oxford, where, as a student of Magdalen, he had passed some years and gained considerable credit. Both universities were in the following year subjected by him to another visitation, having for its express object the more complete establishment of the Catholic religion. In the meantime the burning of Cranmer, Latimer, and Ridley at Oxford, and that of John Hullier, a Protestant scholar and conduct of King's College, on Jesus Green at Cambridge, had brought home to both communities with terrible vividness the stern realities of the religious crisis. The Cambridge martyrs, one and all, died with a fortitude worthy of their cause; and many as have been the passages notable for their touching pathos which men of lofty nature have penned in the anticipation of death, the farewell to which Ridley gave expression, as his university and his ancient college of Pembroke, with its orchard walk, came back to his memory, is unsurpassed in its kind. In January 1557 another visitation of the university took place, the details of which have been preserved to us in a quaint and interesting account by John Mere, the registrary, and one of the esquire bedells of the university. They are chiefly noticeable as illustrations of the ceremonial and procedure observed by the visitors in carrying out their main object. One act, however, conspicuous from its wanton indecency and barbarity, cannot be altogether passed by. The remains of Bucer and Fagius were exhumed, chained like the bodies of living heretics to the stake, and publicly burnt on Market Hill.

The chief result of the visitation was a new body of statutes, generally known as those of Cardinal Pole. They were, however, designed to be only temporary, and proved in their actual result almost inoperative.

From these and similar reactionary or vindictive measures, it is a relief to turn to the one act which,

Dr. Caius refounds Gonville Hall, 1558. during the reign of Mary, conferred a real and permanent benefit on the university. This was the refounding of Gonville Hall by Dr. Caius, an eminent scholar and physician, who, by the practice of his profession, had acquired a considerable fortune. Although a Catholic, his religious prejudices were tempered by long residence abroad, by a wide erudition, and by much observation of men and affairs. He had studied anatomy under Vesalius at Padua, and had himself taught Greek at that famous university. With many of the most eminent scholars of France and Germany he was personally well acquainted. Dr. Caius had received his Cambridge education at Gonville Hall, and by his munificence the college was now reconstituted so as to consist of a master, thirteen fellows, and twenty-nine scholars. Of the fellowships, three represented the original foundation of Edmund Gonville and Bishop Bateman, three the new foundation of Dr. Caius, while the remaining seven derived their endowment from the joint bequests of the other minor benefactors. Himself a native of Norwich, it was his design chiefly to assist Norfolk and Suffolk men; but in other respects the statutes which he gave to the college in 1572 were equally distinguished by liberality and good sense, although, indeed, many of the regulations with respect to general discipline and pastimes must appear, like those of St. John's and Trinity, singularly irksome to a later generation. The three gateways, of Humility, Virtue, and Honour, which adorned the new buildings, were designed by Dr. Caius himself,—the last, in all probability, being in imitation of the ornamental designs of the silversmiths of Italy, with whose work he had become familiar during his residence in that country.

The royal favour, during the reign of Mary, was bestowed chiefly on Oxford; Trinity College, however, received a benefaction, and the building of its chapel was commenced. The queen's death, succeeded within a few hours by that of Cardinal Pole, ushered in a new state of things, and with the acceptance of the chancellorship by Sir William Cecil, it was felt that a new era had begun, and that the period of mere reaction was at an end.

CHAPTER VII.

THE UNIVERSITY DURING THE ELIZABETHAN ERA.

THAT the larger share of patronage bestowed on Oxford during Mary's reign was the result of the greater degree of favour with which Catholic doctrines were there regarded admits of no question. The special reputations of the two universities had greatly changed since the time when Lydgate boasted that 'of heresie Cambridge bare never blame.' The fame of Oxford, as a great centre of theological science and speculation, had long ago departed; while Cambridge, as a home of Reformation doctrine, might rival Wittenberg or Marburg. John Burcher, writing to Bullinger a few months after Bucer's death, and recommending Musculus as his successor, intimates that 'the Cambridge men will not be found so perversely learned as Master Peter found those at Oxford.' By 'not so perversely learned,' he explains, it is his design to indicate that tendency to so-called 'heretical' doctrine evinced by the rising scholarship of the university, which it had been Gardiner's first aim to repress and trample out. It might well appear only natural that Elizabeth should have been inclined to regard with marked

Cambridge more favourable to the Reformation than Oxford.

favour that university where the doctrines which she and her adherents supported found their earliest recognition and their ablest exposition in England. But the preference which she showed for Cambridge is really to be attributed to the good offices of William Cecil,—an influence not less productive of abiding benefit to the university than had been that of Bishop Fisher with the Lady Margaret. It is to Cecil's wise counsel and judicious co-operation from without, combined with Matthew Parker's untiring and unselfish labours within, that we must, in a great measure, attribute the steady, although not altogether uninterrupted, advance which the statistics of the university exhibit down to the close of the century,—an advance which may be broadly illustrated by a comparison of the number of those proceeding to the degree of B.A. in the academic year 1558–9 with that of the years 1570 and 1583. In the first-named year the number was only 28; in the latter years it was 114 and 277 respectively.

Increase of numbers in the university.

The return of the Marian exiles could hardly fail to be attended by circumstances of some difficulty. Their terms of expatriation had been passed amid privations and sufferings which gave peculiar intensity to their sense of wrong; and their conduct, when reinstated in office in their own country, was too often such as to suggest that a desire for retaliation,—to use no stronger term,—was their prevailing sentiment. They had also formed associations which affected not a little their theological sympathies. At Frankfort and at Strassburg, at Basel and at Zürich, they had received hospitality and aid which

Return of the Marian exiles.

were long remembered with gratitude, and which cemented still further their friendship for the theologians of Germany and Switzerland; while, with respect to not a few moot points in the Anglican ritual and the Anglican liturgy, they had exchanged views and arrived at conclusions which served still further to alienate them from all that savoured of the Roman doctrine. Of those who had formerly been active in the university, some of the most eminent, among whom were Sandys, Grindal, and Lever, came back to England, but not to Cambridge. But the two brothers, James and Leonard Pilkington, who had been members of the little church at Frankfort, and Roger Kelke, who had been residing principally at Zürich, together with many others of minor note, were once more to be seen in their former seats in hall and chapel, or moving through the streets of the university, with a sense of recovered influence and possessed by yet more ardent convictions than before. Some of them were avowed disciples of the doctrines taught at Geneva; others had espoused the less gloomy tenets of Zwinglius: both these sections now came more directly under the influence of the Scotch Presbyterianism; and from these several elements our English Puritanism arose. At Cambridge, however, they soon became aware of an opposing force which itself also represented three distinct elements: the influence of Elizabeth, desirous of holding the balance between contending parties, and with a real predilection for the Anglican ritual; that of Cecil, who, though not unfriendly to the more moderate Puritanism, drew back when he clearly saw

Conflict of opinions.

to what lengths the growing demands of that party would lead; and that of a large proportion of the members of the university who supported from genuine conviction the newly defined doctrine and discipline of the English Church, or who were really secretly inclined to Catholicism.

The administering of the oath of supremacy was almost immediately followed by the expulsion of most of the college heads. Three notable exceptions, however, remained. Dr. Pory managed to retain the mastership of Corpus, and subsequently became an active participant in the management of university affairs; Dr. Caius was suffered to remain unmolested at the head of the society which he had himself reconstituted; while at Peterhouse, Dr. Perne once more contrived to find the requirements of commissioners not beyond his conscientious compliance. A divine who, after acting as chaplain to Edward VI., had assented to the Catholic Articles of the year 1555, and who now was willing to subscribe to the Thirty-nine Articles of the English Church, could not, however, altogether escape the imputation of insincerity. The wits of the university coined a new Latin verb, *perno, pernare*, which meant, they affirmed, 'to change often.' It may perhaps be pleaded, in extenuation, that Dr. Perne, throughout the remainder of his career,—that is to say, until his death in 1589,—showed himself an able and judicious administrator; and that his thirty-six years' tenure of the mastership of Peterhouse was marked by a series of genuine services not only to his college and to the university, but also to the

Changes in the government of the colleges.

town and to the wider community of learning at large.

A series of politic measures on the part of the Crown reassured the moderate party in the university, and were approved by all but the most advanced section of reformers. The use of a Latin version of the authorised Prayer-Book in the college chapels was sanctioned.

<small>Other changes favourable chiefly to the study of theology.</small>

It was announced that, in order to give encouragement to meritorious students in theology, all prebends in the royal gift, or in that of the Keeper of the Great Seal, would in future be set apart for bestowal in the universities exclusively. The rights and privileges of the academic community in relation to the town authorities were renewed and extended. It became evident, in every way, that it was the design of Elizabeth and her ministers to make both universities efficient training schools for the clergy, and at the same time to bring them into close connection with the Crown. Such a design was in no small measure justified by the condition of the whole country, for learning in the Church had sunk to its lowest ebb. It was rarely at this time that the country rector or curate understood Latin, while the art of catechising and the cultivation of preaching talent were equally neglected. We have it on the high authority of Lever, that scarcely one in a hundred among the clergy was 'able and willing to preach the Word of God.' Nor was this neglect the result of the distracting influence of other studies. The study of the civil law, as we have already seen, was almost dying out; while the fast-increasing study of the common law found larger opportunities and encouragement in the capital. Medicine, also aided by new foundations in London, was in like manner attracted to the chief centres of population. Theology, with an adequate preparatory arts course, became accordingly the chief concern of the universities; and to train and send forth the well-instructed divine, learned in the original tongues of the Old and New Testaments, and competently read in the most authoritative patristic literature, became for the next three centuries almost the sole professed aim of either Oxford or Cambridge.

In August 1564, the queen's interest in the university was further indicated by a visit extending over five days, and characterised by a series of quaint ceremonies and not a few amusing incidents. In one of the 'acts' or disputations performed in the royal presence, a disputant took part who was destined to exercise no small influence over the subsequent history of the university. This was Thomas Cartwright, afterwards Lady Margaret professor, to whom the distinction may fairly be conceded of having been the founder of the Puritan party in England. The prejudices and antipathies of that party were now beginning to find very marked expression. Under their influence the 'superstitious' painted windows in the college chapels, whereon the use of prayers for the dead was enjoined, were pulled down; and on the appearance of Parker's celebrated *Advertisements*, designed to enforce a uniform church discipline (especially in the use of vestments) a considerable proportion of the

Visit of Queen Elizabeth.

Thomas Cartwright, and rise of the Puritan party.

societies of St. John's and Trinity sought to bring about the disuse of the surplice in the college chapel. These demonstrations were, however, sharply rebuked by Cecil, and Cartwright, the suspected ringleader, thought it prudent to retire for a time to Ireland. On the other hand, those suspected of Romanism were treated with yet greater severity. Dr. Baker, the provost of King's, on being detected harbouring a store of mass-books and Popish vestments, was arraigned before the Visitor of the college, and ultimately compelled to flee from the university. After the massacre of St. Bartholomew the aversion to the Catholic culminated. The acceptance of the oaths of supremacy and uniformity was rigorously enforced where before a merely external compliance had been all that was demanded. The English Catholic was compelled to seek for a university education abroad: at Louvain, or in the rising Jesuit school at Douay, or in the English College in Rome. With what results, as regarded his sympathies not only as a theologian, but as a patriot and a loyal subject, it is not necessary here to explain.

Some time before the year 1569 Cartwright returned to Cambridge. It appears to have been the wish of all parties to condone his past imprudence in consideration of his generally admitted learning and ability, and in that year he was elected Lady Margaret professor. His convictions were, however, as strong and his feelings as ardent as ever; and in his capacity as professor his leanings soon became unmistakably manifest. Elected to his chair in order that he

Cartwright appointed Margaret professor.

might defend the principles and discipline of the Reformed Church of England, he availed himself of the vantage-ground thus afforded him to impugn alike those principles and that discipline. Such conduct was at variance with the conditions implicitly involved in his acceptance of his office, and the effects were immediate and deplorable. The younger and more enthusiastic members of what we may now term the Puritan party rallied round him as their leader, while the seniors of that party signified their concurrence in his teaching by their discourses in the university pulpit or in the college chapel. In a very short time it became only too evident that it was the design of this party to bring about the overthrow of that Church of which Elizabeth and her ministers designed that the universities should be at once the nurseries and the bulwarks. They derided the use both of the surplice and of the square college cap; they refused to kneel at communion; they challenged the interpretation placed by the liturgy on the sacrament of the Lord's Supper; they inveighed against university degrees, and more particularly against theological degrees, declaring it to be an unwarrantable assumption on the part of academic authorities to profess to determine who should and who should not be the religious instructors of the laity; and, finally, while denouncing the whole order of ecclesiastical dignities, themselves put forth theories which glanced not obscurely at the spiritual supremacy of Elizabeth herself as Head or Governor of the Church. The chief authorities in Church and State could not disguise from themselves

Effects of his teaching.

the fact that it was theories such as these, and the controversies by which they were attended, that had already imperilled the interests of more than one Continental university. Before, indeed, Elizabeth's reign was over, the same theories proved almost fatal to the interests of several more. They drove a whole body of professors from Königsberg and seriously diminished the number of its students. They filled Heidelberg with tumult, not unaccompanied by actual bloodshed. They rent Hesse into two rival factions, each with its own university. They entailed scarcely less disastrous results upon the universities of Paris, Marburg, Jena, and Frankfort.

Examples such as these, though present to the minds of only a certain proportion of the seniors of Cambridge at this period, could not fail, wherever recognised, to furnish an argument of considerable weight, the cogency of which it is impossible even now to deny. Among those to whom they seem to have appealed with special force was Whitgift, whose experience of academic life and discipline was considerable. Originally a member of Queens' College in the time of Dr. Mey, he had migrated from thence to Pembroke, where he had been a pupil of John Bradford. From Pembroke he had been elected to a fellowship at Peterhouse, where, under the kindly protection of Dr. Perne, he had succeeded in escaping molestation during the reign of Mary, and ever since the restoration of Protestantism, had been rising steadily in the good opinion of the university and in favour with its all-potent chancellor. A sermon which he preached at St. Mary's, in 1560,

<small>John Whitgift.</small>

seems to have first brought him into general notice, and attracted no little admiration. In 1563 he was appointed to the Lady Margaret professorship; and after a brief tenure of the mastership of Pembroke, was promoted, in 1567, to that of Trinity. In the same year he vacated the chair of the Lady Margaret professorship for that of the Regius professor of divinity. A sermon which he subsequently preached at Court so effectually won the queen's approval that he was forthwith sworn in as one of the royal chaplains. His own religious views at this time seem to have inclined him to Calvinism, and there appears to be no reasonable doubt but that he and the party whom he led were actuated more by a desire to keep the university free from religious controversy than by any arbitrary notion of imposing their own religious views on others. The constitution of the Church having been definitely framed, and the doctrinal teaching of the university being assumed to be in harmony therewith, they foresaw nothing but harm as likely to result from a reopening of those numerous questions which a discussion of the Puritan standpoint involved.

Cartwright's conduct was, in the first instance, made a matter of formal complaint by Chaderton, the president of Queens'. It next met with severe condemnation from Grindal, the archbishop of York, whose sympathy with Puritan views was generally admitted. Ultimately, in order to mark the dissatisfaction of the authorities, when Cartwright himself sought to proceed to the degree of D.D., it was decided by a vote of the *Caput*, or governing body, that he should not be admitted. On

Measures against Cartwright.

THE ELIZABETHAN ERA. 123

this, Cartwright appealed to Cecil, and although that eminent statesman was far from unfriendly to the Puritan cause, he declined actively to intervene as chancellor. The authorities next proceeded to suspend Cartwright from his office as professor, and to withhold the payment of his salary. The final measure was his deprivation, in September 1571, of his fellowship at Trinity by Whitgift.

This rigorous action on the part of the university authorities had, however, been carried into effect in direct opposition to the views of the majority of voters in the regent-house,—in other words, of the younger masters of arts,—and in order to avert a like contest on future occasions, the Heads now proceeded to introduce into the statutes two innovations of primary importance. By the first the election of the *Caput*, by the second the election of the vice-chancellor, were practically withdrawn from the regents and non-regents, and vested in the Heads. After this almost decisive victory over the Puritan party, the authorities and their supporters further proceeded to remodel the statutes of the university. Their innovations were not carried into effect without strenuous opposition on the part of their antagonists, who addressed more than one remonstrance to the Crown; but eventually, in September 1570, the code known as the Elizabethan statutes received the royal assent, having been, as the preamble explicitly declares, designed and framed 'on account of the again increasing audacity and excessive licence of men.' The whole tendency of these statutes was to substitute for what had before been a liberal

Enactment of the Elizabethan Statutes.

and fairly representative academic constitution one which practically transferred the administration into the hands of an oligarchy. This is especially to be noted in the new regulations introduced for the election of the proctors,—functionaries of far greater importance in those days than in the present, and at that time invested with powers and duties which have led to their being styled 'the tribunes of the people.' Before 1570 their election had been, like that of the *Caput*, entirely in the power of the regents. It was now enacted that they should be nominated according to a cycle of colleges, the regents retaining only the right of approving the candidates thus brought forward. At the same time, the functions of the proctors themselves were so materially circumscribed that their office henceforth lost much of its ancient importance. The order of studies, and the succession of lectures and exercises for different classes of students and graduates, were left in nearly the same state, though somewhat more strictly defined, as in the statutes already in force. But the conditions of graduation, at least for the superior degrees, were made generally more severe, both with respect to time and exercises. All graces for dispensations with respect to these latter points were not only forbidden, but declared to be null and void if passed,—a proviso which threatened to deprive the university of what, it can scarcely be doubted, is one of the most graceful and appropriate functions of such a body, namely, that of extending recognition to distinguished merit, in whatever quarter it may present itself. The period of the necessary regency of masters of arts,—that is, the time during which they were required to be actually engaged in teaching,—was extended from two to five years, after which time they became *ipso facto* non-regents. The powers and jurisdiction of the chancellor were but little modified. It was, however, enacted that the proceedings of his court should be regulated by the principles of the civil law; that they should be prompt and expeditious; and that all cases should, if possible, be decided within five days. He possessed the power of punishing all members of the university, whether graduates or undergraduates, by suspension from their degrees, imprisonment, or any lighter punishment, at his sole discretion; but he could not expel a scholar or student, or imprison a doctor or head of a house, without the concurrence of the major part of the heads of houses.

Five years after these statutes had become law, the requirements with respect to time and exercises, in cases where degrees were to be conferred on non-residents, came again under consideration, and were so far modified that it was decided that dispensations might be granted from such requirements in the case of those who were already masters of arts or bachelors of law or physic, 'whose learning and probity of life were known to the university,' but who, 'being hindered by their various employments,' could not be present at the examinations required by statute. Had this concession received no wider interpretation than its authors designed, it would probably have proved a judicious and beneficial enactment; but, as it proved, its permissive character was gradually wrested into a general proviso whereby the requirements for the higher degrees lost nearly all their value and significance. In the case of members of the other university, or of eminent foreigners, the difficulty was met by the expedient of 'mandate degrees,' or degrees conferred by the royal command in response to the petition of the university that the requisite dispensation might be granted, 'any statute to the contrary notwithstanding.'

With this and a few other unimportant exceptions, the Elizabethan statutes continued to be the governing code of the university for nearly three centuries; too often arresting, by unwise and arbitrary restrictions, the progress of improvement in the system of academic instruction; and occasionally, where their provisions stood too manifestly in conflict with external requirements and changes of thought, becoming a dead letter, formally accepted, but practically ignored.

The new statutes were not imposed on the university without demonstrations of the strongest dislike and dissatisfaction on the part of the minority; and Whitgift's position, as their chief promoter, was rendered for a time so irksome and difficult that he even conceived the design of resigning his mastership and quitting the university. Counter-influences, however, and the intervention of Cecil (now Lord Burghley) induced him to forego his purpose, and his residence at Cambridge was prolonged for another six years, greatly to the advantage of the society over which he ruled and of the university at large.

The disposition towards toleration received a further check when the news of the massacre of St. Bartholomew arrived in England. It had for some time been rumoured that Dr. Caius, like

Persecution of Dr. Caius.

Dr. Baker, had in his possession, in his rooms in Caius College, a collection of ornaments, books, and vestments, such as were used in the celebration of the Roman religious services. Respect for his character, attainments, and position had probably hitherto led the authorities to overlook the matter; but he was now compelled to submit to the indignity of having his privacy forcibly invaded by the vice-chancellor and other of the Heads, and seeing the whole collection brought forth and publicly burnt in the court of his own college. That he felt this treatment keenly is plain from his own account of the occurrence; and grieved, as he also appears to have been, at the prevailing indifference to learning that characterised the younger students generally, he retired to London, where he beguiled the closing months of his life (he died 29th July 1573) by writing his *History of the University*. The death of Parker, in May 1575, was a yet more signal blow to the community. Notwithstanding the toils and anxieties of the primacy, and the virulent attacks of the Puritan party, his care for Cambridge had remained undiminished. It was visibly proved by the altered aspect of one of the principal academic thoroughfares, and by a noble benefaction to the public library. On the site now occupied by the senate-house and the open space in front there stood at that time a number of humble tenements, the residences of townsmen, which altogether intercepted the view of the Schools from Great St. Mary's. Of these the greater proportion remained standing until the erection of the senate-house in 1722. By Parker's

His death.

Death of Archbishop Parker.

generosity, however, a sufficient number were now purchased from the authorities of King's College and Corpus to admit of the opening up of a new street, known as University Street, and also as the Regent Walk, which from that time until 1722 formed the main approach to the Schools. In addition to this, says Strype, he repaired the Common Schools, 'greatly fallen then into decay, and wanting both lead, timber, and roofing.' Yet another two years and Whitgift exchanged Cambridge as a sphere of labour for the diocese of Worcester. His departure was sincerely lamented by not a few; and it says much for the general impression produced by his administration, whether as chancellor or as a college head, that on his departure he was attended from the gates of Trinity to the end of the first stage of his journey by a lengthened cavalcade, consisting, according to his biographer, not only of the heads of houses and chief members of the academic body, but, if the narrator may be trusted, of every gownsman or townsman who could manage to borrow a horse.

It was not until after Whitgift's departure and his elevation to the primacy in 1583 that the activity of the Cambridge Puritans reached its culminating point. There were those among them who were still not without hopes of being able to carry into effect, within the Church itself, those modifications and changes which they afterwards embodied in their own organisations as Separatists. Such was at first the design of Walter Travers, a fellow of Trinity, and one of those whom Whitgift had deemed it imperative, for the interests of the college

Increased activity of the Puritans.

and its peace, to compel to withdraw from residence. In 1574 Travers published his celebrated treatise, the *Disciplina*, which Cartwright, upon his retirement to Geneva, proceeded to translate into English. The *Disciplina* went through numerous edi-
<small>The Disciplina of Walter Travers.</small> tions, and in 1644, under the name of the *Directory*, reappeared as a recognised manual of Puritan church government; its primary object was to set forth a system of Church discipline such as the writer conceived was in harmony with Scriptural teaching. That it was a direct blow at the existing organisation of the Church of England and at the Royal Supremacy itself admits of no question. Another member of the university who, like Cartwright and Travers, was compelled to seek
<small>William Ames, Robert Browne, and John Smith.</small> safety in exile, was William Ames of Christ's College, a scholar whose doctrinal tenets alone, if we may accept the statement of his biographer, prevented his election to the mastership. He retired eventually to Franeker, where he was appointed professor of theology, a post which he continued to hold for a space of twelve years, teaching with so much success that students were attracted to that remote university not only from all Flanders, but also from Poland, Hungary, and even Russia.

Others withdrew, not, indeed, under compulsion, but from a sense of being out of sympathy with the prescribed order of things and seeking a freer atmosphere. Among them was Robert Browne, a nephew of Lord Burghley's. He was a member of Corpus College, and along with Harrison, another member of the same society, he emigrated to Middelberg, in Zealand, and on his return to England became the founder of the sect of the Independents. But even at Middelberg the right of private judgment, which Browne had so dogmatically asserted, was turned against himself, and his followers separated into two distinct bodies. Such, again, were John Smith, a fellow of Christ's College, and George Johnson, another member of that foundation, who initiated conjointly a similar movement at Amsterdam. To the former belongs the distinction of having founded the sect known as the General Baptists. Between him and Johnson there soon also arose irreconcilable differences of opinion, and agreement was only restored by the expulsion of the latter from the church at Amsterdam. Of the potency of the disintegrating forces which Cartwright's influence and example had set in motion few at Cambridge could, by this time, have felt much doubt. In 1584, the appearance of an edition of Travers' *Disciplina* (as translated by Cartwright) from the University Press itself, filled Whitgift with alarm and indignation, and he caused the whole impression to be forthwith seized and destroyed.

The foundation of Emmanuel College by Sir Walter Mildmay gave further evidence that the more moderate Puritans, however much they might dislike the use of Latin prayers, despise degrees in divinity, and object to the surplice, were not altogether prepared to desert their university. Sir Walter was a diplomatist of approved fidelity and discretion. He was also treasurer to the royal household, and in the year

Foundation of Emmanuel College, 1584.

1566 succeeded to the office of Chancellor of the Exchequer. He had been educated at Christ's College, and although he left Cambridge without taking a degree, he appears to have retained throughout his life a love for classical learning and a warm interest in the welfare both of his college and of the university. In the month of January 1584 we accordingly find Elizabeth granting to her trusted adviser a charter empowering him and his heirs 'to erect, found, and establish for all time to endure, a certain college of sacred theology, the sciences, philosophy and good arts, of one master and thirty fellows and scholars, graduate or non-graduate, or more or fewer, according to the ordinances and statutes of the same college.' Subsequent reports which reached the ears of Elizabeth roused her suspicions as to the designs even of one whose loyalty had been so long approved. When Sir Walter presented himself on one occasion at Court, his royal mistress openly taxed him with having been engaged in founding a Puritan college. He gravely protested that nothing could be further from his design than to countenance aught which contravened the established laws. He had, he said, but ' set an acorn,' and ' God alone knew what would be the fruit thereof when it became an oak.' The statutes of the new foundation, to which Elizabeth gave her sanction, cannot be said to betray any such design as that imputed to Sir Walter. The conception is that of a training school for the ministry exclusively; while, as regards discipline, the provisions are little more than a transcript of those for Trinity College. That the prevailing tone of the college was intensely Puritan admits, however, of no question. The first master, the eminent Laurence Chaderton (one of the translators of the Bible), who filled the office for thirty-six years, gave on more than one occasion ample proof of his sympathies with the Puritan party. Thomas Hooker, John Cotton, Thomas Shepard, and not a few other names which occupy a conspicuous place in the pages of Cotton Mather's *New England*,—among them the founder of Harvard College,—were some of the earliest who received their education within its walls. At the commencement of the seventeenth century, the practical exemplification which the college gave of the principles laid down in the *Disciplina* was so marked as to evoke a formal protest. The chancel of its unconsecrated chapel looked north. The society used its own form of religious service, discarded surplices and hoods, was neglectful even of the cap and gown, and had suppers on Fridays; while the devout Anglican was scandalised by the reports that reached him of the manner in which its members celebrated the most sacred of all the sacraments. One novel feature in the statutes, especially introduced by the founder himself, was probably a wise innovation. Fellows of the society were forbidden to hold their fellowships for more than a year after admission to their doctor's degree. 'We would not,' were the words of Sir Walter, as embodied in the statute, 'have any fellow suppose that we have given him, in this college, a perpetual abode.' In the reign of King Charles, John Preston, the master, aided by the duke of Buckingham,

<small>Limitation imposed on tenure of fellowships.</small>

succeeded in getting this statute repealed. It was re-enacted by the Long Parliament, but finally set aside after the Restoration. Under Preston's administration, the college enjoyed, in the early part of the seventeenth century, a high reputation for its studious and somewhat austere discipline, and appears to have received the main support of the Puritans. The entries ranged from fifty to seventy per annum, a larger admission, whether relatively to the university total or to subsequent times in the history of the college itself, than has ever been the case since.

No English theologian at this period enjoyed a higher reputation among Continental scholars than William Whitaker, the master of St. John's, and Regius professor of divinity, although carried off at the comparatively early age of forty-six. His reputation rested to no small extent on his writings against Bellarmine,—performances which elicited the highest praise from scholars like Joseph Scaliger and theologians like Andrew Melville. His sympathies were mainly with the moderate Puritans; and St. John's, throughout his mastership, continued to be a noted centre of that party. Secret synods, it was rumoured, were held within its walls, designed for carrying into practice the principles of the *Disciplina*, and attended by Cartwright himself and other nonconforming ministers from Northamptonshire and the adjacent counties.

_{William Whitaker, master of St. John's.}

Within the universities, however, Puritanism had now to contend not only with the Anglican party which supported the Church discipline, but with a growing Arminian party, which, sometimes in alliance with the

_{Rise of an Arminian party in the university.}

Anglican discipline, and sometimes in opposition to it, disavowed the tenets of Calvinism. Foremost among the assertors of these new doctrines was Peter Baro, a Frenchman by birth, who, on the joint recommendation of Burghley and Perne, had been appointed to the Lady Margaret professorship. One of his foremost supporters was William Barret, a fellow of Caius College, who, by a bold attack in a university sermon on Calvinistic doctrine, evoked a memorable discussion, which resulted in the Lambeth Articles. Another eminent member of this party was Richard Bancroft, who, after filling for some time with considerable success the office of tutor in Jesus College, was appointed chaplain to Whitgift. As yet the Calvinistic party was sufficiently strong, not only to carry the promulgation of the Lambeth Articles, but also to oust Baro from his professorship. But the latter measure was not carried without a strong protest from Burghley, and also from Harsnet, afterwards archbishop of York, and the celebrated Andrews, both fellows of Pembroke.

Contest between Arminians and Calvinists.

Such are the chief features in the history of the university in the reign of Elizabeth. It had been decided that Cambridge should be mainly a school of divinity, and it had also been decided that the doctrine taught in her schools should be defined and prescribed beforehand. The results of this policy were such as we can now see to have been inevitable. The main interest having centred in the discussion of theological questions, whatever was taught of liberal learn-

General results of the Elizabethan policy in the university.

ing sank to an almost lifeless tradition, while the fetters placed upon such discussion provoked from time to time a more or less stubborn resistance and bitter controversies. To silence these controversies, deprivation and expulsion were the ordinary expedients, the victims of which, betaking themselves to distant towns or to the Continent, became the founders of organisations whose whole spirit was conceived in opposition to the creed and teaching of the two English universities. It afforded but a slight counterbalancing influence to these unfriendly communities, that Trinity College, Dublin, founded in 1591, was, as Fuller terms it, *colonia deducta* from Cambridge, its statutes being modelled on those of the parent university, while its first five provosts were all Cambridge men.

From such a retrospect, it is a relief to turn to one ably devised measure which, by its operation, so materially improved the condition of the colleges, that the struggling communities whose condition Latimer and Lever had depicted with so much pathos appeared to Peter Baro and other writers towards the close of the century as already in the possession of abundant revenues. For this change the university was mainly indebted to the foresight and ingenuity of Sir Thomas Smith, who, by the Act for 'The Maintenance of the Colleges in the Universities,' made it lawful that in all new leases issued by the colleges it should be made obligatory on the lessee to pay 'one-third part at least' of the old rent '*in corn or in malt.*' At the same time, the wheat was never to be reckoned as

Sir Thomas Smith's Act for the maintenance of colleges.

equivalent in value to more than 6s. 8d. per quarter, nor the barley at more than 5s. The subsequent depreciation in the value of the precious metals, and the rapid rise in the price of corn,—changes which Smith, who was a sagacious economist, had probably to some extent foreseen,—combined to render this proviso an important means of revenue,—the one-third rental payable in corn (which, in conformity with the Act, could only be assessed at a fixed value) rising in time to be a much more fruitful source of income than the remaining two-thirds.

The foundation of Sidney Sussex College in 1596, by Frances, countess of Sussex, the aunt of Sir Philip Sidney, afforded another outward sign of the great revolution of the century, the college having been built on the site of the ancient friary of the Franciscans. In the year 1599 the buildings were completed, and eleven fellows, chosen from different colleges, were appointed. The original statutes were little more than a transcript of those of Emmanuel; but it must not be left unnoted that Sidney was the first Cambridge college which opened its fellowships to students of Scottish or Irish birth,—requiring only that such candidates should previously have studied six years in the university, and should not be below the standing of bachelor of arts.

Foundation of Sidney Sussex College, 1596.

The death of Burghley in the year 1599 deprived the university of its best protector; and though neither Essex nor Robert Cecil was wanting in solicitous care for its interests, the loss remained irreparable. The promul-

Relations between the university and the townsmen.

gation of the Lambeth Articles of 1595 had been followed by a brief lull in theological controversy, succeeded, however, by a long and bitter contention between the academic and the town authorities. The vice-chancellor, Dr. John Jegon, and the Mayor became involved in a singularly undignified dispute concerning precedence. The ill feeling thus excited found notable expression on the part of the students in a college play, entitled *Club Law*, lampooning the Mayor and the burgesses. If the formal plaint of the latter to the Privy Council is to be trusted, they were not only ridiculed on the stage, but also singled out by the graver members of the community as objects of sarcasm and innuendo in the pulpit,—'in publick sermons.' But from these and similar manifestations of feeling, which reflected but little credit on either party, the attention of both the university and the town was now called away by the accession and arrival of the new monarch, and the fresh hopes and expectations to which that event gave rise.

CHAPTER VIII.

FROM THE DEATH OF ELIZABETH TO THE RESTORATION.

THE lively expectations formed alike by the Catholic and the Puritan on James' assumption of the royal authority in England were equally doomed to disappointment; but for a few weeks the feelings of the Anglican party at Cambridge were those of considerable anxiety. Dr. Neville, the master of Trinity College, who bore the congratulations of the archbishops and bishops to the king in Scotland, was outstripped by the Puritan deputation; and although James' answer was reassuring, there was no little misgiving as to how far other influences might not prevail when he had crossed the Tweed. If the 750 ministers who signed the so-called Millenary Petition could have gained their object, the policy which Whitgift and Burghley had striven to carry into effect would have been reversed, and the colleges at both universities would have suffered a serious diminution in their resources by the restoration of the impropriate tithes to their original use. It was not until after the Hampton Court Conference that the Church party at Oxford and at

Expectations of parties at the accession of James.

Cambridge felt that the danger they apprehended was at an end.

The death of Whitgift, in February 1603-4, was a signal loss to Cambridge, but his place was in a great measure supplied by Bancroft, between whom and James a perfect understanding appears at this time to have existed.

Influence of Archbishop Bancroft at Cambridge.

The appearance, in August, of a series of new canons ecclesiastical, imposing uniform compliance in the wearing of the surplice on all colleges and halls, was among the earliest indications of the ascendency of Bancroft's influence. Both Emmanuel and Sidney, sorely against the will alike of their Heads and of the majority of their members, were constrained to give way. 'God grant,' wrote Samuel Ward, the Puritan master of Sidney, in his Diary, 'that other worse things do not follow the so strict urging of this indifferent ceremony!' In the following year, a further step in the requirement of strict theological conformity was made by the demand of a solemn declaration of adherence to the episcopal form of government, and to the liturgies of the Church of England, from all proceeding to *any university degree;* while, in 1613, a royal mandate made subscription to the Three Articles peremptory on the part of all admitted to the degree of B.D., or to that of doctor in any faculty. The primary design of these several measures was undoubtedly to strengthen the connection between the Crown and the universities, and to constitute the latter the special guardians of the theory of the royal supremacy in matters of religious belief. In harmony with this aim was the view that the direct representation of the universities in Parliament was both necessary and desirable. It was chiefly through the efforts of Sir Edward Coke that, in March 1603–4, this privilege was first conferred,—Oxford and Cambridge each receiving the right of returning two burgesses, whose special function it was to be to inform Parliament 'of the true state of the university and of every particular college.' The conduct of the Heads in relation to this new and important privilege exposed them to no little unpopularity. According to the terms in which the privilege had been accorded to the university, it was beyond question that it was designed that the election of the university representatives should be *more burgensium;* but in the year 1614, the privileges of the general body were audaciously challenged, and it was determined by the vice-chancellor, Dr. Corbet, master of Trinity Hall, in conjunction with nine other Heads, that 'every election and nomination of burgesses of the parliament then and thereafter, should be made according to the form of election of vice-chancellor, after the delivery of the king's writ by the sheriff to the vice-chancellor.' In other words, just as the members of the senate had already been virtually deprived of the privilege of choosing the candidates for the office of vice-chancellor, so it was now sought to deprive them of their new privilege of choosing the candidates for the honour of representing them in Parliament. It was not until three successive communications had been addressed to them by their chancellor, at this time the earl of Northampton, that the *Caput* was at length compelled to recognise the fact that the original conditions of the privilege were incompatible with their design. When the next election took place, the prevailing sense of the constituency with respect to the conduct of the Heads found free expression; and as the result, Sir Francis Bacon, the attorney-general, and Sir Miles Sandys were returned by a large majority, while the two Heads who ventured to appear as candidates obtained only seventy-four and sixty-four votes respectively. The great name of Bacon thus stands associated with the political rights of the university, although the services he rendered in this capacity seem insignificant when compared with those which the publication, some ten years later, of his *De Augmentis* rendered to the cause of intellectual freedom and education at large. Much, indeed, as he deprecated the contentions prevailing in the university concerning non-essentials in doctrine, and the narrow spirit of her studies, his loyalty to Cambridge and his zeal for her interests are matters which admit of no question.

The rebuff which the Heads received in their endeavour to tamper with the newly conferred fran-
Arbitrary rule chise was, however, an exceptional ex-
of colleges. perience, and the despotic spirit which they thus collectively exhibited in relation to the university reappears, in not a few instances, and sometimes in a yet more marked degree, in their individual rule of their respective colleges. Occasionally, indeed, a Head's sense of irresponsibility was shown in his supine neglect of the interests of the

society over which he ruled, but far more frequently by the inquisitorial severity with which he sought to impress his own views on all beneath him. According as he was a north or south countryman, a Calvinist or an Arminian, a supporter of the Court and the royal prerogative, or of the still growing Puritan party, his predilections would be manifested with but little reserve. It was thus that each college too often became a narrow exclusive community, where local antipathies and religious or political animosities were fostered and developed, and that catholic interchange of thought and feeling which it is the first function of a university to promote was effectually checked. A passing tribute is consequently all the more due to those few eminent men who, while their rule of the several societies over which they ruled was characterised neither by indifference nor fanaticism, were also distinguished by their care for the general interests and well-being of the whole university. Among their number was Roger Goad, who, from 1570 to 1610, held the provostship of King's. In the earlier years of his long rule he had been fiercely assailed by some of the younger fellows who represented the Puritan faction in that society. He proved, however, completely victorious in the struggle, and his subsequent rule was attended with the utmost advantage and credit to his college and to the university. Dr. Neville, who held the mastership of Trinity from 1593 to 1615, reaped the fruits of the judicious administration of Whitgift and Still. The society was free from domestic dissension. The finances

Eminent heads:
Roger Goad,
Dr. Neville.

were in a satisfactory condition. Theological contention was discouraged and kept in check. On succeeding to his new post, Neville very soon conceived, and lived to see carried to successful completion, the grand design (on which he himself expended no less than £3000) whereby, for a mass of irregular and unsightly buildings, was substituted an erection which an Oxford contemporary somewhat hyperbolically described as—

'the wonderment
Of Christendom and eke of Kent.'

The more general effects of Neville's administration are to be recognised in the great increase which took place in the numbers of the college. In 1617 they had risen to 340, while those of St. John's were only 205,—a disparity much beyond that which obtained towards the close of the century. From this time, however, Trinity may be looked upon as taking up that leading position among the Cambridge societies which only one other society had ever been able even to contest. 'Neville,' says one who was an undergraduate of the college during his mastership, 'never had his like in that orb for a splendid, courteous, and bountiful gentleman.'

Dr. Davenant, at Queens' College, and John Preston, who, after an eminently successful career as a college tutor on the same foundation, succeeded in 1622 to the mastership of Emmanuel, were also able and successful administrators. Not less so were Andrewes and Harsnet at Pembroke,— of whom the former was early distinguished by his

Dr. Davenant, John Preston.

singular ability as an instructor of theological students in the special duty of catechising; while the latter, equally noted for capacity, earned no less distinction, on the one hand by his courageous advocacy of Arminian tenets against the prevailing Calvinism, on the other by his equally courageous denunciation of the spreading belief in witchcraft in opposition to the gloomy creed of Puritanism.

Of the great influence for good or evil wielded by men invested with such authority, we have examples of a very different kind in the rule of Dr. Kelke at Magdalene (1559-1575) and that of Dr. Barwell at Christ's (1582-1609). The misrule of the former nearly brought about the financial ruin of the college. The inefficiency and supineness of the latter would probably have been attended by yet graver consequences, had it not been for the respect and popularity commanded by the teaching of the celebrated William Perkins, who about the same period filled the offices of tutor and lecturer at Christ's College, and was also a much admired and eminently successful preacher.

Although the state of studies throughout the university was such that it could not fail to evoke the censure of the great philosopher of the time, as at once defective and wrongly conceived, it seems to have been in perfect agreement with the views of the pedantic monarch. James delighted in theological disputation; and in such logomachies the Cambridge schoolmen were, from long practice, accomplished adepts. His admiration of these encounters in the schools was, however, surpassed by his delight in witnessing the

College plays: Ignoramus; Pilgrimage to and Return from Parnassus.

dramatic performances in the colleges. With one of these performances, entitled *Ignoramus*, given in Clare Hall on the occasion of a royal visit in March 1615, he was so well pleased that he paid the university another visit two months later, in order to witness the play a second time. Most of these compositions veiled a somewhat deeper design than that of mere amusement; and *Ignoramus* seems to have been conceived by its accomplished author as a means of casting ridicule on the profession of the Common Law, the rapid growth of which was regarded by the civilians of that day with undisguised alarm and jealousy. The common lawyer, with his barbarous dog-Latin and want of all scholarly culture, caring only for gain, and squandering his ill-gotten wealth on sensual pleasures, is the chief character of the piece, the real merits of which but imperfectly atone for its coarseness and vulgarity, its *équivoques* and broad obscenities. It must, however, be admitted that these compositions often afford us an insight into the prevailing tendencies of academic thought and feeling which we should vainly seek elsewhere,—an observation which applies with especial force to one notable trilogy, the *Pilgrimage to Parnassus* and the *Return from Parnassus*, acted in St. John's College about the commencement of the seventeenth century, wherein the ambitions, hopes, hardships, and disappointments of the student life of those days are depicted with considerable force and humour. But, generally speaking, these entertainments were regarded with much dislike by the Puritan party, owing to the gross and licentious tone by which they were often characterised, and which elicited Milton's well-known censure, in his *Apology for Smectymnuus*, on such performances, as singularly unbecoming for youths and men destined to the service of the Church.

Few of the great synods of Protestantism excited more interest at Cambridge than the Synod of Dort (1618–19),—an interest awakened partly by the theological feeling attaching to the questions there debated, and partly to the considerable share which the university obtained in the representation of the English Church on that occasion, no less than four out of the five delegates from Great Britain (viz., Davenant, Samuel Ward, Joseph Hall, and Walter Balcanqual) being Cambridge men. The theological intolerance manifested by that notable assembly had its counterpart in the burning in the Regent Walk,[1] in 1622, of the works of Paræus, an eminent divine of Heidelberg, who had ventured to advance doctrines which impugned the theory of the divine right of kings.

The Synod of Dort.

Before, however, King James died, signs were not wanting that both the doctrines expounded in the Lambeth Articles and the doctrine of divine right were alike destined before long to be rudely challenged. The election in 1626 of the duke of Buckingham as chancellor of the university diverted for a brief period the attention of the community from these questions. The duke was at this very time under impeachment, and his election was accordingly looked upon as dictated by a spirit

Buckingham as chancellor.

---

[1] The main approach to the Schools, a street built in Parker's time, was thus called.

of servility to the Crown which was warmly resented by Parliament. He evinced his sense of the political service which had been rendered him by offering to rebuild the university library, but his munificent project was frustrated by his assassination. The scheme accordingly remained altogether in abeyance until the present century, when the old quadrangle of King's College was purchased in 1829 for the sum of £12,000, and the new buildings,—known, from the name of the architect, as Cockerell's buildings,— were commenced in 1837.

Numerous signs now gave evidence of the approaching change. In 1628 the king found it necessary to suppress Manwaring's sermons, in which the attributes of the royal prerogative were asserted with imprudent boldness; and in the following year it was found politic also to suppress the celebrated *Apello Cæsarem* of Mountague, bishop of Chester. Mountague had published his book four years before, and had received his bishopric from Charles mainly as his reward. The treatise had given rise to a complete controversial uproar, owing to the manner in which the writer sought to combat the Calvinistic tendencies of the Thirty-Nine Articles, maintaining that Calvinism was not the true doctrine of the Church of England. His book was now declared to be the chief cause of the disputes then troubling the Church, and disputations on the Thirty-Nine Articles were forbidden henceforth to be held at either university. In this manner it was sought to arrest all progressive speculation in relation to those studies around which the chief

Signs of the approaching change in both religious and political opinion.

mental activity both at Oxford and at Cambridge revolved. The freedom with which Dr. Dorislaus of Leyden, on his appointment by Lord Brooke to lecture in connection with the new professorship of History,[1] enlarged upon the political rights and privileges of the people, was another significant symptom. In August 1628, the news arrived of the assassination of the chancellor. It was, apparently, not without misgiving that Henry Rich, Lord Holland, acquiesced in the petition of the university that he would consent to occupy the vacant post,—'the condition of man,' he observed in the letter conveying his assent, 'is so frail, and his time so short here.' Within less than a month, Lord Brooke also fell by the hand of an assassin; and it is remarkable that Dr. Dorislaus himself met with a similar fate some twenty years later in Holland, owing to the fact that he was accessory to the proceedings which resulted in the death of Charles I. Other symptoms, and more especially a disregard for the prescribed Anglican discipline, induced Laud in 1636 to declare his intention of visiting both universities by virtue of his right as metropolitan. His assertion of such a right was contested in both cases, but eventually enforced by the royal decision. His visitation of Cambridge, however, never took place, and before long legislation itself pointed in a totally opposite direction. By two enactments, passed in January and April 1640, the House of Commons decided that neither from graduates nor undergraduates should subscription any longer be required.

[1] The persecution to which Dorislaus was subjected induced Lord Brooke to suspend the lectures for a time.

In June 1642 there arrived a royal letter, inviting the university to contribute to the king's defence against Parliament,—such contributions to be repaid with interest at eight per cent. 'justly and speedily as soon as it shall please God to settle the distraction of this kingdom.' The appeal met with a fairly general, although not an enthusiastic, response. St. John's College sent £150; Sidney College, £100; the other colleges, certain sums the amounts of which are not recorded. The townsmen, who mostly sided with the parliamentary party, indulged in reprisals, and fired at the windows of some of the collegians. The colleges sent to London for arms, which, on their arrival, were seized by order of the Mayor. A report became current that Parliament designed a raid upon the colleges for the purpose of depriving them of their plate. Under the pretext that it was desirable to place it in safe custody, they were invited by royal letter to forward it to the headquarters at Leicester. Some of it arrived safely; but the greater portion was intercepted by Cromwell, who forthwith committed three of the Cambridge Heads,—Dr. Beale of St. John's, Dr. Martin of Queens', and Dr. Sterne. of Jesus,—to prison, on account of their complicity in the transaction. In January 1642-3, a parliamentary decree abolished the compulsory wearing of surplices. In the spring of the same year, Cromwell, fearing that the town might be seized by the royalists, occupied it with an army of nearly 30,000 men, and when the panic was over, retained a permanent force of a thousand men to serve as a garrison. In the *Querela Cantabrigiensis*, the composition of an ardent royalist, published in 1647, the sufferings of the scholars and the wanton mischief inflicted by the soldiery during this episode are described in pathetic terms. But the writer's account is unquestionably greatly exaggerated; and as early as March 1642, the House of Lords, at the instance of Lord Holland, and the House of Commons, at that of the earl of Essex, had combined by express edict to shield the university from all spoliation and harm whatever. Oxford, during its occupation by the royalist forces, probably suffered much more severely. As, however, it was decided to make Cambridge a military centre for the parliamentary forces, the customary preparations for defence necessarily involved some encroachment on the college grounds and property. A large quantity of timber and stone, designed for the rebuilding of Clare Hall, was lying near the site; this was now seized and used as material for additional works about the castle. The trees forming the grove about Jesus College, and a considerable portion of those in the other college walks, were felled; the bridges connecting the grounds of St. John's, Trinity, King's, and Queens' with the opposite bank of the river were pulled down; and in January 1643, a large amount of real and irreparable injury was effected by the destruction of a large number of 'superstitious images and pictures' in the halls and chapels of the different colleges. The story of the removal of the glass from King's College Chapel, in anticipation of its destruction by the soldiery, appears to have no foundation in fact; but if the statements of the royalist journalists are to be credited, Lord Grey and Cromwell resorted in 1643 to something like compulsion to induce the Heads to contribute funds 'for the public use.' In the month of May in the same year, Dr. Richard Holdsworth, the vice-chancellor, was committed to prison for having authorised the reprinting at the university press of the Royal Declarations, which had been already printed at York. After this, we hear of but few instances of contumacy; but a petition to Parliament in the following June represents the condition of the university as pitiable in the extreme, 'the numbers grown thin and the revenues short.' The general state of both Oxford and Cambridge appears, indeed, to have been so unfavourable to the pursuit of study that the Assembly of Divines petitioned Parliament that a college might be opened in London, where students might for a time receive instruction under more desirable conditions; and in 1649 a new Academy was actually inaugurated in Whitefriars by one Sir Balthazar Gerbier for the teaching of all manner of arts and sciences. In the same year, Cromwell gave his sanction for the foundation of the University of Durham, but this design was not carried into effect for nearly two centuries.

In February 1643-4, it was ordered by both Houses of Parliament that the Solemn League and Covenant should be tendered and accepted in the university. The measure resulted in the expulsion of a majority of the Heads and fellows of colleges. Among

Changes consequent upon the imposition of the Solemn League and Covenant.

those thus ejected were Dr. John Cosin, master of Peterhouse (afterwards bishop of Durham); Dr. Parker, the master of Clare; Richard Crashaw, the poet, fellow of Peterhouse; Cowley, the poet, fellow of Trinity; and Seth Ward, fellow of Sidney, and afterwards bishop of Salisbury. Among their successors, one or two acted with exemplary moderation; as, for instance, the celebrated Cudworth, who was appointed to the mastership of Clare Hall, and in 1654 to that of Christ's; while the scarcely less eminent Whichcote, who was now made provost of King's, not only himself declined to take the Covenant, but succeeded in obtaining a like exemption for all the fellows on that foundation. With characteristic liberality, he also allowed his predecessor, Samuel Collins, a stipend from the dividend which he himself received. Others, however, like Thomas Hill, the master of Trinity, and William Dell, the master of Caius, not only sought to give an exclusively sectarian character to the societies over which they ruled, but advocated changes which would have resulted in a complete modification of both the teaching and the organisation of the university. Dell, indeed, not only disapproved of university degrees, but considered that it would be much better if the instruction given at Oxford and Cambridge could also be imparted in the large towns of the west and the north, so that students might no longer be under the necessity of undertaking such long and perilous journeys in the pursuit of knowledge. His project, if carried into effect, could hardly in those days have failed to denationalise the two universities and narrow the general standard of culture. Oliver Heywood, at that time an undergraduate at Trinity, tells us with much complacency how, under the influence of his Puritan instructors, he had already come to prefer writers like Perkins, Preston, Bolton, and Sibbes to Aristotle and Plato. The contempt of the soldiery for 'carnal learning' became more and more marked; and in the month of July 1652 Cromwell found it necessary to forbid the quartering of soldiers in the colleges, and also 'the offering of injurie or violence to any of the students.' The Barebones Parliament even went so far as to discuss the question of suppressing the universities altogether. During the Protectorate, when the university was represented in Parliament by Richard Cromwell, a more tolerant spirit prevailed; and on 21st May 1659 it was resolved, in response to a petition from the army, that 'the universities and schools of learning shall be so countenanced and reformed as that they may become the nurseries of piety and learning.' The Presbyterians in London and elsewhere also subscribed for the maintenance of forty scholars in each university. On the removal of Richard Cromwell, however, another reaction took place. It was proposed to remodel the universities 'after the Dutch fashion'; to reduce the colleges to three in each university, for the respective faculties of divinity, law, and physic, each with its own professor; and to require 'all students to go in cloaks.' The alarm created by these proposals was dissipated by the news of Monk's march for London; and on the 23rd January 1659-60 Parliament published a Declaration to the effect that 'they would uphold the public universities and schools of the land, and not only continue to them the privileges and advantages they then enjoyed, but would be ready to give them such further countenance as might encourage them in their studies, and promote godliness, learning, and good manners among them.'

As regards the prevailing tone within the university itself, it would appear that Puritanical strictness was already on the wane; and Samuel Pepys, who entered as a sizar at Trinity in 1650, mentions in his *Diary* that, when revisiting Cambridge in February 1659–60, he was informed that the 'old preciseness' had almost ceased to exist.

CHAPTER IX.

FROM THE RESTORATION TO THE ACCESSION OF GEORGE I.

THE Restoration was hailed by both the university and the town with signs of genuine enthusiasm and delight, and was commemorated by the former by the publication of a volume of congratulatory verses.[1] In May and June 1660, two successive orders of the House of Lords restored the earl of Manchester to the chancellorship, and the ejected Heads to the rule of their several colleges. The fee-farm rents, which had been purchased in order to supply the deficiency caused by the stoppage of the pensions from the royal treasury, were presented to King Charles with fervent assurance of 'the tender care and loyal affection' of the university. The use of the surplice in College chapels was enjoined by a royal manifesto; but it was ordered that subscription to the Three Articles should not be made compulsory on admission to degrees. It is evident, indeed, that

Changes at the Restoration.

---

[1] Compositions of this kind had before this time become customary in the university on the occurrence of any especially noteworthy event; it was in a similar collection (on the death of Edward King) that the *Lycidas* of Milton first appeared.

considerable freedom in such matters still prevailed; for at Emmanuel the surplice was not resumed, while the Liturgy and the Directory were used on alternate weeks in the chapel services.

In the House of Commons, on the occasion of passing a bill for the establishment of a General Letter Office, an amusing discussion took place as to whether the name of Oxford should continue to have precedence over that of Cambridge. The difficulty of deciding the question was ultimately met by passing the proviso without naming either, but referring to them simply as 'the two universities.' In 1662 the Act of Uniformity was again put in force, by requiring that all Heads, fellows, chaplains, and tutors of colleges, and all professors and readers in the university, should subscribe a declaration to the effect that they held armed resistance to the Crown to be unlawful under any pretext whatever, and also promising conformity to the Liturgy of the Church of England as by law established. It soon became evident that it was by no means the royal intention to look upon these expressions of loyalty and submission as merely formal, and the use made by Charles of the universities as a means of gratifying his supporters and favourites was marked and frequent. Between the 25th June 1660 and the 2nd of the following March mandate degrees,—*i.e.*, degrees conferred, at the royal request, on those who were academically unqualified through not having fulfilled the statutable conditions of admission, —were bestowed as follows:—D.D., 121; D.C.L., 12; D.M., 12; B.D., 12; M.A., 2; B.C.L., 1. In

May 1662 a yet more arbitrary exercise of the prerogative took place. The fellows of Queens' College had elected Symon Pattrick, afterwards bishop of Ely, to the presidency of their college, but the election was nullified by a royal mandamus, which called upon them to accept Dr. Sparrow, a man of inferior ability and reputation.

In the year 1665 the two universities, together with the royal library, acquired by Act of Parliament the right of receiving a copy of every book printed within the realm.

Side by side with the disputatious theology and the political vicissitudes of the age, two movements were now going on which were destined materially to influence the studies of the university. Of these, the one which, at the time, undoubtedly attracted the larger share of attention was the rise of that remarkable school of divines since known as the Cambridge Platonists. Among its most eminent representatives were Benjamin Whichcote (1610–1683), whose appointment to the provostship of King's has been already noted; John Smith, a fellow of Queens' (1618–1652), who, although dying at the early age of thirty-four, left behind him a volume of *Discourses* which are still read and admired for their eloquence and superiority to the narrow formalism of his time; Ralph Cudworth (1617–1688), master of Christ's College, the author of the once well-known *Intellectual System of the Universe;* Henry More (1614–1687), a fellow of the same society, in whom the Platonising influences of the school reached their fullest develop-

[margin: Rise of the Cambridge Platonists: Whichcote, John Smith, Cudworth, and Henry More.]

ment; and Culverwell (b. *circa* 1617), a member of Emmanuel College, and author of the eloquent *Discourse of the Light of Nature*. Others of the same school, and scarcely less distinguished, were Worthington, Rust, Patrick, Fowler, Glanvil, and Norris. In most cases, the inspiration and tendencies of this remarkable school would appear to have been derived from the Cartesian philosophy; and a pamphlet published in 1662, professing to give some account of the movement under the designation of 'the new sect of Latitude men,' refers expressly to Descartes as the philosopher who had been most successful in the endeavour to explain 'that vast machine, the universe.' While repudiating the scholastic Aristotle, these Cambridge thinkers sought, much like the Christian Platonists of the second and third centuries, to prove that religion and philosophy were perfectly reconcilable. So far were they from placing themselves in opposition to the scientific tendencies of their age,—tendencies to which the foundation of the Royal Society had given a remarkable impulse,—that it was their aim to show that these tendencies, if rightly controlled, might be made eminently serviceable, by being regarded as auxiliary to revealed religion. 'God,' said Whichcote, 'hath set up two lights to enlighten us in our way: the light of reason, which is the light of His creation; and the light of Scripture, which is after-revelation from Him. Let us make use of these two lights, and suffer neither to be put out.' Whatever may be our estimate of the method of these several thinkers, it must be admitted that they rendered a genuine service to their age by the example they one and all gave of a spirit which stood in marked contrast to the intolerant sectarianism by which they were surrounded. Their hope for humanity was associated not with the triumph of any one religious sect, but with the universal diffusion of Christian principles, as exemplified in a virtuous life, and in mutual charity, forbearance, and toleration. 'There is nothing more unnatural to religion,' was one of Whichcote's aphorisms, 'than contentions about it.' On the other hand, their own example was often of a kind tending rather to the encouragement of the contemplative than of the practical virtues; and the life of Henry More at Christ's College was that of an amiable recluse. His writings, largely tinged with mysticism, are of a purely speculative and somewhat morbid character. They are animated, however, by a gentle glow and fervour of thought, which appealed with considerable effect to the religious public of his day, and his *Divine Dialogues*, more especially, attained to a wide popularity. A leading London bookseller declared that, for twenty years after the return of Charles II., More's works 'ruled all the booksellers in London.' More's admiration of the Cartesian philosophy was expressed in characteristically enthusiastic terms. 'All the great leaders of philosophy who have ever existed,' he wrote to Descartes himself, 'are mere pigmies in comparison with your transcendent genius.' More was buried in the chapel of his college, where, in less than a year, Cudworth was laid beside him.

The second movement, which though less noted in its commencement was far more permanent in its after effects, was that associated with the increased attention now given to natural philosophy, which paved the way for the rejection of the Ptolemaic theory and changed the conception of the universe. As early as the year 1639, Horrocks, a young sizar of Emmanuel, had written in favour of the Copernican theory and had watched the transit of Venus. Oughtred, a fellow of King's College (who, in 1647, published his *Easy Method of Geometric Dialling*), Seth Ward, a fellow of Sidney, and Wallis, a fellow of Queens', both of whom became Savilian professors at Oxford, were also avowed Copernicans. The year 1663 was marked by the foundation of the Lucasian professorship of mathematics by Henry Lucas, who had formerly represented the university in Parliament. During the first five years (1664–1669) the chair was filled by Isaac Barrow, and for the next thirty-three years by Isaac Newton. Both Barrow and Newton were fellows of Trinity College, where the former succeeded, in 1673, to the mastership. At the time when Newton entered, the college appears to have been, like the other foundations, at a low ebb, and in 1664 there were no less than forty-four vacancies in the scholarships. To one of these he was elected, Barrow being his examiner in Euclid. In the following year, the Great Plague of London extended to Cambridge, compelling not only the abandonment of Sturbridge fair at Midsummer, but also the discontinuance of sermons at St. Mary's and of the customary acts in the Schools. The admissions to the degree of B.A. fell this year to the lowest point reached throughout the century. Among those who thus involuntarily quitted Cambridge was Newton, who retired to his home at Woolsthorpe, an episode in his career rendered memorable by the well-known incident of the falling apple, and his consequent generalisation of the law of gravity. Barrow, in his lectures on optics, published in 1669, acknowledges the aid he received from his friend and fellow-collegian. In the course of the next fifteen years Newton's reputation became widely spread; and Halley of Oxford, in pursuing his investigations in connection with Kepler's law, found, on visiting Cambridge in August 1684, that assistance from the Lucasian professor which he had failed in obtaining in any other quarter.

On the death of Charles II. and the accession of his brother, the double event was celebrated, according to custom, in a collection of verses by different members of the university. Among the contributors were Thomas Baker, the eminent antiquary, and Matthew Prior, the poet, both fellows of St. John's College; Joshua Barnes of Emmanuel College; and Charles Mountagu, afterwards earl of Halifax. The reign of Charles was not unmarked by various measures designed to raise the standard of discipline in the university, and concurrently the education of the clergy at large. Archbishop Sancroft, formerly a fellow of Emmanuel, whose efforts on behalf of learning were both constant and judicious, ordered that no one should be ordained a deacon or a priest who had not taken 'some degree of school' in one of the universities of the realm. In 1674 a royal injunction censured the custom, prevalent among the clergy, of dressing the hair in the manner then

Attempted reforms of discipline during the reign of Charles II.

fashionable, and of wearing perukes. It was also ordered that the practice of reading sermons should 'be wholly laid aside,' and that preachers should deliver their sermons, whether in Latin or English, by memory and without book.

At the desire of Charles himself, the university in the same year elected the duke of Monmouth to the chancellorship. Monmouth was deposed from his office by his father in 1682; and after his rebellion, in 1685, his picture was burnt by the yeoman bedell and his name erased from all the lists of university officers. 'Fickle Cambridge' was taunted for its servility by one of its own members, George Stepney of Trinity College, who recalled

<small>Monmouth as chancellor.</small>

> 'With what applause they once received his Grace,
> And begged a copy of his god-like face.'

The disposition shown in the preceding reign to assert the royal right of interference was carried by James to a point which eventually roused both universities to strenuous resistance. At Trinity College, every fellowship, as it fell vacant, was regularly filled by some royal nominee. In December 1686, the death of Dr. Minshull caused a vacancy in the mastership of Sidney College. It was forthwith filled up by the appointment, by virtue of the king's mandate, of Joshua Bassett, a fellow of Caius College, and a reputed papist, who at the same time received the royal dispensation from the oath required by college statute. In the next year matters reached a climax. The occasion arose out of another mandate calling upon the university to admit a Bene-

<small>Mandate elections to fellowships.</small>

dictine monk, one Alban Francis, a man of no acquirements, to the degree of master of
arts. It was urged in James' defence,
that his design in thus bringing Catholics into the
university was simply to bring about a better feeling between Protestants and Romanists; that such
mandates were very rarely refused; and that quite
recently a Mahometan, the secretary of the ambassador from Morocco, had been admitted without
hesitation to a like distinction. On the other hand,
it was contended that an important difference was
involved in the bestowal of degrees on strangers not
designing to reside, and on such as, like brother
Francis, were proposing to take up their abode in
the university, and who, by virtue of their degree,
would acquire the right of voting in congregation.
The general alarm seems to have been greatly enhanced by the belief that these steps were only the
prelude to the introduction of the Jesuits into the
university. And when we consider what had been
the experiences of Paris and other universities consequent upon the intrusion of that Order, the distrust
and the alarm of Cambridge will scarcely appear
unreasonable. It was held by some that compliance
might in this instance be yielded to the royal mandate, if it were at the same time expressly declared
that the admission of Francis was not to constitute
a precedent. But eventually it was decided by the
Caput not to bring the question before the university,
but simply to advise the vice-chancellor not to admit
Francis, and in the meantime to petition the king
to recall his mandate. James, with his habitual

The case of Alban Francis.

obstinacy, having refused to do this, the question was at length referred to the regents and non-regents (as the electoral body of that time was designated), and by that assembly it was decided that the 'admission of Mr. Francis without the usual oaths was illegal and unsafe,' and their decision was forthwith forwarded to London. The result of this courageous demonstration was, that the university authorities were summoned before the Lords Commissioners in London. They were represented by a deputation, consisting of the vice-chancellor (Dr. Peachell) and eight others, which appeared before the Commissioners on 21st April 1687. They were cross-questioned and brow-beaten by the Lord Chancellor Jeffreys, and then dismissed; and, in the course of a few days, Peachell was called upon not only to resign the vice-chancellorship, but also the mastership of Magdalene. At the same time, certain clauses in the statutes of Sidney College, requiring that the master should 'detest and abhor Popery' were struck out. The dissenters of Cambridge did themselves little credit on this occasion by openly applauding James' tyrannical conduct. In the following year, after the Prince of Orange had already landed at Torbay, the king endeavoured, when it was too late, to re-establish friendly relations with the university, by annulling the foregoing acts.

The accession of Queen Mary called into prominence opposition of another kind. Sancroft, after having declined the chancellorship of the university, was deprived of his archbishopric in consequence of his refusal to take the oath of allegiance. The office of chancellor was now

Changes consequent upon the accession of Queen Mary.

A.D. 1660 TO 1714. 165

filled by the duke of Somerset, known in his own day as the 'Proud Duke,' who held the office continuously for the lengthened period of sixty years. In March 1690-1 a royal letter, addressed to the vice-chancellor and senate, directed that all persons admitted to degrees under letters mandatory should pay fees, subscribe the common form and words, and perform (or give sufficient caution for the performance of) all statutable acts and exercises. In 1689, the oaths of supremacy and allegiance were abrogated by Act of Parliament, and others substituted for them. The new oaths met, however, with considerable opposition, and at St. John's College no less than twenty of the fellows refused compliance. A mandamus issued in 1693 for their removal from their fellowships was for a long time evaded on various pleas; and it was not until the year 1717 that twenty-two fellows of this single college were eventually deprived. Among their number was
Thomas Baker. Thomas Baker, who continued notwithstanding to reside in college, his high character and eminent services to learning pleading effectually in his favour. During his lifetime he presented twenty-three volumes of his manuscript collections to Harley, earl of Oxford, which are included in the Harleian collection now preserved in the British Museum; eighteen others were bequeathed by him to the university library in Cambridge, and the whole series is of the highest value in relation to the history both of the university and the colleges at large. Baker died suddenly in his college rooms on 2d July 1740. His *History of St. John's College,*

since edited and published by Professor John E. B. Mayor, is a highly valuable contribution to our knowledge, not only of the history of the college, but of the university and learning at large.

The central figure in the university, from his appointment to the mastership of Trinity in 1700 down to his death in 1742, was Richard Bentley. That society, towards the close of the seventeenth century, had somewhat declined from its original reputation. In the earlier part of the century, it had supplied from among its resident fellows no less than six of the translators engaged upon the Authorised Version, and had educated a larger proportion of the episcopal bench than any other society. In polite learning it had produced John Donne, the most admired poet of that century, and also Abraham Cowley. The administration of Pearson, who was master from 1662 to 1673, and that of Barrow, who held the same office from 1673 to 1677, had contributed in no slight degree further to raise the college in the general estimation. Their successors, the Hon. John North and the Hon. John Montagu, were less successful; and the effects of mandate elections, which Charles and James II., presuming on the fact that the college was a royal foundation, had almost systematically enforced, had lowered the standard of attainments among the fellows. In numbers the college was at this time below St. John's.[1] Bentley himself had been educated at the latter foundation, where his

Richard Bentley, master of Trinity.

---

[1] The university at large appears to have declined in numbers; in 1622 the total number of residents was 3050; in 1672, it was 2522.

name appears as last of twenty-three sizars who matriculated 6th July 1676. But the proviso in the statute relating to elections to fellowships, which limited to two the number of fellows from any one county, excluded him as a Yorkshireman from a fellowship. He retired from the university; and it was not until he had been appointed King's Librarian at St. James's, that his valuable services in aiding and advising in the restoration of the University Press, and his *Dissertation on Phalaris*, re-established his connection with Cambridge. In 1699, on the unanimous recommendation of the University Commissioners,

His efforts in the cause of science. he was appointed to the mastership of Trinity. He undoubtedly presented a rare combination of qualifications for the office. He had from the first taken the warmest interest in Newton's epoch-making discoveries, and had publicly extolled them in his Boyle Lectures delivered in London in 1692; and he now sought by every means to stimulate the exertions of Cotes, of Whiston, and other rising disciples of the great philosopher. Through his interest, Cotes, who had been elected to a fellowship in 1705, was appointed first Plumian professor, while still only bachelor of arts; and to aid him in the prosecution of his researches, Bentley caused an Observatory to be erected

His improvements in the College. over the King's Gate (as the chief entrance to the college was then termed), and furnished it with the best astronomical instruments obtainable.[1] It was mainly owing to his persuasions, again, that, at an interval of twenty-seven

[1] The Observatory was taken down in 1797.

years from the first appearance of the work, Newton was eventually induced to publish, in 1713, a second edition of the *Principia*. The improvements effected by Bentley in the external appearance of the college were also considerable. Writing in 1710 to the bishop of Ely, he says :—' It has been often told me by persons of sense and candour, that when I left them, I might say of the College what Augustus said of Rome, *Lateritium inveni, marmoreum reliqui*. The College chapel, from a decayed, antiquated model, made one of the noblest in England ; the College hall, from a dirty, sooty place, restored to its original beauty, and excelled by none in cleanliness and magnificence.'

<small>Uffenbach's impressions of the libraries of the colleges.</small> It is singular to note that Uffenbach, the German *savant*, who visited the university in the same year that Bentley wrote his letter, should have described the hall of Trinity as ' very large, but ugly, smoky, and smelling so strong of bread and meat, that,' he says, ' it would be impossible for me to eat a morsel in it.' The same keen-eyed traveller, in visiting the other colleges, could not but be struck by the indifference evinced for the higher interests of learning. At Caius College he found the manuscripts placed in ' a miserable garret under the roof,' and lying ' thick with dust ' on the floor. At Magdalene all the books were ' entirely overgrown with mould.' At St. John's the collection of coins was lying covered with dust in ' a poor drawer, unlocked, and left open.' At Trinity Hall, the library appeared to him ' very mean, consisting only of a few law books.' At Emmanuel, the books, though ' respectable in number,' stood ' in

entire confusion.' At Peterhouse, the manuscripts were 'buried in dust' and in the greatest disorder. At the University Library, a rare codex of Josephus being 'torn at the end,' the library-keeper obligingly presented him with a leaf! In the libraries of Trinity, St. John's, and Corpus Christi, on the other hand, Uffenbach found something that repaid him for his toil and even commanded his admiration.

Notwithstanding, however, this too prevalent apathy, we find the reputation of the university at this period upheld by names which, in the respective provinces of science and learning, were inferior only to those of Newton and Bentley. Cotes, although carried off at the early age of thirty-four, lived long enough to leave behind him the impression of rare ability, and also some important contributions to mathematical knowledge. Whiston, notwithstanding the vagaries which characterised his *Theory of the Earth* (an attempt to harmonise the Bible and the Newtonian discoveries), discharged his duties as Lucasian professor with credit, even though appearing as the successor of Newton. Joshua Barnes, who filled the chair of Greek from 1695 to 1712, has, although exposed to Bentley's severest criticism, probably rather gained than lost ground in the estimation of scholars since his own day. Davies, the president of Queens' and the editor of Cicero,—Sike, who through Bentley's interest was appointed to the Regius professorship of Hebrew,—and Wotton, a fellow of St. John's, a scholar gifted with a marvellous memory and of varied attainments,—were also of more than usual

[margin: Cotes, Whiston, Joshua Barnes, &c.]

eminence. Laughton, who in 1694 was appointed tutor of Clare Hall, materially contributed to the reputation of that society by the ability with which he enforced discipline, and by the success which attended his efforts to promote the study of the Newtonian philosophy. Covel, the octogenarian master of Christ's College, was equally distinguished by his acquirements as a linguist, his urbanity, and his knowledge of the world.

Religious controversy, which at Cambridge would appear to have slumbered for a time, was revived in the reign of Queen Anne by the disputatious spirit of Whiston. He commenced as a champion of orthodoxy, denouncing the chief divines of the university as sceptics, and putting forth with overweening confidence the results of his own investigations in Church history. His conclusions, as unfolded in his *Primitive Christianity Revived*, seem to have landed him, in the first instance, in Arianism, but finally led him to join the General Baptists. His Arian tenets led to his banishment from the university in 1710, and his deprivation of his professorship. He was subsequently prosecuted for heresy in the Court of Arches, but pardoned after the accession of George I., although he persistently refused to retract any of the opinions which he had advanced; while the controversies which his writings had evoked long continued to agitate the university and wider circles beyond.

<small>Controversy revived by Whiston.</small>

CHAPTER X.

FROM THE ACCESSION OF GEORGE I. TO THE END OF THE EIGHTEENTH CENTURY.

NEITHER Newton's later career nor that of Bentley can be held to have added to the estimation in which both are regarded by posterity. The former, although hardly to be considered mentally unsound, was subject for some years to a melancholy which impaired his intellect, and his *Observations* on Daniel and the Apocalypse can scarcely be looked upon otherwise than as a misapplication of his powers. Bentley published in 1711 his ill-considered edition of Horace, abounding with unjustifiable 'emendations,' and in 1731 his almost ludicrous edition of *Paradise Lost;* while his overbearing conduct towards the other Heads and some of the officers of the university led to his arrest in his own Lodge (23rd September 1718), at the suit of Middleton, and to his deprivation of his degrees by the senate of the university. In 1720 an unsuccessful attempt was made, by an application to the King's Bench, to deprive him of his professorship. He was restored to his degrees after five years' and a half deprivation; but in 1729 articles were

Later years of Newton and Bentley.

preferred against him, as administrator of the college, by the Visitor, Dr. Greene, bishop of Ely. Although Bentley succeeded in frustrating the design of the bishop, new articles were preferred against him by Colbatch, a fellow of the college, whereby it was sought to bring about his removal from the mastership. A memorable struggle, extending over ten years, thereupon ensued; and it was not until Bishop Greene had died, at the age of fourscore, and Bentley was himself in his seventy-seventh year, that these proceedings were brought to a conclusion. Bentley contrived to throw his own legal expenses, amounting to £4000, entirely on the college, and the society became for a time considerably embarrassed in consequence. Although the coolness and consummate ability with which he fought the battle moved the admiration even of his antagonists, it was impossible to deny that his administration was in some respects highly culpable. Under the pretext of liability to catch cold, he scarcely ever appeared in college chapel, where the attendants at length discontinued lighting the candles in his stall; and he appropriated without scruple the college funds to his personal use and advantage. His desire, indeed, to set himself above the laws was sufficiently shown in another capacity, for, as archdeacon of Ely, during the thirty-seven years that he held the office, he never once personally inspected the churches and parsonages of the diocese.

Among the smaller foundations, St. Catherine's, in the latter part of the seventeenth century, had gained considerably both in numbers and reputation owing

to the influence of John Lightfoot, who was master
from 1650 to 1675. In 1672 its num-
bers (including the servants of the college)
amounted to 150. Thomas Sherlock, who
held the mastership for the brief period 1714 to
1719, was at that time one of the most
influential members of the university. By
his opposition to Bentley, however, he seems to have
incurred the bitter hostility of the latter, who was
wont to designate him as 'Cardinal Alberoni.' Sherlock's controversial writings, chiefly against Hoadly,
Collins, and Woolston, characterised as they were
alike by breadth of judgment and yet firm adherence to the orthodox standpoint, have caused him
to be termed 'the representative Churchman of his
age.' In his capacity as vice-chancellor, it devolved
upon him, in 1715, to present to George I. the
address of the senate, conveying the thanks of that
body for the royal munificence, whereby the library
of Dr. John Moore, bishop of Ely, had been purchased, after his death, and bestowed on the university. By this means the University Library was
augmented by some 30,000 volumes. In 1724
King George, having observed that 'no encouragement or provision' had hitherto been made in the
university for 'the study of modern history or modern languages,' founded the
Regius professorship of History. The
office was first filled by S. Harris, a
master of arts of Peterhouse, and from
1768 to 1771 was held by the poet Gray. The
Woodwardian professorship of Geology, founded in

Growth of St. Catherine's College.

Dr. Sherlock.

Foundation of the Regius professorship of History and of the Woodwardian professorship of Geology.

1727, was first filled by the celebrated Conyers Middleton, another of Bentley's antagonists, who published in 1719 his 'Full and Impartial Account' of the proceedings which led to Bentley's deprivation of his degrees. Bentley afterwards prosecuted Middleton for libel; but although he gained a verdict, the sympathy of the university with his antagonist was shown by the latter being appointed in 1721 principal university librarian.

On the 6th July 1730 the new Senate House, which had occupied eight years in construction, was opened by the ceremonies of a Public Commencement, and in the course of another ten years it became the arena for the university examinations, and especially for the Tripos. The origin of this name is somewhat peculiar. The very different notions which prevailed among the Reformers had led to a singular travesty of the ancient observance of Ash Wednesday. In mediæval times, the expression *stare in quadragesima,*—to stand (as a determiner) in Lent,—denoted a solemn ordeal. Among the Protestants of the days of Elizabeth,—who lost no opportunity of evincing their contempt for the notions which had found favour among their Catholic forefathers,—the grave ceremony was converted into a ludicrous farce. The questionists who aspired to the dignity of bachelor of arts, found themselves, on repairing to the Schools, confronted by a certain 'ould bachilour' (old, that is to say, in academic status rather than in years), to whom the university for the nonce delegated its functions. The 'bachilour' was seated on a *three-legged stool*

The Tripos: origin of the term.

(from whence the term *tripos*), and it was his function to dispute not only with the 'eldest son' (the foremost of the questionists), but also with the questionists' 'father,' the delegate of the college, on whom it devolved to present the candidates. As the united ages of the three disputants often failed to represent a total of threescore years and ten, the levity of youth availed itself, only too readily, of the recognised licence of the occasion,—especially as the examiner himself, on his stool, invariably led the way in the congenial task of giving vent to gibes, personalities, and general opprobrium. Even amid the marked absence of restraint which characterises the earlier years of the Restoration, the senior proctor sometimes found himself called upon to exhort the Tripos to remember, while exercising his privilege of humour and satire, 'to be modest withal.' Long after 'Mr. Tripos' himself had been abolished, the tripos-verses, —which were originally compositions in Latin verse, having reference to the *quæstiones* propounded for disputation,—were recognised in his place, as an authorised observance, and preserved the tradition of his Fescennine freedom of criticism. In 1740, the authorities, after condemning the excessive licence of the Tripos, announced that the *Comitia* at Lent would in future be conducted in the Senate House, and all members of the university, of whatever order or degree, were forbidden to assail or mock the disputants with scurrilous jokes or unseemly witticisms. About the year 1747-8, the moderators (*i.e.*, the two masters of arts selected to supervise the disputations) initiated the practice of printing the honour lists on the back of the sheets containing the tripos-verses, and after the year 1755 this became the invariable practice. By virtue of this purely arbitrary connection, these lists themselves became known as the Tripos, and eventually the examination itself, of which they represented the results, also became known by the same designation. About the same time, the questions propounded for the examination appear to have been restricted to mathematics, and before the year 1770 Latin had given place to English both in the paper work and in the *viva voce*.

The establishment of the first Tripos is itself a matter requiring explanation and involved in some obscurity. It would seem that for some years, at least, after its institution, the sole test of a candidate's qualifications still continued to be that afforded by his performance in the Schools as a disputant,—as participant, that is to say, in a public Act. The abler and more ambitious students who sought to acquire a reputation in this way habitually frequented the Schools, taking part in a much larger number of disputations than were required by statute; and the distinction they had thus already acquired made it a matter of no great difficulty, when Lent approached, for the examiners to draw up a first list of Wranglers and Senior Optimes,[1] whose *seniority*, or order of merit, as bachelors, was thus 'reserved' (to use the technical expression) from the first Act (or *Comitia*), which was always

Establishment of the first Tripos.

---

[1] The Senior Optimes were first placed in a separate division from the Wranglers in the Tripos of 1753,—but the reasons which led to this alteration are not on record.

held on Ash Wednesday,—the questionists having previously sworn to abide by the decision of the proctors with respect to their order of merit. Then followed the Lenten disputations, and every day saw certain selected disputants (the 'respondents') defending a chosen thesis against the 'opponents,' who were generally four in number.[1] It does not appear that the performances of the Wranglers and Senior Optimes during this time in any way affected *their* position on the published list, but at the conclusion of the exercises the examiners drew up a *second list*, in which the Junior Optimes were assigned their order of seniority according to the manner they had acquitted themselves in their respective acts. And at the conclusion the senior proctor announced that all the determiners (as the questioners were called) had finally determined and were actually bachelors of arts. The πολλοί or Poll Men had no seniority reserved to them until the Great Commencement. On that occasion, which was on the first Tuesday in July, the bachelor (in common with the masters of arts and doctors in each faculty) was admitted to his degree and became full bachelor.

Apart from the crude and superficial manner in which the merits of candidates were thus tested,—

'Proctor's Optimes.' success in a disputation being frequently gained by assurance and ready invention, rather than by genuine attainments,—the earlier

[1] 'I was *third* opponent only, and came off with "*optime quidem disputasti*," i.e., "You've disputed excellently indeed" (quite as much as is ever given to a third opponency'). (W. Goode to his parents, 6th November 1790.) From this conventional use of *optime* the name of the second and third divisions arose.

C. H.　　　　　　　　　　　　　　　　　　　M

Tripos lists were subject to another disturbing influence which still further detracted from their value as a trustworthy gauge of merit. This arose from the practice of inserting names, known as 'proctor's optimes,' which were assigned a place in the honour list by mere favour, the candidates not having really undergone any examination whatever. The injustice thus done to the best men was often singularly glaring. Bentley, for example, who was third wrangler in 1680 (the examination, at that time, was not limited to mathematics), appeared as sixth in the official list, three proctor's optimes having been placed above him. This peculiar exercise of the proctorial prerogative does not appear to have been had recourse to after the year 1797, although it was not formally abolished until 1827. In the printed Calendars, the names of the Honorary Senior Optimes from 1747 were inserted in the first three issues, but discontinued in the fourth.

Originally the examination for the mathematical tripos was limited to two days and a half; while the maximum number admissible to rank as wranglers and senior optimes was twenty-four,—a limit not invariably observed. The examination commenced before breakfast, and after half an hour had been allowed for that meal, was resumed at half-past nine, and continued until eleven. Then ensued an interval of two hours, after which the examination was resumed from one to three, and then again, after half an hour's interval for tea, until five. The Senate House examination then terminated, but in the evening the more pro-

The original examination for the Mathematical Tripos.

mising candidates were invited to a further exhibition of their powers in the rooms of the senior proctor. Here problems were set, and the overtaxed powers of the competitors were stimulated, not very judiciously, with fruit and wine. It was probably the severity of the brief contest, while it lasted, which led Sir William Hamilton, himself a student of extraordinary powers, to condemn the ordeal as imposing too great a strain upon the brains of the examined. Otherwise, the character of the competition would appear scarcely to bear comparison with that of the present day; Paley is said to have gained his senior wranglership in 1763 on little more than twelve months' reading. A distinguished writer on the subject of university education (himself a senior wrangler) has observed that in these times a student might 'not infrequently have entered the university quite ignorant of mathematics, his training having been obtained in other branches of learning, and yet have ultimately obtained the highest place in the examination. Thus Atwood, who came from Westminster School, was third wrangler in 1769, and Pollock, who came from St. Paul's School, was senior wrangler in 1806; it can scarcely be doubted that both of these before they entered the university must have been almost exclusively engaged in the classical studies which were characteristic of their famous schools. . . . For ten years prior to 1847 the examination for the mathematical tripos continued six days. A change then took place, it being determined that the duration should be extended to eight days. The first three days were to be devoted to the elementary subjects; then an interval of rather more than a week was interposed, after which those who had passed in a satisfactory manner through the three days' test were examined during five days in the higher subjects.'[1]

Although the emulation excited and developed by the institution of its earliest tripos was undoubtedly the source of the reputation which Cambridge had by this time acquired as a school of mathematical science, there were those, even in the last century, who from time to time clearly perceived and lamented some of the collateral results of this exclusive devotion to one particular study. The Craven scholarship, founded in 1647, and the Battie, founded exactly a century later, represented at this period the only channels whereby the classical scholar could obtain recognition of his attainments. Those who possessed no aptitude for mathematics, however studiously inclined, found, accordingly, so little encouragement to exert their powers, that they were too often content to join the throng of idlers. The proportion of these was abnormally large, the conditions imposed for obtaining the ordinary degree affording scarcely any guarantee of attainment. So late as 1822, the Calendar gives 'the statutable exercises before admission *ad respondendum quæstioni*' as 'two acts and two opponencies'; 'these,' it adds, 'in part are sometimes dispensed with, and kept by what is termed " huddling."'

The signal merit of Porson, who was first chancellor's medallist and third senior optime in 1782,

Sidenote: Subordination of other studies to mathematics.

[1] Todhunter, *Conflict of Studies*, pp. 194 and 202.

was recognised by his election to a fellowship at Trinity in the same year,—at that time an almost unprecedented distinction. His scruples with regard to taking holy orders did not, however, suffer him long to retain the emolument, and his extraordinary merit as a scholar obtained but inadequate recognition by his appointment, in 1790, as Regius professor of Greek,—the salary amounting only to some £40 a year. It was not, indeed, until he obtained the post of librarian to the London Institution that he found himself in circumstances of comparative comfort. The Porson Prize was founded after his death from the residue of a sum which had been collected for his support during his lifetime by some of his warm admirers. Of his attainments as a scholar it is unnecessary here to speak, and the remarkable elegance with which he wrote the Greek character is well known. A Greek fount, cut at the University Press under his directions, still exists, and was used so recently as in printing Dr. Lightfoot's edition of *Galatians*.

So early as the year 1772, Dr. Jebb of Peterhouse had sought to raise the average standard of attainment by proposing to make it compulsory on all students, without exception, to pass a specified annual examination. The subjects were to comprise 'the law of nature and of nations, chronology, set periods of history, select classics, metaphysics, limited portions of mathematics and natural philosophy, moral philosophy, and metaphysics. In their final examination all were to be required to show a knowledge of the four Gospels in Greek and of Grotius' *De*

Dr. Jebb proposes to institute an annual compulsory examination.

Veritate.'[1] The scheme was opposed on various grounds, and especially by Dr. Powell, the master of St. John's, who had recently set an excellent example by instituting examinations in his own college. Another critic characterised the new proposals as 'tending to reduce the whole university into the state of one vast and unwieldy college.' Eventually Dr. Jebb's scheme was completely defeated; and the unpopularity he incurred by bringing it forward was such that in 1776 his vote, as a member of the Senate, was declared to be forfeited, and he eventually quitted the university. Efforts at reform in other directions gave, however, promise of being attended with better success. In the same year that Dr. Jebb brought forward his proposals, questionists were released from the obligation to sign the Thirty-nine Articles; and in 1787, Dr. Priestley, the philosopher (who had not at that time embraced the Unitarian persuasion), in a letter to Mr. Pitt, expressed himself sanguine as to the result of an endeavour which was then being made in the university to bring about the admission of Dissenters into the colleges. The conservative reaction which, when the French Revolution had run its course, set in all over Europe, did not fail, however, materially to influence the universities; and both at Oxford and Cambridge there now ensued a spirit of systematic opposition to all reforms and innovations whatever.

[1] In order to obviate one difficulty, Dr. Jebb proposed that noblemen and fellow-commoners should be allowed to pass a different examination,—a proposal which necessarily drew down a good deal of criticism on his whole scheme.

It can hardly be doubted that the tendencies of theological thought in the university, throughout the eighteenth century, were to a great extent affected by the bias given to its studies. They were characterised by that spirit of 'common sense' and those somewhat mediocre aims which prevailed in society at large, and also by that dislike of enthusiasm and of all beliefs which did not commend themselves to the practical reason, which especially distinguished the school of Sherlock, Edmund Law, and Paley. Appeals to the emotional nature on the part of the divine, and the setting up of too lofty ideals of life and conduct, whether in religion or in morality, were alike discouraged. These views found marked expression in the writings of Edmund Law, originally a member of Christ's College, but who from 1756 to 1788 was master of Peterhouse, and from 1764 to 1769 professor of casuistry. In most respects he was an avowed disciple of Locke, whose influence is plainly manifest in his *Considerations on the Theory of Religion*, which he published in 1745. The work went through numerous editions, and although marred by some singular puerilities and defective critical knowledge, is notable as putting forward a philosophic conception of humanity, which it exhibits as subject to laws of development and divinely destined to be continuously progressive. Among the young students of Christ's College was one whose merits Law seems early to have discerned, and whom he warmly befriended and aided. This was William Paley, who entered the college as a sizar, and became senior wrangler in 1763, and subsequently fellow and tutor of his college. His *Moral and Political Philosophy* was published in 1785, his *Horæ Paulinæ* in 1790, his *Evidences of Christianity* in 1794, and his *Natural Theology* in 1802. In these writings, especially the first and last, the influence of his patron is frequently discernible; while the influence which they in turn exercised over the character and tendencies of Cambridge thought and education for nearly a century can scarcely be overestimated. Richard Watson, who was second wrangler in 1759, and afterwards Norrisian professor, and John Hey, who was senior wrangler in 1755, and was appointed Regius professor of divinity in 1771, were also divines of the same school.

It was in no small measure as a reaction against this class of thinkers that the Evangelical school, the school of Toplady and John Newton, took its rise. That movement somewhat resembled the earlier Puritanism, although wanting alike its grandeur of conception and intellectual force. Berridge, a fellow of Clare Hall, was distinguished by his aversion from the new studies, declaring that the cultivation of human science involved the neglect of the Bible. The two Milners, however, represented a somewhat less narrow spirit. Joseph Milner, of Catherine Hall, who was gold medallist in 1766, published, between the years 1794 and 1812, his *History of the Church of Christ*. The work was modelled, it is said, on a *Plan of Ecclesiastical History* previously put forth by John Newton, and although the result of considerable labour, was rendered almost worthless by the singular canon of treatment laid down by the writer, who declared at the outset his determination to recognise no elements save those which he regarded as genuinely religious. His uncritical deference to patristic authority was also another serious defect. Joseph's brother, Isaac, of Queens' College, who was senior wrangler in 1774, and subsequently president of his college and Lucasian professor of mathematics, held very similar views.

In the year 1769 a change was made in the costume of the undergraduates. Down to that time they had worn round caps lined with black silk, and with a brim of black velvet for pensioners, or black silk for sizars. At their own petition, they were now allowed to adopt a square cap, the duke of Grafton, who was chancellor, having given his consent, with the concurrence of the Heads. The innovation, which in the days of Cartwright and Whitgift would have thrown the whole university into an uproar, seems to have been effected in the quietest manner possible.

<small>Introduction of square caps for undergraduates.</small>

In the year 1796 there appeared the first University Calendar. Its publication was not official, but represented the private venture of one G. Mackenzie, a bachelor of arts of Trinity. In the preface he modestly characterises the volume as one which, it might be presumed, would be 'neither useless nor uninteresting to the members of the university.' 'The public,' he goes on to say, 'has not sufficiently been made acquainted with the emoluments to be obtained at the several colleges;

<small>First publication of the University Calendar.</small>

the principal object of the CAMBRIDGE CALENDAR is to supply this defect, by stating the number of the fellowships, scholarships, and exhibitions at each, with their respective endowments; to render which complete, a list of the livings belonging to each college is added, the values of which are taken from Bacon's *Thesaurus*.' In giving an outline of the origin of the university, Mackenzie inclines to the belief that it had been founded by 'one Cantaber, a Spaniard, about 370 years before Christ;' and he regards it as beyond dispute that it was restored by King Sigebert in the year 630. In the following year the volume was edited by J. Beverley, one of the esquires bedell. The project would seem to have been at first regarded with little favour by the authorities, and was but languidly supported by the university at large, for in 1798 the Calendar failed to appear. Isaac Milner, in his capacity as president of Queens', was uncourteous enough, on one occasion, to withhold the requisite information. But in 1799 the volume reappeared, and ever since that time has been published with due regularity, although never invested with official authority. The earlier editions were in paper boards, with a bluish-grey cover, bordered by a running pattern of arrow-heads. A comparison of the volume for 1887 with that of the first issue, ninety-one years before, brings home to us with singular force the remarkable progress of the university during the present century.

CHAPTER XI.

FROM THE COMMENCEMENT OF THE CENTURY TO THE PRESENT TIME.

THE commencement of the century saw the foundation of Downing College. Its founder, Sir George Downing, died in 1749, and, having no legitimate offspring, devised extensive estates in Cambridgeshire, Bedfordshire, and Suffolk to a cousin, with remainder in trust for other relatives. In the event of there being no succession, by issue, to these other relatives, the devised estates were to be appropriated to the foundation of a college in the university of Cambridge. The contingency contemplated having actually occurred, a charter was obtained in the year 1800 for the foundation of a college for students in law, physic, and other useful arts and learning, such college to be called Downing College, and to consist of a master, two professors, and sixteen fellows. In pursuance of these instructions, a site near Maid's Causeway, known as Doll's Close, was originally purchased, but was subsequently exchanged for the present grounds. In 1805 statutes were given for the college, which were superseded by another code in 1860. The carrying out of the entire scheme was attended with costly litigation, and only two sides of

Foundation of Downing College, 1800.

the handsome quadrangle contemplated in the original plan have as yet been erected.

The great struggle in which England was engaged on the Continent told unfavourably on the numbers of students at both universities during the earlier years of the century; but between 1812 and 1822 the number of names on the boards at Cambridge increased by considerably more than a third, —an increase much beyond what had taken place in the preceding half-century. The authorities, who were little disposed to initiate reforms, gladly construed the fact into evidence that the condition of the university was regarded by the public at large with satisfaction. 'The question of utility,' wrote Dr. Monk, the Regius professor of Greek, in 1818, when repelling the suggestion that Cambridge would do well to profit in certain respects by the example of other universities, 'the question of utility must be determined in a great degree by the opinion of the public, which is shown pretty clearly in the increased numbers of students who have, of late years, flocked to this place.'

Increase in the numbers of the university.

The growing sense that classical studies demanded further recognition was shown by the institution of two additional scholarships,—the Davies in 1804, and the Pitt in 1813. And although a scheme brought forward by the master of Trinity (Dr. Wordsworth) in 1821 for examining the students in classics and the elements of theology was rejected in the Non-Regent House, on the 28th May 1822 a grace passed the Senate for the establishment of an annual voluntary classical examination. The scheme provided that the examina-

Institution of the Classical Tripos.

tion should last for four days,—from half-past nine to twelve in the morning, and from one to four in the afternoon. Translations were to be required of passages selected from the best Greek and Latin authors, as well as written answers to questions arising immediately out of such passages. No *original* composition, either in Greek or Latin, was to be required.

The beneficial operation of this scheme was, however, to a great extent marred by the condition imposed on all candidates, that they should have 'obtained an honour at the mathematical examination of the preceding January.' When, accordingly, the class-list of the first examination, held in 1824, was published, out of seven names that appeared in the first class, three were wranglers and four were senior optimes; of the four who obtained a second class, two were senior and two were junior optimes ; of six who obtained a third class, three were wranglers and three were junior optimes. For more than a quarter of a century,—that is, until its abolition in 1850,—this unwise restriction continued in force, and in some instances effectually prevented classical scholarship of no common order from obtaining due recognition. It serves to illustrate the influence which tradition and custom exercise over even very vigorous intellects, that Whewell, at that time fellow and tutor of his college, and afterwards the advocate of numerous and important innovations and reforms, put forth, in 1835, a pamphlet,[1] in which he dwelt with complacency on

Restriction originally imposed on candidates, and its removal.

[1] *Thoughts on the Study of Mathematics as a Part of a Liberal Education.* By William Whewell, M.A. 1835.

the condition of studies at Cambridge, and insisted on the value of mathematical studies as 'the principal means in the cultivation of the reasoning faculty.' His views were controverted with much force and some acrimony by Sir William Hamilton in a notable article in the *Edinburgh Review*, wherein the writer declared that Cambridge 'stood alone,' in making, 'in opposition even to the intentions of its founders and legislators, mathematical science the principal object of the whole liberal education it afforded,'—that 'the stream of opinions and the general practice of the European schools and universities allowed to that study, at best, only a subordinate utility as a means of liberal education,'—and finally denounced the existing system as 'leaving the immense majority of the *alumni* without incitement, and the most arduous and important studies void of encouragement and reward, and maintaining a scheme of discipline more partial and inadequate than any other which the history of education records.'

<small>Sir W. Hamilton and Adam Sedgwick on the still existing defects.</small>

Such strictures, proceeding from a Scotch professor of logic and metaphysics, would probably not have sufficed, unaided, to produce much effect. But the passing of the Reform Bill had awakened a widespread desire for the removal of palpable defects and obsolete restrictions in connection with institutions of every kind, and it was impossible for the more liberal element in the university not to be aware that there was much in the existing discipline and organisation that called for amendment. Adam Sedgwick, the Woodwardian professor, a fellow of Trinity College, published in 1833 his *Discourse on the Studies of the University of Cambridge*. In the preface, he criticised with considerable freedom the narrow spirit in which both mathematical and classical studies were pursued. In the one case, he adverted in terms of undisguised disapprobation to 'those severe physical studies, during which the best faculties of the mind are sometimes permitted to droop and wither;' in the other, he demurred to the amount of attention devoted to mere verbal criticism, and ventured to think that 'in straining after an accuracy beyond our reach students were taught to value the husk more than the fruit of ancient learning; while he had even the rare courage to ask whether 'the imagination and the taste might not be more wisely cultivated than by a long sacrifice to what, after all, ended but in verbal imitations.' He pleaded also for more systematic attention to the lessons of ancient history as distinguished from its literature, and urged, with arguments much resembling those employed about the same time by Arnold of Rugby, the general advantages of historical studies. In referring to philosophy, he criticised with considerable effect the unfavourable results which appeared to follow from a too exclusive attention to the utilitarian teaching of Locke and Paley.

In the meantime, as the requirements of the older tripos became more and more severe, partly from the increasing competition, partly from the development that was taking place in every branch of mathematical science, the restriction imposed on candidates for classical honours was found proportionably more irksome. In each of the

<small>Removal of restriction on the Classical Tripos.</small>

years 1849 and 1850 there appeared in the first class of the classical tripos no less than six names for which, in the preceding mathematical tripos, it was necessary to seek low down among the junior optimes, —a significant proof either of the perfunctory manner in which the prescribed condition had been complied with, or else of the inaptitude of the candidates for their enforced curriculum of study. At last, in 1850, the restriction was altogether removed, and the only mathematical attainments required from classical students were those imposed as 'additional subjects' at the previous examination. And since 1885 these also have practically been no longer imperative, owing to the admission of French or German as an alternative. With this change, the number of classical students presenting themselves at the mathematical examination, or *vice versâ*, became gradually fewer. In the years 1860, 1870, and 1880 the numbers of the classical tripos were 62, 76, and 75 respectively; and of these, the numbers of those who had already obtained mathematical honours were 11, 5, and 2. A certain reaction against these exclusive tendencies is, however, already discernible, owing to the recent division of the respective triposes into parts.[1]

Concurrently with this growth of a more liberal conception in relation to the studies of the university came the revival of the movement for the entire or partial abolition of religious tests. In 1834, a petition signed by sixty-two of the leading resident members of the university was sent up to the House of Commons, suggesting 'the expedi-

Movement in favour of the abolition of university tests.

---

[1] See *infra*, p. 208.

ency of abrogating, by legislative enactment, every religious test exacted from members of the university before they proceed to degrees, whether of bachelor, master, or doctor in arts, law, or physic.' The petitioners recalled the 'informal and unprecedented manner in which these restrictions had been imposed on the university in the reign of James I., and urged that, just as the Test Act had been recently repealed by the legislative bodies of the United Kingdom, so a corresponding measure seemed imperative in order to bring the university, as a *lay corporation*, into harmony with the social system of the State.' This appeal was met by a counter protest, signed by 258 members of the Senate (the great majority of whom were non-residents). A bill was subsequently, however, brought into the House of Commons for the 'removing of religious tests upon the taking of degrees in the universities of Oxford and Cambridge,' which passed the house by a majority of 174, but was thrown out in the House of Lords, on the second reading, by a majority of 102. It is to be observed that the proposed measure affected only the university,—the petitioners disclaiming all intention of thereby 'interfering, directly or indirectly, with the private statutes of individual colleges.' Among its most distinguished supporters were the historians, Thirlwall and Kemble, the former at that time fellow of Trinity ; Dr. Lee, the professor of Hebrew, Adam Sedgwick, Babbage, the Lucasian professor, and Peacock, afterwards dean of Ely. It was opposed by nearly all the Heads of Houses, the master of Caius (Dr. Davy) and the master of Corpus (Dr. Lamb) being the only two who signed the original petition; and it was unanimously opposed by the theological professors. The advocates of the measure were, however, sanguine of success; and Dr. Lamb, in the preface to his volume of *Documents*, published four years later, declared it to be 'evident to all who observed the signs of the times that these religious tests could not long be retained in the universities.' But it was not until another generation had passed away that, in the year 1871, religious tests were finally abolished alike in the university and in the colleges.

Although Whewell's name does not appear in connection with the above movement, and the views to which he gave expression in his pamphlet of 1835 indicated a far too complacent estimate of the condition of Cambridge studies at that time, he was a steady promoter of reform in other directions. When acting as Moderator in 1820, he had succeeded in introducing the Continental form of mathematical notation.[1] On being elected, in 1838, to the professorship of Moral Philosophy, he made what had before been regarded as a sinecure a chair of active teaching associated with examinations. He subsequently appears as taking an active part in bringing to successful issue the measures which will shortly demand our attention,—the institution of two new Triposes.

Dr. Whewell as a reformer.

In the year 1846, the whole scientific world received with interest the intelligence of the discovery of the planet Neptune by Mr. (now Professor) Adams,—a

[1] A comparison of the papers set in the mathematical triposes of 1818, 1819, and 1820 will illustrate this statement.

like result having been obtained almost simultaneously, although quite independently, by Leverrier.

Foundation of the Adams Prize. This brilliant achievement was commemorated soon after by several members of St. John's College (of which Mr. Adams was at that time a fellow) by the foundation of the Adams Prize.

Within four years from the publication of Sedgwick's *Essay*, a criticism of similar design, but conceived in a very different spirit, appeared from the pen of another fellow of the same society.[1] Obscurity has since overtaken both the writer and his treatise; and it must be admitted that his arguments are urged with an acrimony which probably contributed not a little to deprive them of their legitimate effect. When, however, we take into consideration the fact that this expression of opinion appeared just half a century ago, the discernment with which it singles out the defects in the range and character of the existing course of studies must be considered not a little remarkable. Whether it be in dealing with the obsolete and useless restrictions which demanded abolition, or with ancient rights and privileges which had unwisely been permitted to fall into disuse, or with the branches of learning which called for encouragement and development, the writer urges his views with a cogency of argument and breadth of judgment which leave it to be regretted

Walsh's Historical Account.

[1] *A Historical Account of the University of Cambridge and its Colleges, in a Letter to the Earl of Radnor.* By Benjamin Dann Walsh, M.A., Fellow of Trinity College. 1837.

only that his language was not at the same time more guarded and conciliatory.

In advocating a considerable extension of the range of studies, Walsh recommended the institution not of two, but of five new triposes: (1) ancient and modern history, political economy, moral and political philosophy, and the history of the human mind; (2) natural history in all its branches; (3) geology, mineralogy, chemistry, electricity, &c.; (4) the principal Oriental languages; (5) the principal languages of modern Europe.

His proposals for the future.

We have now briefly to point out how all these studies have since received the recognition demanded by the writer, although not precisely in the same connection as that which he suggests.

Appointment of a syndicate in 1848.

On the 9th February 1848 a grace was carried in the Senate, by a majority of 26 to 7, for the appointment of a Syndicate 'to consider whether it is expedient to afford greater encouragement to the pursuit of those studies for the cultivation of which professorships have been founded in the university.' As the result of their deliberations, the Syndics, in a report published on the 8th of the following April, 'while admitting the superiority of the study of mathematics and classics over all others as the basis of general education, and acknowledging, therefore, the wisdom of adhering to our present system in its main features,' gave it nevertheless as their opinion 'that much good would result from affording greater encouragement to other branches of science and learning which were daily acquiring more importance and a higher estimation in the world.' They accordingly recommended the establishment of two new Honour Triposes: the one to include Moral Philosophy, Political Economy, Modern History, General Jurisprudence, and the Laws of England; the other, Anatomy, Comparative Anatomy, Physiology, Chemistry, Botany, and Geology. Among those composing the Syndicate appear the names: W. Whewell, H. Philpott, Henry S. Maine, James Challis, J. J. Smith, C. Merivale, and W. H. Thompson.

Institution of the Moral Sciences and Natural Sciences Triposes.

Such were the circumstances under which the MORAL SCIENCES TRIPOS and the NATURAL SCIENCES TRIPOS were founded, the first examination in connection with each being held in the year 1851.

Of the movement to which these triposes owed their origin, Whewell undoubtedly represented the leading spirit. His influence was described by Sir James Stephen, writing in the same year, as that of 'one dominant mind, informed by such an accumulation of knowledge and experience as might have become a patriarch, and yet animated by such indomitable hopefulness and vivacity as might have been supposed to be the exclusive privilege of boyhood.'[1]

These important extensions of the curriculum of study were accompanied by efforts in the direction of reform with respect to general discipline and organisation. Dean Peacock's *Observations on the Statutes of the University*, published in 1841, supplied an admirable elucidation of the existing code, regarded from a historical point of view, together with a masterly criticism of actual

Movements in favour of further reforms.

[1] Preface to *Lectures on the History of France.*

defects and practical suggestions for their remedy. In 1844 the society of Trinity College obtained, at their own instance, new statutes from the Crown. Their example was followed, with a like result, in 1849, by St. John's; and it now began to be very generally recognised that the time had come for a broader and more thorough reform both of the colleges and of the university at large,—a view which was shared with an influential minority within the academic community by a considerable proportion of the educated classes without. The increase in the numbers of the students at the two universities, although considerable at Cambridge, had not been commensurate with the growing wealth and population of the nation. The Dissenters, now that religious disabilities had been abolished in almost every other quarter, demurred at an exclusiveness which debarred them from the substantial rewards of academic success and from all share in the academic government. On the eve of the Royal Commission of 1850 one of their principal organs drew attention to the fact that while the undergraduates at Oxford and Cambridge scarcely numbered 3000,[1] there were, in the two universities of Valencia and Valladolid, which together represented little more than a fourth of the university students in Spain, nearly the same number. In other words, the most bigoted and unprogressive country in Europe, with but half the population, could reckon very nearly four university students to every one that was to be found in liberal and enlightened England!

The growing feeling was marked by the appoint-

[1] The number of undergraduates in Cambridge in 1850 was 1742.

ment of a Syndicate (7th March 1849) for the
Proposed revision of the university statutes. purpose of revising the statutes of the university; and in June 1850 a memorial, signed by many distinguished graduates of Oxford and of Cambridge, and by some of the most eminent members of the Royal Society, was addressed to Lord John Russell, First Lord of the Treasury, setting forth 'that the present system of the ancient English universities had not advanced, and was not calculated to advance, the interests of religious and useful learning to an extent commensurate with the great resources and high position of those bodies,— that the constitution of the universities of Oxford and Cambridge and of the colleges (now inseparably connected with their academical system) was such as in a great measure to preclude them from introducing those changes which were necessary for increasing their usefulness and efficacy,'—and under these circumstances, believing that the aid of the Crown was the only available remedy for the above defects, the memorialists prayed that his lordship would advise Her Majesty to issue Her Royal Commission of Inquiry into the best methods of securing the improvement of the universities of Oxford and Cambridge.

On the 31st of the following August, the Commission petitioned for was appointed; and on the
Appointment of the Commission of 1850. 30th August 1852, the Commissioners presented their report, in which they recommended the codification of the ordinances of the Senate, and drew attention to the fact that the statutes of Queen Elizabeth contained many directions which had become obsolete, as being no longer suited to the

existing course of study. The printing and publication of the ancient statutes of the university, and also those of most of the colleges, which took place during the labours of the Commission, have since proved of material service in connection with the investigation of the history of the university. The main features of the reforms advocated were thus summed up by the Commissioners themselves:—

'We have proposed the restoration in its integrity of the ancient supervision of the university over the Substance of their report. studies of its members, by the enlargement of its professorial system,—by the addition of such supplementary appliances to that system as may obviate the undue encroachments of that of private tuition,—by opening avenues for acquiring academical honours in many new and distinct branches of knowledge and professorial pursuit,—by leaving to more aspiring students ample opportunity to devote themselves to those lines of acquirement in which natural bias has given them capacity, or in which the force of circumstances has rendered it urgent upon them to obtain pre-eminence; while yet not denying to the less highly gifted the social advantage of a university degree. Still following the same lead, though here, no doubt, passing beyond the immediate limits marked out by internal reformations, we have recommended the removal of all restrictions upon elections to fellowships and scholarships, and we have pointed out the means by which, without any real injury to the claims of particular schools, all fellowships and scholarships may be placed on such a footing as to be brought universally under the one good rule of unfettered and open competition. In a like spirit we have regarded the existing distribution of collegiate emoluments. We recognise the prevailing practice by which fellowships are looked upon as just rewards of eminent merit, and as helps and encouragements to the further prosecution of study or general advancement in life. But, at the same time, bearing in mind that the fellows of colleges were by the original constitution of the university in the position of teachers, and had laborious duties assigned to them, arising out of the old scheme of academical instruction, while in modern times the fellowships are frequently held by non-residents, and rarely contribute in any direct way to the course of academical instruction, though their emoluments far exceed their original value, we have thought, that in consideration of this practical exemption from the performance of such educational duties, it is no more than reasonable and equitable, in return, that an adequate contribution should be made from the corporate funds of the several colleges towards rendering the course of public teaching, as carried on by the university itself, more efficient and complete.'

The scheme of reform thus described was for the most part embodied in the new statutes which came into operation in 1858, whereby the university was liberated from the obsolete and irksome restrictions to which for nearly three centuries it had been subjected by the Elizabethan code.

Consequent enactment of statutes of 1858.

But notwithstanding this important advance, it soon became apparent that more was still required to satisfy the growing demands of the age, and that, in the opinion of some of the ablest judges, much still remained to be effected, in relation to the studies pursued. In 1867 there appeared, under the editorship of Dr. Farrar, the now well-known *Essays on a Liberal Education.*

<small>Reforms in the curriculum of studies advocated in the *Essays on a Liberal Education.*</small>

The volume was essentially a Cambridge manifesto, all save one of the seven writers being members of the university,[1] and well qualified by practical experience as teachers both in the university and at the public schools to form a competent opinion with respect to the subjects of which they severally treated. Their condemnation of the existing system of education, and especially of the method pursued in classical studies, was unanimous. The traditional arguments in favour of these studies were called in question with unprecedented freedom. It was denied that the training afforded by the study of the classics was the best aid to the mastery of English. It was suggested that the analysis of language, involving as it did a considerable strain on the reflective faculty, would be best taught in the most familiar language, and therefore in the vernacular. The discontinuance of both Greek and Latin verse composition, and of Greek prose, was strongly urged, as the time hitherto devoted to such attainments, it was maintained, would be far more advantageously given to natural science and the study of the chief models of English literature.

In the following year (1868) a volume put forth by Mr. Mark Pattison, and another by Mr. Goldwin

---

[1] The contributors were C. S. Parker (Oxford), H. Sidgwick, John Seeley, E. E. Bowen, F. W. Farrar, J. M. Wilson, J. W. Hales, W. Johnson, Lord Houghton.

Smith, advocated further measures of reform for Oxford; and in the same year appeared the Report drawn up by Mr. Matthew Arnold on *Schools and Universities on the Continent,*— all alike pointing to the conclusion that, in the opinion of these writers, it would be well if the two great English universities were more closely assimilated to the universities of Germany. In 1869 some advance was made in this direction by the enactment of a statute admitting students as members of the university without making it imperative that they should be entered at any hall or college. It was, however, still required that they should be resident either with their parents or in duly licensed lodgings—the authorities thus retaining a certain control and supervision, the absence of which in German universities is a generally admitted defect.

<small>Other expressions of opinion.</small>

In framing the new college codes, which were introduced coincidently with the new statutes of 1858, the Commissioners had encountered considerable opposition within the university, and the changes introduced by them were consequently in some cases only tentative and generally incomplete. In the autumn of 1871 a committee of the fellows of Trinity College was formed for the special purpose of considering all those portions of the statutes which dealt with elections to fellowships and with their tenure. A fatal accident, in 1866, had deprived the society of the guidance of Dr. Whewell, but his successor, Dr. Thompson, well supplied his place. He supported the committee in their work with firmness, and with admirable skill

<small>Example set by Trinity College of a reformation of college statutes.</small>

and tact. Their scheme, when submitted to the general body of fellows, met with almost entire approval, and was finally adopted at a meeting on 13th December 1872. The meeting, as described by one who took part in the proceedings, 'lasted, with two short adjournments, from 11 A.M. to midnight, and was one which those who were present will not easily forget. . . . Almost the first act of the governing body of the College, in November 1877, was to adopt the draft statutes of 1872 as the basis of their work. The result was, that the settlement of the various questions respecting elections to fellowships and their tenure, adopted by Trinity in 1872, are now the basis of the statutes of all the colleges in the university.'[1]

The committee at Trinity had commenced their investigations about the same time that a more general inquiry into the administration of the revenues was initiated from without. In October 1871 the advisers of the Crown having made known to Parliament their opinion that a complete inquiry ought to be instituted into the revenues and property of the two universities, a Royal Commission (5th January 1872) was appointed for the purpose of carrying out the proposed inquiry.

Appointment of the Royal Commission of 1872.

The general results of the labours of this Commission are to be found embodied in the first volume of the *Universities Commission Report*, published in 1874. Prior to its publication, the evidence brought to light had induced a highly influential body in the university to assume

Memorial to the Prime Minister in 1874.

---

[1] The late Rev. Coutts Trotter, vice-master of Trinity, in the *Cambridge Review*.

the initiative by memorialising the Prime Minister. The memorial was signed by only 2 of the 17 heads of colleges, but it included 26 of the 33 professors, 20 out of 26 college tutors, 66 out of 84 lecturers, and 28 out of 57 resident fellows,—the total number of signatures being 142, or nearly half the electoral roll.

The memorialists, under the conviction that the following reforms would 'increase the educational efficiency of the university, and at the same time promote the advancement of science and learning,' recommended that:

<small>Recommendations of the memorialists.</small>

1. No fellowship should be tenable for life, except only when the original tenure is extended in consideration of services rendered to education, learning, or science, actively and distinctly in connection with the university or the colleges.

2. A permanent professional career should be as far as possible secured to resident educators and students, whether married or no.

3. Provision should be made for the association of the colleges, or of some of them, for educational purposes, so as to secure more efficient teaching, and to allow to the teachers more leisure for private study.

4. The pecuniary and other relations subsisting between the university and the colleges should be revised, and, if necessary, a representative board of university finance should be organised.

It was mainly on the basis of the foregoing recommendations that the *Universities of Oxford and Cambridge Act* of 1877 was drawn up, and, as approved by the Queen in Council in 1882,

<small>Universities Act of 1877.</small>

became the Code under which both universities and their colleges are now regulated. By its provisions all restrictions in elections to fellowships have been finally removed, but fellowships are no longer tenable for life unless associated with some college or university office; the colleges have been required to contribute a specified percentage of their incomes towards the funds of the university, and the incomes of fellows under the new statutes have been subjected to a corresponding reduction. A system of intercollegiate lectures has greatly extended the usefulness of the collegiate instruction, and also led to its increased efficiency.

Contemporaneously with these several stages of reform, the studies of the university itself have been to a great extent remoulded and new triposes have been established.

The examinations for the Civil Law Classes had been held so far back as 1815, but in 1858 these were superseded by the institution of a LAW TRIPOS. The advantages resulting from the extension thus given to the range of studies had by this time become too patent to be called in question even by those who had originally been disposed to resist such innovations. A *Quarterly Reviewer*, writing in 1868, was fain to admit that 'a too luxuriant growth of mathematical competition ... had been checked by a series of successful efforts to give vigour and reputation to classical and other subjects.' 'The Classical Tripos,' he observed, 'already contains nearly as many names as the mathematical, and its value is rising every day.' The marked suc-

Institution of the Law Tripos in 1858.

cess that had attended the institution of a school of Law and Modern History at Oxford partly suggested that of the Law and History Tripos in 1870, when the final examination in these subjects was for the first time accepted as qualifying for the degree of B.A. or LL.B.

Changed to the Law and History Tripos in 1870.

As thus constituted, the Tripos was not, however, of long duration, for a Syndicate having been appointed, 23d May 1872, to take into consideration what modifications were desirable, ultimately decided to recommend the establishment of two Triposes, one to be called the Law Tripos, the other the HISTORICAL TRIPOS.

This divided in 1872 into the Law Tripos and the Historical Tripos.

They also gave it as their opinion that History, 'as the subject of an independent Tripos, required to be placed on a wider basis than its subordinate position in other Triposes had hitherto allowed,' and accordingly proposed that 'Ancient and Mediæval History should have their due place in the Tripos, as well as Modern History, so that History might be placed before the student as a whole.' They further recommended that the study of history should be accompanied with the chief theoretical studies which find their illustration in history.

These proposals having received the sanction of the Senate, the first examinations for the two Triposes were held in 1875. The subjects for the Historical Tripos included English History, three special periods, selected respectively from the divisions known as Ancient, Mediæval, and Modern, the principles of Political Philosophy and General Jurisprudence, Constitutional Law and Constitutional History, Political

Economy and Economic History, and International Law in connection with selected Treaties.

Ten years' experience, however, led those who had the best opportunities for forming a competent judgment as to the practical working of this scheme to advocate certain changes which were embodied in a Report (27th October 1885) and adopted by the Senate.

By these new regulations the number of subjects was reduced from eight to seven, and greater stress is now laid on a knowledge of Original Authorities, and of the Constitutional History of England. According, again, as the tastes and aptitudes of the student incline him either to fuller research or to the study of theoretical generalisations, he is permitted to choose between a second special subject and the alternative papers on (1) Political Economy, and (2) the General Theory of Law and Government and the Principles of International Law.

Changes in the Historical Tripos, to take effect after 1888.

By a scheme which came into operation in 1881, the Classical Tripos also underwent material modification,—the examination being divided into two parts, to be taken in different years. Of these, the first part represents an examination similar to that of the original tripos, but includes questions on Greek and Roman antiquities. The second part is subdivided into five subjects, of which the first represents pure scholarship and is compulsory, while a selection of one (or two) is admitted in relation to the other four, which consist of Philosophy, ancient Greek and Roman History and Law, Archæology, and Comparative Philology.

Changes in the Classical Tripos from 1881.

THE PRESENT CENTURY. 209

The requirements for the THEOLOGICAL TRIPOS (first held in 1874) have, in like manner, undergone certain modifications, which first came into effect in 1884. The general tendency of these changes has been: first, a reduction of the required amount of reading, which had before been of too heterogeneous a character; secondly, the provision for further special study in certain specified subjects, viz., the Old and New Testaments, Church History, and Doctrine; thirdly, to both enable and induce those who had already taken honours at other triposes to present themselves for examination in the second part of this tripos.

Changes in the Theological Tripos from 1884.

In 1878 the SEMITIC LANGUAGES TRIPOS first came into operation, having as its main subjects Arabic, Hebrew, Syriac, Biblical Chaldee, and the Comparative Grammar of the Semitic Languages. In the following year was held the first examination for the INDIAN LANGUAGES TRIPOS, which, taking Sanskrit as its basis, is restricted mainly to Persian and Hindustani and the Comparative Grammar of the Indo-European Languages; and in 1886 was held the first examination for the MEDIÆVAL AND MODERN LANGUAGES TRIPOS, which, after testing the candidate's acquaintance with French and German, gives alternative papers in (*B*) French, with Provençal and Italian; (*C*) German, with Old Saxon and Gothic; (*D*) English, with Anglo-Saxon and Icelandic.

Institution of the Semitic Languages Tripos, the Indian Languages Tripos, and the Mediæval and Modern Languages Tripos.

In connection with the growth of the studies fostered by the Natural Sciences Tripos, it remains to note the

C. H. O

remarkable increase in the activity of the medical school during the last ten years. In 1865 the number of M.D. and M.B. degrees conferred was 6, in 1875 it was 12, in 1887 it was 57. The university has recognised and furthered this increase by the foundation of new professorships in Physiology, Pathology, and Surgery, and of lectureships in other branches of professional study. Clinical lectures at Addenbrooke's Hospital, first introduced by Dr. (Sir George) Paget in 1841, furnish the necessary element of practice; and if we may judge from a *Report of the Visitors of University Examinations appointed by the General Medical Council* (1886), the medical degrees and examinations of the university now stand second to none in the kingdom as regards professional repute and distinction. In the present year (1888) over 300 undergraduates are pursuing medical study in the university.

The fundamental changes introduced into the constitution of both the university and the colleges has not failed, as might have been anticipated, to give rise to counter efforts, indicating on the part of their supporters a desire to retain to some extent the principles of the older system. In 1882 Selwyn College was founded, in memory of the eminent bishop of Lichfield, better known by his zeal and self-devotion as bishop of New Zealand. The design of the foundation, as set forth in its charter, is to provide persons 'desirous of academical education, and willing to live economically, with a college wherein sober living and high culture of the mind may be combined with Christian training, based upon the principles of the Church of

Foundation of Selwyn College, 1882.

England.' At the close of 1886 there were ninety-five undergraduates in residence, and it was in contemplation to build additional rooms, so as to enable the College to receive 120, the number for which it was originally planned. Thirty-seven of its members had graduated, of whom fifteen had gained honours.

The foundation of Ridley Hall, in 1881, by members of the Evangelical Church party, may be looked upon as an extension of the same idea, the Hall being designed to supply residence and tuition in theology for those who have already graduated in the university, and are intending to enter holy orders. The students are thus enabled to continue to reside in Cambridge instead of entering at one of the various theological colleges in other parts of England.

Foundation of Ridley Hall.

Although many of the changes above described were regarded with much apprehension by not a few sincere well-wishers to the university, and encountered no little opposition, it cannot be said that the alarm they excited has been justified by the sequel. At no period in its history has the reputation of the University of Cambridge stood so high as it now stands. At no period has discipline been maintained with so little difficulty, or the general conduct of the students been so satisfactory. While as regards the evidence afforded by the test of mere numbers, it is sufficient to note the steady increase that has taken place during the past quarter of a century. In the year 1862–3, the total number of undergraduates (which had been on the decline for some years previously) was 1526;

Growth of the university during the last quarter of a century.

in 1886–7 it was 2979; in the former year, the number of matriculations was 448; in the latter, 1009.

The accompanying chart is designed to represent the number of B.A. degrees conferred in the university since the year 1500. It is to be observed, that the ordinate corresponding to any particular year represents, not the actual number of degrees conferred in that year, but the average number for five consecutive years of which that year is the middle.

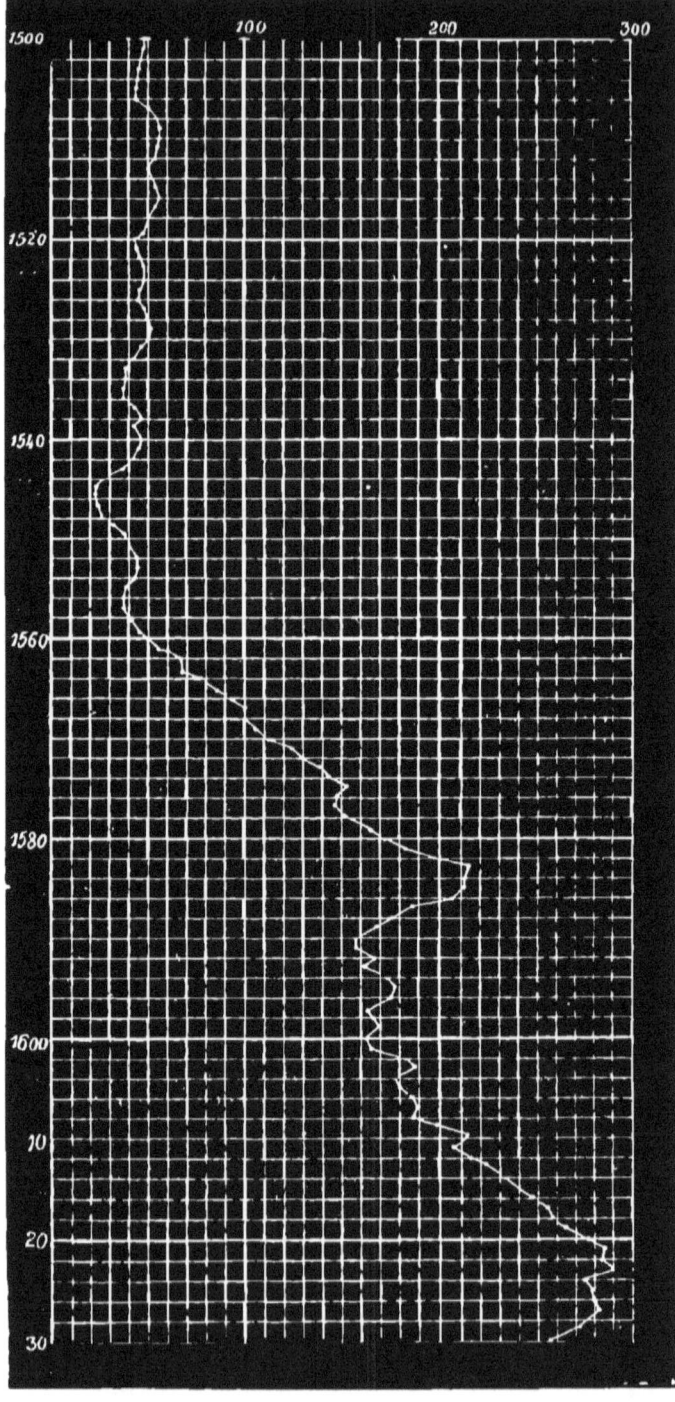

[*To face page* 212.—(1)

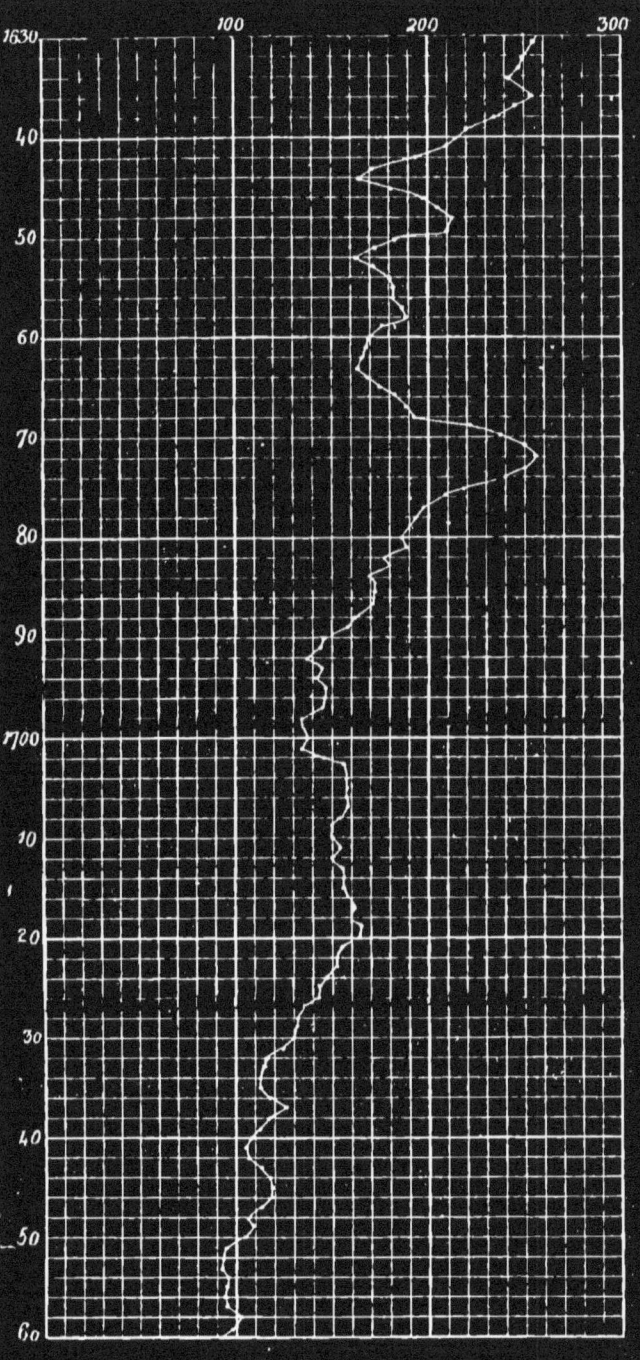

CHAPTER XII.

CAMBRIDGE IN RELATION TO NATIONAL EDUCATION.

THE facts contained in the preceding chapter are sufficient to show the advance which the university has made during the last half-century towards regaining its ancient national character and extending the range of its culture. It now remains to give some account of two concurrent movements which have served to bring the university into closer connection with education generally throughout the country. By the one, the Local Examinations, it has performed a national service by gradually raising the standard of instruction, alike in public and private schools; by the other, the University Extension Lectures, it has rendered no less service by placing instruction, after the standard and method which belong to academic teaching, within the reach of students of all classes and ages throughout the land.

<small>Institution of the LOCAL EXAMINATIONS.</small>

The LOCAL EXAMINATIONS was the earlier movement, having received the sanction of the Senate in the year 1858. On the 11th of February in that year a Grace was passed to the following effect:—

1. That there be two Examinations in every year, commencing at the same time, one for students who

are of not more than fifteen (raised to sixteen, 19th March 1858) years of age, and the other for students who are of not more than eighteen years of age.

2. That the Examinations be held in such places as the Syndics, to be appointed as hereafter mentioned, may determine.

3. That the subjects of examination be the English language and literature, History, Geography, the Latin, French, and German languages, Arithmetic, Mathematics, Natural Philosophy, and such other branches of learning as the Syndics may determine.

4. That every candidate be examined also in Religious Knowledge, unless his parents or guardians object to such examination.

A Syndicate was appointed, 17th February 1858, for the purpose of carrying the foregoing scheme into effect.

The design of the Examinations thus instituted, as originally conceived, was to provide an adequate test and stimulus for the schools which lie between the great Public Schools and the National Schools, and to raise their standard of instruction. For some years they were accordingly known as the Middle Class Examinations. Their success, however, has been greater than perhaps even the most sanguine supporter of the scheme ventured to anticipate, and the range of their influence much beyond what was at first contemplated. An eminently beneficial competition of one school with another, and one scholar with another, has been evoked, which has served not only to raise the whole standard of national education, but also to bring a large number of schools

Original scope of the Examinations.

THE LOCAL EXAMINATIONS. 215

directly under the influence of the universities. The certificates granted to successful candidates have also been recognised by other educational bodies as satisfactory tests of efficiency, and are accepted by several professions in lieu of their own preliminary examinations, and also by the university in lieu of the Previous Examination. The growth of the movement has been steady and continuous. The number of boys presenting themselves for examination in December 1858 was 370; in December 1878 it was 3916, that of girls (to whom the scheme had subsequently been extended), 2480; in December 1887 the number of boys was 5630, that of girls, 3976. Centres have now been established in countries as remote as New Zealand and Trinidad.

Ten years after the commencement of the above movement (29th October 1868) the sanction of the Senate was given to a similar scheme for the examination of women who should have completed the age of eighteen years, the carrying out of the design being entrusted to the same Syndicate as that already appointed in connection with the original scheme. To the stimulus thus imparted to female education must be attributed, in no small measure, those projects which soon after came into operation for a more thorough and extended scheme of education for women. 'The certificates' (the Secretary to the Examinations reports) 'are of great value to governesses and teachers, and are becoming almost indispensable for those who purpose making tuition their vocation, and the careful training the candidates have gone through cannot but have a

Extension of the design to older students.

beneficial effect on the character of the instruction they give.'

In 1873 men above the age of eighteen were also admitted to these examinations.

In 1871 another Syndicate was appointed for the purpose of concerting arrangements, in conjunction with the Masters, for the examination of those schools which were professedly preparatory for the universities. In their Report the Syndics recommended that the University should undertake the examination of the Highest Grade Schools, as they were termed, in a twofold manner: first, by an examination which would enable the examiners to report on the *general* character and efficiency of the teaching; secondly, by examining individually all boys who should offer themselves for the purpose on leaving school, and grant 'leaving certificates,' which should certify, in the event of the examination having proved satisfactory, that the candidates had reached a standard adapted (1) for boys under nineteen, (2) for boys under sixteen. The case of those leaving school early in order to enter into business, and that of those remaining later with the intention of entering the professions or proceeding to one of the universities, would both, it was considered, thus be met.

<small>Further extension to Highest Grade Schools.</small>

In June 1873 a Joint Board, composed of members of the universities of Oxford and Cambridge, was formed for the purpose of agreeing upon some general plan of examination, and also securing a certain uniform standard for the 'leaving certificates.' In the following year it was

<small>The certificates invested with a university value.</small>

decided that a certain university value should be assigned to these certificates, by excusing successful candidates from the whole or part of the Previous Examination.

In 1876 it was decided to extend the operations of the Joint Board so as to include Girls' Schools of the Highest Grades, and also girls individually.

Inclusion of Girls' Highest Grade Schools.

The UNIVERSITY EXTENSION MOVEMENT originated in a course of lectures delivered in 1867 by Professor James Stuart to women in Liverpool, Manchester, and Sheffield. The lectures were first delivered in connection with a society then recently started, called 'The North of England Council for the Higher Education of Women,' the president of which was Mrs. Josephine Butler, and the secretary, Miss A. J. Clough. The subject was 'Natural Philosophy,' and the lectures were eight in number. These were followed by a course by the same lecturer at Crewe in 1868, and a third course at Rochdale. Syllabuses were given out, to which weekly papers of questions were appended, the written answers being examined and corrected by the lecturer. The experiment was attended with signal success. The women who joined the classes in 1867 were in all about 600; the workpeople at Crewe about 500 to 800; those at Rochdale about 1000. Other courses, on Meteorology and Political Economy, followed, in which Professor Stuart was aided by Mr. T. Aldis and Mr. L.

The University Extension Movement.
Its first origin.
Professor James Stuart's Lectureships.

Cumming. These courses were held in the same four towns, or sometimes in connection with different groupings of towns. In 1871 the success of the movement had become so evident that certain gentlemen at Nottingham (Mr. R. Enfield, the Rev. F. Morse, the Rev. J. B. Paton) were induced to place themselves in communication with Professor Stuart on the subject. His observations had already suggested to him the necessity of ensuring continuity of effort in order to render success permanent, and the desirability, for that purpose, of forming a sort of 'peripatetic university'; and eventually four memorials (from the West of England Council, the Co-operative Society at Rochdale, the workmen at Crewe, and the Committee at Nottingham), together with a fly-sheet drawn up by Professor Stuart, were forwarded to Cambridge. The ground taken by the memorialists assumed that education, as carried on at the universities, is not necessarily restricted to high and abstruse subjects, but is capable of being applied to all subjects alike; that although in its completeness the university curriculum calls for the devotion of the whole time and energies of the student, there is no reason why a less amount of the knowledge and mental discipline which is thus offered should not also prove highly useful when brought within the reach of those who cannot attain to these advantages by residence in the university; and finally, that it is a matter of national importance that such instruction should be so brought within the reach of all classes. As the result of these memorials a Syndi-

Adoption of his scheme at Nottingham.

Joint Memorial to the University.

cate was appointed by the Senate to take the whole matter into consideration. They ultimately recommended that the scheme proposed should receive a probationary trial for three years; and as the result three lecturers were appointed, the Rev. V. H. Stanton, Mr. Birks, Mr. T. O. Harding, to lecture at Derby, Nottingham, and Leicester. After this the utility of the movement and its success seemed to be placed beyond doubt, and the Extension Lectures have developed into what has been described as an 'itinerant teaching organisation,' connecting the chief centres of our higher education with the nation at large. By this means it has been sought to educate the adult as well as the young; to bring instruction home to those whose avocations preclude their gaining it in the busy hours of the day; and not merely to provide the instruction, but systematically to superintend it, and to test its value by regularly ascertaining the results. That these aims have corresponded to a real and widespread want is sufficiently proved by the extent to which individuals of all classes of society have availed themselves of the advantages thus held out. Although mainly designed for adults, the lectures have, in many places, been largely attended by the senior pupils in schools, especially in girls' schools; while young people who have recently left school, ladies, persons of both sexes engaged in business, artisans and labourers, have all, in greater or less proportion, been represented in the classes, and in some instances an enthusiasm has been excited greatly beyond the most sanguine expectations of the lecturers themselves. So early as the year

Adoption of the scheme by the Cambridge Syndicate.

Its remarkable success.

1877 the present bishop of Chester (Dr. Stubbs) augured 'very great things' from the movement, if it were only conducted 'on sound principles, apart from party organisation, and in the hands of competent teachers'; and it may safely be asserted that the success since realised has been largely owing to the strict observance of these principles.

The genuine character of the work is attested by the manner in which the other universities have followed the example thus set. The university of Oxford has adopted a like scheme on independent lines. The *London Society for the Extension of University Teaching* is a direct offshoot from the Cambridge scheme. The university of Durham has, at its own instance, been associated with Cambridge in the work carried on in the north. The universities of Glasgow and Victoria, and the three local colleges in Wales, have initiated corresponding organisations. While Firth College, Sheffield, and University College, Nottingham, owe, in a great measure, their existence to the desire for higher education thus awakened.

Its adoption at Oxford, in London, and elsewhere.

It may also safely be asserted that the experience gained since the commencement of the movement has been of the highest value in relation to the theory and practice of education, and it has not been without a reflex influence on the work of the universities themselves. Foremost among these results we must place *the development of a special method*. The lectures have generally been delivered once a week, and the adoption of a printed and interleaved syllabus has now become an almost invariable

Method of instruction introduced with the movement.

rule. The learners have thus been furnished with an outline, to which they have been able to add their own notes from the lecture. At the foot of the outline of each lecture questions have been appended, and the written work in answer to these has supplied, at the conclusion of the following lecture, the subject-matter for a conversation class,—the instruction of the previous week being thus driven home in a less formal but not less effective manner. In the opinion of the most experienced lecturers, indeed, this portion of the work constitutes the most vital part of the system.

Another feature is the improved method which has gradually obtained of conducting the examinations.

<small>Method of examination.</small> In order, as far as possible, to check the practice of cramming, no student is permitted to enter for the examination whose work with the lecturer has not reached a certain standard of merit. The result of the examination has also invariably represented the twofold impression of the lecturer and of the examiner. It has been the practice for the former to send in an alphabetical list, distinguishing by an asterisk the names of those who have done good work on the weekly papers; while the latter has drawn up a corresponding list, placing an asterisk against the names of those who have acquitted themselves most creditably in their work on his independent examination paper. The order of merit has then been finally decided by a comparison of the work of those whose names are thus distinguished in *both lists*. It can hardly be doubted that the general adoption of a like plan would go far towards preventing those disheart-

ening failures which sometimes almost suffice to produce a feeling of mistrust with respect to examinations altogether.

A further development of the whole scheme has recently received the sanction of the Queen in Council, whereby students at an affiliated lecture centre are placed on the same footing as students at an affiliated college; so that those who have passed through a continuous course of study extending over three years, together with certain prescribed examinations, will be excused the Previous Examination at Cambridge, and be admitted to a tripos or degree examination after two years' residence.

Further development of the scheme.

In the session 1885–6 over eight thousand students attended the lectures at about fifty centres. In March 1887, a largely attended Conference was convened at Cambridge to discuss the question of affiliating these centres to the university, together with other matters. The Conference assembled in the Senate House; and the vice-chancellor (Dr. Taylor), in opening the proceedings, adverted to the largeness of the gathering, and observed that the day would be 'a memorable one in the records of the university, and perhaps in the annals of the education of the country at large.' Professor Westcott, in a speech of remarkable interest, noted that the movement 'had begun wisely and vigorously, had progressed steadily, . . . and had now found acceptance in every other English university.' The marquis of Ripon instituted a felicitous contrast (which the earlier pages of the present volume will

Conference at Cambridge in connection with the movement.

serve to illustrate) between those mediæval times when
'there was gathered round this university a vast multi-
tude of poor students who came from various parts of
the country,' and the present day, when we see the
university 'endeavouring to take its best teaching
into every part of the country, to the homes of the
people.'

INDEX.

ABÉLARD, schools taught by, 3; a pupil of William of Champeaux, 7.
Act for the maintenance of colleges, 135; universities, of 1877, 205.
Adams, Prof., discovery of the planet Neptune by, 194.
Adams prize, institution of, 195.
Age of students on admission, earliest evidence respecting limitation on, 48.
Ainslie, Dr., abstract by, of early code of Pembroke Hall, 36-38.
Alane, Alex., elected King's scholar, 88; persecution of, on account of his lectures, *ib*.
Alcock, Jo., bp. of Ely, founds Jesus College, 59; his character, *ib*.
Alcuin of York, assistance rendered by, to Charles the Great, 3.
Alfred, King, said to have been educated at Ely, 10; mythical founder of Oxford University, 11.
Ames, Wm., compelled to quit the university, 129; becomes a professor at Fraueker, *ib*.
Andrewes, Lanc., bp. of Winchester, protests against expulsion of Baro from his professorship, 134; his success as instructor in the art of catechising, 144.
Aquinas, Thos., study of, at Cambridge, 60, 61.
Aristotle, the New, 8; study of the original, 94.
Arles, school at, 2.
Arminianism, growth of, in the university, 133.
Arthur, Thos., a leading Reformer, 81.
Arundel, Archbp., suppression of Lollardism by, 51; refusal of, to credit the alleged privileges of the university, *ib*.
Ascham, Roger, testimony of, 87; *Scholemaster* of, 91; description by, of improvement in Cambridge studies, 94; description by, of customary pronunciation of Greek, *ib*.; controversy of, with Gardiner, 95; testimony of, on evils of patronage, 102.
Audley, Sir Thos., endows Magdalene College, 90; founds the same, 96.
Augustinian friars, establishment of, at Cambridge, 17.
Avignon, Wm. Bateman an official at the papal court at, 40.

BACHELOR, meaning of the term, 25; 'commencing,' meaning of term, 24; B.A., smallness of number of admissions to, in 1665, 160; B.D., requirements imposed on those of status of, 105.
Bacon, Lord, returned as representative of the university in Parliament, 141; attachment of, to the university, *ib*.; censure of, on academic studies, 144.
Bacon, Sir Nich., benefactor of C. C. College, 44.
Baker, Dr., provost of King's, compelled as a Catholic to flee, 119.
Baker, Thos., ejection of, from fellowship, 165; manuscript collections of, *ib*.; death of, *ib*.
Balsham, Hugh de, ordinance of, 30; sympathies of, 31; introduces secular scholars into the Hospital of St. John, 32.
Bancroft, Ri., archbp. of Canterbury, a leading member of the Arminian party in the university, 134; understanding between, and King James, 139.
Barbarossa, privileges bestowed by, on universities of Italy, 5.
Barnes, Robt., prior of Barnwell, a leading Reformer, 81; his sermon at St. Edward's, 82; his arrest and recantation, *ib*.
Barnes, Josh., reputation of, as a Greek scholar, 169.
Barnwell, foundation of priory at, 14.
Barnwell Process, the, 52.
Baro, Peter, ejection of, as an Arminian, from the Lady Margaret professorship, 134.
Barret, Wm., f. of Caius, attack on Calvinism by, 134.
Barrow, Isaac, master of Trinity, examines Newton in Euclid, 160; aided by Newton in his work on optics, 161.
Barwell, Dr., maladministration of, as master of Christ's College, 144.
Bassett, Josh., f. of Caius, appointed to mastership of Sidney College, 162.
Bateman, Wm., bp. of Norwich, career and character of, 40; Trinity Hall founded by, 40; death of, at Avignon, 42.
Battie scholarship, foundation of, 180.
Benedictines, foundation of, in Cambridge, 96.

INDEX. 225

Benet, Thos., M.A., burnt as a Protestant martyr, 83.
Bentley, Rl., influence of, as master of Trinity, 166; formerly of St. John's, *ib.*; career of, prior to his appointment to the mastership, 167; encouragement extended by, to scientific studies, *ib.*; improvements effected by, in Trinity College, 168; criticism of Barnes by, 169; misplaced literary activity of, 171; contentions of, with the university, *ib.*; deprivation of, of his degrees, *ib.*; contentions of, with fellows of Trinity, 172; suit gained by, *ib.*; faults of, as administrator, *ib.*; prosecution of Middleton by, 174; position of, in tripos, 178.
Berridge, Jo., dislike of, to scientific studies, 184.
Bill, Wm., master of Trinity, a leader in the university, 91.
Bilney, Thos., the first leader of the Reformation in Cambridge, 80.
Boethius, knowledge of the *Organon* of Aristotle preserved by writings of, 8.
Bologna, origin of university of, 4; becomes a centre for the study of law, 5; obtains State recognition, 9.
Books, presentation to university library of all, printed within the realm, *see* Parliament.
Browne, Robt., of C. C. College, quits Cambridge, 129; becomes the founder of the sect of Independents, 130; schism among his followers, *ib.*
Bucer, Martin, appointment of, to Regius professorship of Divinity, 105; character of his theology, 106; his death, *ib.*; exhuming of remains of, 110.
Buckingham College, conversion of, into Magdalene, 96.
Buckingham, fourth duke of, election of, to the chancellorship, 146; proposal of to rebuild university library, *ib.*; assassination of, 148.
Burcher, Jo., account by, of 'Cambridge men' in letter to Bullinger, 113.
Burghley, Lord, protests against ejection of Baro from his professorship, 134; loss to the university by death of, 136. *See* also Cecil.
Bury, Simon de, first warden of King's Hall, 47.

CAIUS COLLEGE, founding of, in 1558, 110; statutes of, 111; gateways of, *ib.*
Caius, Dr., maintains superior antiquity of university of Cambridge, 11; description by, of state of the university at accession of Elizabeth, 102; refounds Gonville Hall, 110; not molested on accession of Elizabeth, 116; harsh treatment of, as a suspected Catholic, 127; retirement of, to London, *ib.*; death of, *ib.*
Caius, Thos., maintains superior antiquity of university of Oxford, 11.
Calendar, University, first publication of, 185.
Cambridge, town of, burnt, 10; early importance of, 12; early reputation of, for learning, 16; townsmen, dispute of, with the university, 137; occupation of,

by Cromwell, 149; selection of, as a military centre in the Civil War, 150.
Cambridge, university of, alleged foundation of, by Cantaber, 11; placed after Oxford by Parliament, 11; migration to, from Oxford, 12; introduction of the Mendicants at, 16; migrations of students to, in thirteenth century, 17; riots between students in, 18; destruction of original documents of, 20; modelled on the university of Paris, 21; organisation of, in thirteenth century, 30; alleged ancient privileges of, 51; these called in question by the bishops of Ely, *ib.*; character of the teaching in, at close of fifteenth century, 60; never chargeable with heresy, 79; becomes a chief centre of the Reformation, 81; impoverished state of, 93; improved condition of, 94; unsatisfactory condition of, at accession of Elizabeth, 103; increase of, during reign of Mary, 108; visitation of, in 1557, 110; less favoured than Oxford during Mary's reign, 113; less 'perversely learned' than Oxford, *ib.*; progress of, during reign of Elizabeth, 114; three religious parties in, 115; chief aim of, for three centuries, 118; chief features of, during reign of Elizabeth, 134; compelled to contribute in aid of Parliamentary forces, 151; state of, during the Civil War, 151; dangers of, under the Commonwealth, 153; depressed state of, in 1665; increase in numbers of, after 1812, 188; different views of studies of, 189-191; recent growth of, 211.
Canon Law, mediaeval course of study in, 26; study of, discouraged at Jesus College, 59.
Cap, square, objected to by the Puritan party, 120; when first worn by undergraduates, 185.
Caput, the, decision of, against Cartwright, 122; election of, withdrawn from the regents, 123.
Carmelites, establishment of, at Cambridge, 17; their premises purchased by Queens' College, 90.
Cartesian philosophy, influence of, on the Cambridge Platonists, 158.
Cartwright, Thos., Margaret professor, the Puritan party founded by, 118; retirement of, to Ireland, 119; return of, to Cambridge, *ib.*; elected professor, *ib.*; effects of teaching of, 120; deprivation and departure of, 122.
Castle, the, at Cambridge, 13.
Catholic party at the universities, flight of, to the Continent, 119.
Cecil, Wm., lectures at St. John's College on Greek, 91; election of, to chancellorship of the university, 112; good offices of, with Elizabeth, on behalf of the university, 114.
Chaderton, Wm., pres. of Queens', complaint of, against Cartwright, 122.
Champeaux, Wm. of, his school at Paris, 7.
Chancellor of the university, the, authority of, as defined by the Elizabethan statutes, 125.

C. H. P

Charles the Great, restoration of education by, 3.
Charles I., college contributions in aid of, 149.
Charles II., university verses on death of, 161; abuse of mandate degrees by, 156.
Chedworth, Jo., second provost of King's College, 58.
Cheke, Sir Jo., revives the study of Greek, 91; friendship of, with Smith, 92; appointed first Regius professor of Greek, 94; advocates a changed pronunciation of Greek, ib.; protects the university at Court, 97; one of the commissioners of 1549, 104.
Christ's College, foundation of, 68; early statutes of, ib.
Civil law, alleged tuition of, by Vacarius at Oxford, 12; mediæval course of study in, 26; foundation of Regius professorship of, 94; decline of the study of, 106; proceedings of chancellor's court regulated by, 125.
Clare, Countess of, refounds University Hall, 45.
Clare Hall, foundation of, 45; destructive fires at, 46; modern buildings of, ib.; distinguished members of, 47; proposed amalgamation of, with Trinity Hall, 107; material for rebuilding of, seized by Parliament, 150.
Classical authors, study of, in sixteenth century, 94.
Clergy, the, design of Elizabeth to make the university a training school for, 117.
Club Law, a college play lampooning the townsmen, 137.
Coke, Sir Edw., obtains for the universities the privilege of returning two burgesses to Parliament, 140.
Colleges, early architectural development of, 31; introduction of sons of the wealthier classes into, 100; Act for the maintenance of, 135; description of, by Uffenbach in 1710, 168.
Collins, Sam., provost of King's, liberality shown to, by Whichcote, 152.
Commission of 1547, 97; of 1549, 104; of 1850, 199; of 1872, 204.
Common Law, jealousy with which it was regarded by the civilians, 145.
Controversy, theological, effects of, in the universities, 121.
Corbet, Dr., master of Trinity Hall, invasion of the electoral privileges of the university by, 140.
Corpus Christi College, destruction of documents at, 19; foundation of, 43; early statutes of, 44; buildings of, ib.
Cosin, Jo., master of Peterhouse, ejection of, 152.
Cotes, Roger, election of, to Plumian professorship, 167.
Covel, Jo., master of Christ's College, character of, 170.
Cowley, Abr., ejection of, from fellowship, 152.
Cranmer, Archbp., his suggestion with respect to the Divorce, 83; his position not impartial, 84; burning of, at Oxford, 109.
Crashaw, Ri., ejection of, from fellowship, 152.
Craven scholarship, foundation of, 180.
Croke, Ri., of King's College, early career of, 75; appointed public orator, ib.; addresses delivered by, ib.; visits the Continental universities to obtain opinions on the Divorce, 84.
Cromwell, Oliver, commits certain Heads to prison, 149; occupation of the town by, ib.; forbids the quartering of soldiers in colleges, 153.
Cromwell, Ri., represents the university in Parliament, 153.
Cromwell, Thos., succeeds to the chancellorship, 85; motives which led the university to elect him, ib.
Cudworth, Ra., appointment of, to mastership of Clare Hall, 152; Intellectual System of, 157.
Culverwell, a distinguished Platonist, 158.
Cursory, see Lectures.

DAVENANT, Dr., his successful administration of Queens' College, 143.
Davies, Jo., pres. of Queens', classical scholarship of, 169.
Davies scholarship, foundation of, 188.
De Burgh, see Clare, Countess of.
Degrees, statistics of, illustrating the progress of the university, 114; mandate, 126; conformity to Church of England required on admission to all, 139.
Dell, Wm., master of Caius, scheme of, for the instruction of the large towns, 152.
Descartes, extravagant estimation of, among Cambridge Platonists, 158, 159.
'Determining,' meaning of the expression, 24.
Dialectic, see Logic.
Directory, the, see Travers.
Disciplina, the, of Travers, translated by Cartwright, 130; seizure of, at University Press, ib.
Dispensations from exercises prescribed by statute, 125.
Disputations, effects of, 23.
Divinity, foundation of Regius professorship of, 94.
Divorce, the royal, effects of, at Cambridge, 83; irregular means by which the decision of the university was obtained, 84.
Documents, consequences resulting from destruction of, 20.
Doket, Andrew, first president of Queens' College, 57.
Dominicans, establishment of, at Cambridge, 16; Edmund Gouville, a friend of, 36; foundation of, at Thetford, 38.
Dorislaus, Dr., appointment of, to professorship of history, 148; assassination of, ib.
Dort, synod of, delegates to, from Cambridge, 146.
Downing College, foundation of, 187.
Durham, university of, foundation of, sanctioned by O. Cromwell, 151.

EDUCATION, theories of, at the earlier colleges, 48.
Edward I., assent of, to introduction of secular scholars at St. John's Hospital, 33.
Edward II., assent of, to foundation of Michaelhouse, 35; designed foundation of King's Hall by, 47.
Edward III., assent of, to foundation of the College of the Annunciation, 38; building of King's Hall by, 47.
Edward IV., Elizabeth Woodville, consort of, gives a code to Queens' College, 57.
'Edward's College,' proposed foundation of, 107.
Elizabeth, Queen, visit of, in 1564, 118.
Ellisley, Thos., first master of C. C. College, 44.
Ely, early education at, 10; made an episcopal see, 11, 16; relations of, to Cambridge, 11; influence of monastery at, on Cambridge, 16; monastery at, controlled by the bishop, 16.
Ely, archdn. of, supervises 'the glomerels,' 23.
Ely, bishops of, claim of, to visitatorial rights over the university, 51.
'Ely, scholars of,' fellows of Peterhouse originally so termed, 34.
Emmanuel College, foundation of, 130; code of, 131; Puritan character of, 132; limitation of tenure of fellowships at, ib.; reputation of society of, 133; state of discipline at, after the Restoration, 156.
Erasmus, influence of, at Cambridge, 67; residence of, at Queens' College, 73; patronage of Ri. Croke by, 74; effects produced at Cambridge by publication of his New Testament, 80.
Essays on a Liberal Education, publication of, 202.
Eton College, foundation of, 54.
Examinations, first efforts to introduce general, 181, 182.

FAGIUS, PAUL, appointed reader in Hebrew, 105; death of, ib.; exhuming of remains of, 110.
Fellows of colleges, earliest mention of, 33; required to study, 46.
Fellowships, limitation imposed on tenure of, at Emmanuel College, 132.
First-fruits, payment of, a serious burden on the university, 85.
Fisher, Jo., bp. of Rochester, debt of Cambridge to, 67; academic career of, ib.; entertains Erasmus at Queens' College, 68; his efforts on behalf of St. John's College, 70; his statutes for Christ's and St. John's Colleges, 71; excommunication of Peter de Valence by, 80; feeling of the university after execution of, 85.
Forman, Thos., pres. of Queens', a leading Reformer at Cambridge, 81.
Fox, Edw., bp. of Hereford, joins in discussion on the Divorce, 84; memorable admission made by, 89.
Francis, Alban, contest respecting conferring degree on, in obedience to royal mandate, 163; decision against admission of, 164.
Franciscans, establishment of, at Cambridge, 16; befriended by Marie de St. Paul, 36; materials from their house taken to build Trinity College, 90.
Franks, the, decline of learning among, 3.
French, admission of, as an alternative for mathematics, 192.
Frost, Hy., founds the Hospital of St. John, 15.
Fuller, Thos., on fires in the university, 20.

GARDINER, STE., joins in discussion on the Divorce, 84; prohibits changed pronunciation of Greek, 95; restored to chancellorship of the university, 107; death of, 109.
Geology, Woodwardian professorship of, filled by Conyers Middleton, 174.
Gerbier, Sir Balthazar, inauguration of new Academy by, 151.
German, admission of, as an alternative for mathematics, 192.
'Germany,' name given to the meeting-place of the Cambridge Reformers, 82.
Goad, Rog., provost of King's, able rule of, 142.
Gonville, Edm., founder of Gonville Hall, 36; descent and character of, 38.
Gonville Hall, foundation of, 38; early statutes of, 39; removal of, from original site, 41; new code given to, by Bp. Bateman, 42; refounding of, 110. See also Caius College.
Gratian, appearance of Decretum of, 5.
Gray, Wm., bp. of Ely, his collection of classical manuscripts, 66.
Gray, the poet, Regius professor of History, 173.
Greek, study of, discouraged in the Latin Church, 2; institution of daily public lectures on, 86; expedient for paying the lecturer, 93; proposed change in pronunciation of, 94; its final adoption, 95.
Greek type, first use of, in England, at Cambridge, 77.
Grindal, Archbp., censure of, on Cartwright, 122.
Guilds at Cambridge, foundation of C. C. College by, 43.

HADDON, Walter, a distinguished member of King's College, 92.
Hall, early use of term as synonymous with college, 36.
Halley, Edm., aided by Newton in his researches, 161.
Hamilton, Sir Wm., strictures of, on examination for the mathematical tripos, 179.
Harsnet, S., archbp. of York, protest of, against expulsion of Baro from his professorship, 134; liberal-mindedness of, 144.
Harvard College (U.S.), founder of, educated at Emmanuel College, 132.
Heads of colleges, attempt of, to deprive the university of the suffrage, 140; arbitrary rule of, 141.

INDEX.

Hebrew, university lecturer on, how paid, 93; study of, enjoined on masters of arts, 105.
Henry V., appropriation of revenues of alien priories by, 54.
Henry VI., foundation of King's College by, 54.
Henry VII., bequest of, for completion of King's College chapel, 68.
Henry VIII., refusal of, to sanction plunder of the universities, 86; decision of, at Hampton Court, in favour of Cambridge, 97; nominal founder of Trinity College, 98.
Hey, Jo., theological sympathies of, 184.
Heywood, Oliver, prefers the Puritan writers to Plato, 153.
Hill, Thos., master of Trinity, illiberal rule of, 152.
History, foundation of professorship of, by Lord Brooke, 148; foundation of Regius professorship of, 173; first professors, 173; study of, advocated by Sedgwick, 191.
Holdsworth, Dr. Ri., vice-chancellor, committal of, to prison for reprinting the Royal Declarations, 151.
Horrocks, Jer., watches the transit of Venus, 160.
Hullier, Jo., conduct of King's, burning of, on Jesus Green, 109.

Ignoramus, performance of, before King James, 145.
Injunctions, the Royal, of 1535, 86.
Institution of a Christian Man, The, chiefly a Cambridge production, 89.
Intercollegiate teaching, first proposal for, 205.
Irishmen, first admission of, to fellowships at Sidney College, 136.
Irnerius, teaching of, at Bologna, 4.

JAMES I., expectations at accession of, 138; deputation of the university to, *ib.*; delight of, in theological disputation, 144; and in college plays, 145.
James II., pushes exercise of royal right of interference to extremes, 162; retracts when too late, 164.
Jebb, Dr., proposal of, to institute annual examinations, 181.
Jegon, Dr. Jo., vice-chancellor, dispute of, with the Mayor, 137.
Jesus College, foundation of, 59; first statutes of, *ib.*; the only college where, after 1549, grammar was still taught, 104.
Johnson, Geo., of Christ's College, expulsion of, from Church at Amsterdam, 130.
Josselin, secretary to Archbp. Parker, 44; his history of C. C. College, *ib.*

KELKE, ROG., master of Magdalene, a Marian exile, 115; maladministration of, as master, 144.
Kilkenny, Wm. de, foundation of first university exhibitions by, 14.
King's College, foundation of, 54; early code of, *ib.*; exceptional independence which its founder seeks to secure for it, 55; completion of chapel of, 68.

King's Hall, foundation of, 47; statutes of, 48; dissolution of, 98.

LAMB, Dr., prophesies the abolition of tests, 194.
Lambert, Jo., a leading Reformer, 81.
Lambeth Articles, controversy generated by the, 134.
Latimer, Hugh, joins the Reformers at Cambridge, 82; becomes a special object of attack, 83; burning of, at Oxford, 109.
Latin, knowledge of, where first acquired in mediæval times, 22; institution of daily public lecture on, 86; gives place to English at examinations, 176.
Laud, Archbp., design of, to visit the university, 148.
Laughton, tutor of Clare Hall, a promoter of the Newtonian philosophy, 170.
Law, Edm., master of Peterhouse, character of his theology, 183.
Lectures, 'cursory,' meaning of the expression, 28; meaning of 'ordinary,' *ib.*; twofold character of, in mediæval times, 62.
Leo X., proclamation of, affixed to doors of the Schools, 80.
Lever, Thos., testimony of, respecting alienation of funds designed for Trinity College, 99; respecting the rapacity of the courtiers, 102.
Library, *see* University Library.
Lightfoot, Jo., influence of, as master of St. Catherine's, 172.
Local Examinations, institution of, 213; extension of scope of, 215; extension of, to highest grade schools, 216.
Logic, the study of, acquires new importance, 6; attention devoted to, by William of Champeaux, 7; importance attached to, in mediæval times, 23.
Lollardism, presence of, in the universities, 50; repression of, by Arundel, 51.
Lombard, Peter, a pupil of Abélard, compiles the *Sentences*, 7.
Lucasian professorship, foundation of, 160.
Lutheran books, evidence of existence of, at Cambridge, 77; importation of, into the eastern counties, 80; burnt on Market Hill, 81.
Lydgate, Jo., vindication of Cambridge from heresy by, 79.

MACKENZIE, G., of Trinity, starts the University Calendar, 185.
Madew, Jo., master of Clare, a leader in the university, 91.
Magdalene College, endowed from monastic property, 90; foundation of, 96; original statutes of, *ib.*; losses of, 144.
Magister Glomeriæ, function of, 23.
Manchester, earl of, restored to the chancellorship, 155.
Mandate degrees, royal abuse of, 156; royal letter respecting, 165.
Map of Cambridge in 1574, 89.
Margaret of Anjou founds Queens' College, 56.
Margaret, the Lady, countess of Rich-

mond, appoints Bishop Fisher her confessor, 67; founds professorship of Divinity, ib.
Margaret, Lady, preachership, foundation of, 67.
Margaret, Lady, professorship, foundation of, 67.
Marie de St. Paul, foundress of Pembroke Hall, 36.
Marian exiles, the, sentiments with which they returned to Cambridge, 114.
Martin V., Pope, supports the university in its repudiation of the jurisdiction of the bishops of Ely, 52.
Martin (St.), monastery of, at Tours, 3.
Mary I., Queen, state of university during reign of, 108.
Master of arts, original significance of the term, 25; studies of, 57; usual career of, 63.
Mathematics take the place of grammar in the *Trivium*, 104.
Matriculation of students, statute requiring, 95.
Mayor, Prof. J. E. B., edition of Baker's *History of St. John's College* by, 165.
Medicine, the study of, promoted by the Saracens, 4; original course requisite for degree of doctor of, 27; development in the Cambridge school of, 210.
Mendicants, the, influence of, at the universities, 31; traces of their overthrow at Cambridge, 89.
Mere, Jo., registrary of the university, 110.
Merton College, Oxford, early statutes of, 33.
Merton Hall, probable date of, 15.
Merton, Walter de, code given by, 33.
Methods of instruction and examination, new, introduced in connection with university extension movement, 220, 221.
Mey, Jo., services of, as member of University Commission, 97.
Michaelhouse, foundation of, 35; Fisher appointed to mastership of, 67; dissolution of, 98.
Middelberg, a centre for Puritan secessionists from the university, 130.
Middleton, Conyers, relations of, to Bentley, 174; appointment of, as university librarian, *ib*.
Mildmay, Sir Walt., foundation of Emmanuel College by, 130; his motives questioned by Elizabeth, 131; limitation imposed by, on tenure of fellowships, 132.
Millenary Petition, the, scope of, prejudicial to the universities, 138.
Millington, Wm., first provost of King's College, 55; his ejectment from his post, *ib*.
Milner, Isaac, theological views of, 185.
Milner, Joseph, *History of the Church*, by, 184.
Milton, Jo., his censure on college plays, 146.
Monasteries, dissolution of, a gain to the colleges, 90.
Monk, Dr., on the increasing numbers of the university, 188.

Monmouth, duke of, election of, to chancellorship, 162; deposition of, *ib*.
Montacute, 8L., bp. of Ely, gives statutes to Peterhouse, 33.
Monte Cassino, teaching at monastery of, 2, 4.
Moral Philosophy, activity of Whewell as professor of, 194.
More, Hen., a distinguished Platonist, 157; popularity of works of, 159.
Mountague, Ja., suppression of the *Apello Cæsarem* of, 147.

'NATIONS,' division of Continental universities into, 18.
Neville, Dr., master of Trinity, deputed to congratulate King James I., 138; munificence of, as master, 143.
New College, Oxford, code of, a model for that of King's College, 54.
New England, early divines of, educated at Emmanuel College, 132.
Newton, Sir Isaac, early Cambridge career of, 160; retirement of, on the outbreak of the plague, 161; growth of academic reputation of, *ib*.; publishes second edition of *Principia* at Bentley's persuasion, 167; later career of, 171.
Nicholson, Sygar, early printer in Cambridge, 77.
Nonjurors, mandamus for ejection of, from fellowships, 165.
Norfolk, natives of, prominent among the Cambridge Reformers, 81.
Norfolk, ninth duke of, restored to highstewardship of the university, 107.
'North and South,' division of the English universities into, 18.
Northampton, migrations from Oxford and Cambridge to, 18.
Northampton, earl of, discountenances the pretensions of the *Caput*, 140.
Northumberland, first duke of, arrest of, in King's College, 107.
Numbers, decline of, in the university, in latter part of seventeenth century, 166, *note*.

OATH of supremacy, consequences of administering of, 116.
'Opponent,' the, in disputations, 23; four in number, 177.
Optime, senior and junior, explanation of term, 177; senior, when first divided from wranglers, 176, *note;* proctor's, 177.
Orders, religious, early admission of, to degrees in the university, 17.
Oughtred, Wm., f. of King's, a supporter of the Copernican theory, 160.
Oxford, town of, burnt, 10; schools at, *ib*.
Oxford, university of, probably older than Cambridge, 11; placed before Cambridge by Parliament, *ib*.; influenced by the Renaissance earlier than Cambridge, 66; decline of, during the Reformation period, 113.

PAGET, Wm., high steward, a leading Reformer, 81.
Paley, Wm., befriended by Law, 183; writings of, 184.

230   INDEX.

Paræus, burning of the works of, 146.
Paris, commencement of university of, 6; teachers of, obtain State recognition, 9; model for Oxford and Cambridge, 11; migrations from, to England, 17.
Paris, schools of Abélard at, 3; study of logic at, 7.
Paris, Matthew, statements of, respecting Oxford. 12.
Parker, Matt., archbp. of Canterbury, his secretary, Josselin, 44; map of Cambridge executed by direction of, 89; appointed dean of college at Stoke, 93; election of, to mastership of C. C. College, 97; services of, to the university, *ib.*; resignation of headship, by, 108; death of, 127; benefactions of, to the university, *ib.*
Parliament, university acquires the privilege of returning members to, 140; Act of, requiring presentation of printed books to the university, 157.
Parr, Kath., the real foundress of Trinity College, 98.
Paschal II., Pope, constitutes Ely an episcopal see, 11.
Pattrick, Symon, election of, to presidency of Queens', 157; the same nullified by the Crown, *ib.*
Paynell, Wm., innovations on subjects for lectures by, 81.
Peachell, Jo., master of Magdalene, examined before Commissioners, 164; deprivation of, *ib.*
Peacock, Dean, publication of *Observations* of, 197.
Pecock, Reginald, illustration of fifteenth century tendencies afforded by, 52.
Pember, Robt., tutor of Ascham, 91.
Pembroke Hall, foundation of, 36; earliest extant statutes of, *ib.*
Pensioner, the college, early existence of, 69; enactment of restrictions on admission of, 87, 99.
Perkins, Wm., ability of, as tutor at Christ's College, 144.
Perne, Dr., master of Peterhouse, manages to retain his post, 116; his character, *ib.*
Peterhouse, foundation of, 33; earliest code of, *ib.*; original buildings of, 35.
Physic, foundation of Regius professorship of, 94.
Picot, the Norman sheriff, founds the church of St. Giles, 13.
Pilgrimage to Parnassus, performance of, in St. John's College, 145.
Pilkington, Jas., one of the Marian exiles at Frankfort, 115.
Pilkington, Leon., one of the Marian exiles at Frankfort, 115.
Pitt scholarship, foundation of, 188.
Plague, Great, of 1349, effects of, 40; extension of, to Cambridge, 160.
Platonists, the Cambridge, 156; character of their philosophy, 158.
Plays, college, dislike with which they were regarded by the Puritans, 145.
Pole, Card., elected chancellor of the university, 109; statutes of, 110.
Poll men, 177.

Ponet, Jo., a distinguished member of Queens' College, 92.
Porson, Ri., election of, to fellowship at Trinity, 181; appointment of, to professorship of Greek, *ib.*
Porson prize, foundation of, 181.
Pory, Dr., permitted, though a Catholic, to retain the mastership of Corpus, 116.
Powell, Dr., institutes examinations at St. John's, 182.
Prayer-Book, a Latin version of the, used in college chapels, 117.
Precedence, question of, between the two universities, how solved, 156.
Preston, Jo., successful rule of, at Emmanuel College, 133; success of, as college tutor at Queens', 143.
Proctors, the, 'the tribunes of the people,' 124; nominated by a cycle of colleges, *ib.*; curtailment of functions of, *ib.*
Puritanism, takes its rise at Cambridge, 118; design of, in the university, 120; increased activity of, 128; development of, at Emmanuel College, 132; and at St. John's, 133; decline of, in the university, noted by Pepys, 154.
Pythagoras, School of, 15.
Quadrivium, the, course of study comprised in, 25; modification of, 104.
Queens' College, first foundation of, 56; original statutes of, 57; Fisher appointed president of, 67; purchases the premises of the Carmelites, 90; services of, to learning, at the time of the Reformation, 92.
Querela Cantabrigiensis, the, a royalist manifesto, 150.
REDMAN, Jo., first master of Trinity, a leader in the university, 91; services of, as commissioner, 97; master of King's Hall, 99.
Reformation, the, unfavourable effects of, on the university, 93, 102.
Reformers, the, in the university, 81; include many of the best scholars, 82; invited to Cardinal College, *ib.*; their influence at Oxford, 83.
Regent Walk, the, the chief approach to the Schools, 146.
Regents, the, the teachers of the university, 27; extension of period of their teaching, 125.
Regius professorships, foundation of, 94.
Renaissance, the, earliest influences of, at Cambridge, 66; further progress of, 69.
'Respondent,' the, in disputations, 23.
Return from Parnassus, performance of, in St. John's College, 145.
Rhetoric, study of, in mediæval times, 24.
Ridley Hall, foundation of, 211.
Ridley, Nich., bp. of London, when master of Pembroke, learns by heart the Pauline Epistles, 92; one of the commissioners of 1549; burning of, at Oxford, 109; his pathetic remembrance of his college, 110.
SALERNO, university of, its origin, 2.
Salisbury, John of, his surprise at excessive attention given to study of logic, 7.
Sancroft, Archbishop, efforts of, to pro-

mote university education among the clergy, 161; chancellorship declined by, 164.
Sandys, Dr., bp. of London, arrest of, as vice-chancellor, 107.
Saracens, the, originated a more scientific study of medicine, 4.
Scholar, earliest use of the term in its modern academic sense, 38.
Scholars required to place themselves under supervision, 18, 30; complaints of, of absence of patrons, 103.
Schoolmen, abolition of the, as text-books, 87.
Schools of the Roman Empire, disappearance of, 2.
Schools, the university, when built, 28.
Scotchmen, first admission of, to fellowships, at Sidney College, 136.
Sedgwick, Adam, *Discourse* of, 191.
Selwyn College, foundation of, 210.
Senate House, the new, building of, 174; examinations first held in, *ib.*
Sentences, the, of Peter Lombard, 7; abolition of, as a text-book, 86.
Sermons, reading of, forbidden to the clergy, 162.
Seville, school at, 2.
Shaxton, bp. of Sarum, a leading Reformer at Cambridge, 81.
Sherlock, Thos., bp. of London, master of St. Catherine's, influence of, in the university, 173; writings of, *ib.*
Siberch, Jo., first printer of Greek at Cambridge, 76.
Sidney Sussex College, foundation of, 136; original statutes of, *ib.*; first Cambridge college to admit Irishmen and Scotchmen to fellowships, 136; contribution of, in aid of Charles I., 149; vacancy in mastership of, filled up by royal mandate, 162; clauses in statutes of, against Popery struck out, 164.
Sike, H., appointed through Bentley's interest professor of Hebrew, 169.
Sizars, earliest apparent institution of, 34.
Smith, Jo., f. of Christ's, becomes founder of the General Baptists, 130.
Smith, Jo., f. of Queens', *Discourses* of, 157.
Smith, Sir Thos., friendship of, with Cheke, 92; pupils of, *ib.*; advocates changed pronunciation of Greek, 94; controversy of, with Gardiner, 95; elected vice-chancellor, *ib.*; protects the university at Court, 97; brings about the foundation of Trinity College, 98; appointment of, as Regius professor of Civil Law, 106; Act of, for the maintenance of colleges, 135.
Somerset, eleventh duke of, election of, to chancellorship, 165.
Somerset, the Protector, chancellor of the university, 107.
Sophister, meaning of the term, 23.
Sparrow, Dr., imposed as president upon Queens' College by the Crown, 157.
Stafford, Geo., success of his lectures on the New Testment, 81.
Stamford, migration from Oxford to, 18.
Stanley, Jas., gives original statutes of Jesus College, 59.

Stanton, Hervey de, founds Michaelhouse, 35.
Stare in quadragesima, explanation of expression, 174.
Statutes (of the colleges), reformation of 204. *See also* under names of colleges.
Statutes (of the university): *Statuta Antiqua*, 20; statute of 1276, 30; of 1538, 93; of 1544, 95; statutes of 1549, 104; repeal of same, 108; of 1557, 110; Elizabethan, of 1570, 123; revision of, petitioned for, 199; of 1858, enactment of, 201.
St. Benet, præ-Norman church of, 13.
St. Catherine's Hall, foundation of, 58; statutes of, *ib.*; reputation of, in seventeenth century, 173.
St. Giles, foundation of church of, 13; canons of, move to Barnwell, 14.
St. John the Evangelist, foundation of Hospital of, 15; introduction of secular scholars at, 32; suppression of, 70.
St. John's College, foundation of, 70; alienation of estates bequeathed to, *ib.*; different codes of, given by Fisher, 71; eminent members of, at the time of the Reformation, 91; Puritan synods secretly held at, 133; contribution of, in aid of Charles I., 149; *History* of, by Baker, 165; new statutes granted to, by the Crown, 198.
St. Mary's (Gt.), destruction of documents at, 19; university gatherings held in, 28.
St. Rhadegund, nunnery of, foundation of, 15; suppression of, 59.
Stephen, Sir Jas., description of Whewell by, 197.
Stuart, Prof. Jas., lectures by, the origin of the University Extension Movement, 217.
Students, non-collegiate, statute for admission of, 203.
Studium generale, generally used to denote a university in mediæval times, 1.
Subscription, abolition of, by Parliament in 1640, 148; again required in 1662, 156.
Supremacy, oath of, abrogated by Parliament, 165.
Surplice, the, opposition to, in the university, 119, 132; wearing of, enjoined, 139; compulsory wearing of, abolished, 149; wearing of, enjoined at the Restoration, 155.
Tests, movement for the abolition of, 192; rejection of Bill for, by the House of Lords, 193; chief supporters of the Bill, *ib.*; final abolition of, 194.
Theology, course of study in, in mediæval times, 26.
Thompson, Dr., master of Trinity, service rendered by, in preparation of improved college statutes, 203.
Three Articles, the, subscription to, required on admission to the doctorate, 139; not to be compulsory on admission to degrees, 155.
Town and gown, earliest frays between, 19.
Travers, Walt., designs of, as a moderate Puritan, 128; expulsion of, from his fellowship, by Whitgift, *ib.*; the *Disciplina* of, 129; reappearance of same, as the *Directory*, *ib.*

Trinity College, claim of, to represent the earliest Cambridge college, 35; partly built out of materials from the Franciscan precincts, 90; foundation of, 98; first fellows of, partly from St. John's, 99; original statutes of, *ib.*; benefaction to, from Mary I., 111; increase in numbers at, during Neville's administration, 143; rebuilding of, *ib.*; state of, at time of Newton's entry, 160; improvements effected in, by Bentley, 168; new statutes granted to, by the Crown, 198; statutes of, further remodelled, 203.

Trinity College, Dublin, modelled on the university of Cambridge, 135.

Trinity Hall, foundation of, 40; early buildings of, 42; fire at, 43; proposed amalgamation of, with Clare Hall, 107.

Tripos, the, origin of the term, 174; establishment of first, 176; mathematical, original examination of, 178; classical, foundation of, 188; changes in examination for classical, 191-2; moral sciences, foundation of, 197; natural sciences, foundation of, *ib.*; law, foundation of, 206; historical, foundation of, 207; changes in same, 208; changes in classical, *ib.*; theological, foundation of, and modification of, 209; Semitic languages, foundation of, *ib.*; Indian languages, *ib.*; mediæval and modern languages, foundation of, *ib.*

Tripos verses, origin of, 175.

Trivium, course of study included in, 22; modification of, 104.

Tyndale, Wm., a leader of the Reformers in the university, 81.

UFFENBACH, description of Cambridge colleges by, in 1710, 168.

Undergraduate course of study in mediæval times, 22.

Undergraduates, numbers of, in 1850, 198, *note*; recent increase in, 211.

Uniformity, Act of, again put in force, 156.

Universities, features of the earliest, 9.

University Extension Movement, origin of, 217; growth of, 218; new methods introduced by, 220; conference in connection with, 222.

'University,' original meaning of term of, 1.

University Hall, Clare Hall originally so called, 45.

University Library, the duke of Buckingham offers to rebuild, 147; enlargement of, in 1837, *ib.*; right of, to copies of books printed within the realm, 157; presentation to, by George I., of library of Bishop Moore, 173.

University Press, the, first publications of, 77; royal licence given for, *ib.*; subsequent inactivity of, 78; seizure of Travers' *Disciplina* at, 130.

VACARIUS, alleged teaching of, at Oxford, 12.

Valence, Peter de, attack on doctrine of indulgences by, 80.

Verse composition, discontinuance of, recommended, 202.

Verses, occasional, production of, a common practice, 155.

Vice-chancellor, election of, vested in the Heads, 123.

Vives, Lud., on academic disputations, 62.

WALLIS, Jo., f. of Queens', a supporter of the Copernican theory, 160.

Walsh, B. D., *Historical Account* of, 195; innovations advocated by, 196.

Ward, Sam., master of Sidney, deplores the requirement to wear the surplice, 139.

Ward, Seth, ejection of, from fellowship, 152; a supporter of the Copernican theory, 160.

Warham, Arch., testimony of, respecting influence of Cambridge at Oxford, 83.

Watson, Ri., theological sympathies of, 184.

West, Nich., f. of King's, modifies early statutes of Jesus College, 59.

Westcott, Prof., speech of, at University Extension Conference, 222.

Whewell, Dr., views of, controverted by Sir W. Hamilton, 190; reforms introduced by, 194; influence of, described by Sir James Stephen, 197; death of, 203.

Whichcote, Benj., provost of King's, refusal of, to take the Covenant, 152; a representative of the Cambridge Platonism, 157; notable sayings of, 158, 159.

Whiston, Wm., encouraged by Bentley, 167; his *Theory of the Earth*, 169; his discharge of duties of Lucasian professor, *ib.*; theological controversy raised by, 170; his *Primitive Christianity*, *ib.*; banishment of, from the university, and final career, *ib.*

Whitaker, Wm., master of St. John's, European reputation of, 133; Puritan sympathies of, *ib.*

White Horse Inn, the, a meeting-place of the Reformers, 81.

Whitgift, Archbp., early academic career of, 121; deprives Cartwright of his fellowship, 123; proposed retirement of, from Cambridge, 126; departure of, for Worcester, 128; orders seizure of Travers' *Disciplina*, 130; death of, 139.

Wolsey, Card., visit of, to Cambridge, 75; surrender of the university statutes to, 76; founds Cardinal College, 82; invites thither some of the young Cambridge Reformers, 83.

Woodlark, Robt., founds St. Catherine's Hall, 58; rule of, as third provost of King's College, *ib.*

Woodville, Eliz., first code of Queens' College given by, 57.

Wotton, Wm., remarkable attainments of, 169.

Wyclif, influence of, at Oxford, 50. *See also* Lollardism.

Wykeham, Wm. of, his despair of the monasteries, 59.

YORK, school at, 2.

AUGUST 1889.

GENERAL LISTS OF WORKS
PUBLISHED BY
MESSRS. LONGMANS, GREEN, & CO.
LONDON AND NEW YORK.

HISTORY, POLITICS, HISTORICAL MEMOIRS, &c.

Abbey and Overton's English Church in the Eighteenth Century. Cr. 8vo. 7s. 6d.
Arnold's Lectures on Modern History. 8vo. 7s. 6d.
Bagwell's Ireland under the Tudors. Vols. 1 and 2. 2 vols. 8vo. 32s.
Ball's Legislative Systems in Ireland, 1172-1800. 8vo. 6s.
— The Reformed Church of Ireland, 1537-1886. 8vo. 7s. 6d.
Boultbee's History of the Church of England, Pre-Reformation Period. 8vo. 15s.
Buckle's History of Civilisation. 3 vols. crown 8vo. 24s.
Churchill's (Lord Randolph) Speeches. 2 vols. 8vo. 24s.
Cox's (Sir G. W.) General History of Greece. Crown 8vo. Maps, 7s. 6d.
Creighton's Papacy during the Reformation. 8vo. Vols. 1 & 2, 32s. Vols. 3 & 4, 24s.
De Redcliffe's (Viscount Stratford) Life. By Stanley Lane-Poole. 2 vols. 8vo. 36s.
De Tocqueville's Democracy in America. 2 vols. crown 8vo. 16s.
Doyle's English in America: Virginia, Maryland, and the Carolinas, 8vo. 18s.
— — — The Puritan Colonies, 2 vols. 8vo. 36s.
Epochs of Ancient History. Edited by the Rev. Sir G. W. Cox, Bart. and C. Sankey, M.A. With Maps. 10 vols. Fcp. 8vo. price 2s. 6d. each. See p. 3.
Epochs of Modern History. Edited by C. Colbeck, M.A. With Maps. 19 vols. Fcp. 8vo. 2s. 6d. each. See p. 3.
Epochs of Church History. Edited by the Rev. Mandell Creighton, M.A. 14 vols. Fcp. 8vo. price 2s. 6d. each. See p. 3.
Freeman's Historical Geography of Europe. 2 vols. 8vo. 31s. 6d.
Froude's English in Ireland in the 18th Century. 3 vols. crown 8vo. 18s.
— History of England. Popular Edition. 12 vols. crown 8vo. 3s. 6d. each.
— Short Studies on Great Subjects. 4 vols. crown 8vo. 24s.
Gardiner's History of England from the Accession of James I. to the Outbreak of the Civil War. 10 vols. crown 8vo. 60s.
— History of the Great Civil War, 1642-1649 (3 vols.) Vol. 1, 1642-1644, 8vo. 21s. Vol. 2, 1644-1647, 8vo. 24s.
Godolphin's (Earl of) Life. By the Hon. Hugh Elliot. 8vo. 15s.
Greville's Journal of the Reigns of King George IV., King William IV., and Queen Victoria. Cabinet Edition. 8 vols. crown 8vo. 6s. each.
Historic Towns. Edited by E. A. Freeman, D.C.L. and the Rev. William Hunt, M.A. With Maps and Plans. Crown 8vo. 3s. 6d. each.

London. By W. E. Loftie.	Bristol. By the Rev. W. Hunt.
Exeter. By E. A. Freeman.	Oxford. By the Rev. C. W. Boase.
Cinque Ports. By Montagu Burrows.	Colchester. By the Rev. E. C. Cutts.
	Carlisle. By the Rev. M. Creighton.

LONGMANS, GREEN, & CO., London and New York.

General Lists of Works.

Lecky's History of England in the Eighteenth Century. Vols. 1 & 2, 1700-1760, 8vo. 36s. Vols. 3 & 4, 1760-1784, 8vo. 36s. Vols. 5 & 6, 1784-1793, 36s.
— History of European Morals. 2 vols. crown 8vo. 16s.
— — — Rationalism in Europe. 2 vols. crown 8vo. 16s.
Longman's Life and Times of Edward III. 3 vols. 8vo. 28s.
Macaulay's Complete Works. Library Edition. 8 vols. 8vo. £5. 5s.
— — — Cabinet Edition. 16 vols. crown 8vo. £4. 16s.
— History of England :—
Student's Edition. 2 vols. cr. 8vo. 12s. | Cabinet Edition. 8 vols. post 8vo. 48s.
People's Edition. 4 vols. cr. 8vo. 16s. | Library Edition. 5 vols. 8vo. £4.
Popular Edition. 2 vols. cr. 8vo. 5s.

Macaulay's Critical and Historical Essays, with Lays of Ancient Rome In One Volume :—
Authorised Edition. Cr. 8vo. 2s. 6d. | Popular Edition. Cr. 8vo. 2s. 6d.
or 3s. 6d. gilt edges.

Macaulay's Critical and Historical Essays :—
Student's Edition. 1 vol. cr. 8vo. 6s. | Cabinet Edition. 4 vols. post 8vo. 24s.
People's Edition. 2 vols. cr. 8vo. 8s. | Library Edition. 3 vols. 8vo. 36s.

Macaulay's Miscellaneous Writings. 2 vols. 8vo. 21s. 1 vol. crown 8vo. 4s. 6d.
— Miscellaneous Writings and Speeches. Student's Edition. Cr. 8vo. 6s. Popular Edition. Crown 8vo. 2s. 6d.
— Miscellaneous Writings, Speeches, Lays of Ancient Rome, &c. Cabinet Edition. 4 vols. crown 8vo. 24s.
— Writings, Selections from. Crown 8vo. 6s.
— Speeches corrected by Himself. Crown 8vo. 3s. 6d.
Magnus's Outlines of Jewish History. Fcp. 8vo. 3s. 6d.
Malmesbury's (Earl of) Memoirs of an Ex-Minister. Crown 8vo. 7s. 6d.
May's Constitutional History of England, 1760-1870. 3 vols. crown 8vo. 18s.
Merivale's Fall of the Roman Republic. 12mo. 7s. 6d.
— General History of Rome, B.C. 753-A.D. 476. Crown 8vo. 7s. 6d.
— History of the Romans under the Empire. 8 vols. post 8vo. 48s.
Nelson's (Lord) Letters and Despatches. Edited by J. K. Laughton. 8vo. 16s.
Pears' The Fall of Constantinople. 8vo. 16s.
Porter's History of the Corps of Royal Engineers. 2 vols. 8vo. 36s.
Seebohm's Oxford Reformers—Colet, Erasmus, & More. 8vo. 14s.
Short's History of the Church of England. Crown 8vo. 7s. 6d.
Showers' A Missing Chapter of the Indian Mutiny. 8vo. 8s. 6d.
Smith's Carthage and the Carthaginians. Crown 8vo. 10s. 6d.
Taylor's Manual of the History of India. Crown 8vo. 7s. 6d.
Todd's Parliamentary Government in England (2 vols.) Vol. 1, 8vo. 24s. Vol. 2, 30s.
Tuttle's History of Prussia under Frederick the Great, 1740-1756. 2 vols. crown 8vo. 18s.
Walpole's History of England, from 1815. 5 vols. 8vo. Vols. 1 & 2, 1815-1832, 36s. Vol. 3, 1832-1841, 18s. Vols. 4 & 5, 1841-1858, 36s.
Wylie's History of England under Henry IV. Vol. 1, crown 8vo. 10s. 6d.

LONGMANS, GREEN, & CO., London and New York.

General Lists of Works.

EPOCHS OF ANCIENT HISTORY.
Edited by the Rev. Sir G. W. Cox, Bart. M.A. and by C. Sankey, M.A.
10 volumes, fcp. 8vo. with Maps, price 2s. 6d. each.

The Gracchi, Marius, and Sulla. By A. H. Beesly, M.A. With 2 Maps.
The Early Roman Empire. By the Rev. W. Wolfe Capes, M.A. With 2 Maps.
The Roman Empire of the Second Century. By the Rev. W. Wolfe Capes, M.A. With 2 Maps.
The Athenian Empire from the Flight of Xerxes to the Fall of Athens. By the Rev. Sir G. W. Cox, Bart. M.A. With 5 Maps.
The Rise of the Macedonian Empire. By Arthur M. Curteis, M.A. With 8 Maps.
The Greeks and the Persians. By the Rev. Sir G. W. Cox, Bart. With 4 Maps.
Rome to its Capture by the Gauls. By Wilhelm Ihne. With a Map.
The Roman Triumvirates. By the Very Rev. Charles Merivale, D.D. With Map.
The Spartan and Theban Supremacies. By Charles Sankey, M.A. With 5 Maps.
Rome and Carthage, the Punic Wars. By R. Bosworth Smith. With 9 Maps.

EPOCHS OF MODERN HISTORY.
Edited by C. Colbeck, M.A. 19 volumes, fcp. 8vo. with Maps. Price 2s. 6d. each.

The Beginning of the Middle Ages. By the Very Rev. R. W. Church. With 3 Maps.
The Normans in Europe. By Rev. A. H. Johnson, M.A. With 3 Maps.
The Crusades. By the Rev. Sir G. W. Cox, Bart. M.A. With a Map.
The Early Plantagenets. By the Right Rev. W. Stubbs, D.D. With 2 Maps.
Edward the Third. By the Rev. W. Warburton, M.A. With 3 Maps.
The Houses of Lancaster and York. By James Gairdner. With 5 Maps.
The Early Tudors. By the Rev. C. E. Moberly, M.A.
The Era of the Protestant Revolution. By F. Seebohm. With 4 Maps.
The Age of Elizabeth. By the Rev. M. Creighton, M.A. LL.D. With 5 Maps.
The First Two Stuarts. By Samuel Rawson Gardiner. With 4 Maps.
The Thirty Years' War, 1618-1648. By Samuel Rawson Gardiner. With a Map.
The English Restoration and Louis XIV., 1648-1678. By Osmund Airy.
The Fall of the Stuarts. By the Rev. Edward Hale, M.A. With 11 Maps.
The Age of Anne. By E. E. Morris, M.A. With 7 Maps and Plans.
The Early Hanoverians. By E. E. Morris, M.A. With 9 Maps and Plans.
Frederick the Great and the Seven Years' War. By F. W. Longman. With 2 Maps.
The War of American Independence, 1775-1783. By J. M. Ludlow. With 4 Maps.
The French Revolution, 1789-1795. By Mrs. S. R. Gardiner. With 7 Maps.
The Epoch of Reform, 1830-1850. By Justin McCarthy, M.P.

EPOCHS OF CHURCH HISTORY.
Edited by the Rev. Mandell Creighton. Fcp. 8vo. price 2s. 6d. each.

The English Church in other Lands. By the Rev. H. W. Tucker.
The History of the Reformation in England. By the Rev. George G. Perry.
The Church of the Early Fathers. By Alfred Plummer, D.D.
The Evangelical Revival in the Eighteenth Century. By the Rev. J. H. Overton.
A History of the University of Oxford. By the Hon. G. C. Brodrick, D.C.L.
A History of the University of Cambridge. By J. Bass Mullinger, M.A.
The English Church in the Middle Ages. By Rev. W. Hunt, M.A.
The Arian Controversy. By H. M. Gwatkin, M.A.
Wycliffe and Movements for Reform. By Reginald L. Poole.
The Counter-Reformation. By A. W. Ward.
The Church and the Roman Empire. By the Rev. A. Carr.
The Church and the Puritans, 1570-1660. By Henry Offley Wakeman.
The Church and the Eastern Empire. By the Rev. H. F. Tozer.
Hildebrand and His Times. By the Rev. W. R. W. Stephens.
The Popes and the Hohenstaufen. By Ugo Balzani.

LONGMANS, GREEN, & CO., London and New York.

BIOGRAPHICAL WORKS.

Armstrong's (E. J.) Life and Letters. Edited by G. F. Armstrong. Fcp. 8vo. 7s.6d.
Bacon's Life and Letters, by Spedding. 7 vols. 8vo. £4. 4s.
Bagehot's Biographical Studies. 1 vol. 8vo. 12s.
Burdett's Prince, Princess, and People: the Public Life and Works of T.R.H. the Prince and Princess of Wales. 8vo. 21s.
Carlyle's Life, by J. A. Froude. 8vo. Vols. 1 & 2, 1795-1835, 32s. Vols. 3 & 4, 1834-1881, 32s.
— (Mrs.) Letters and Memorials. 3 vols. 8vo. 36s.
English Worthies. Edited by Andrew Lang. Crown 8vo. each 1s. sewed; 1s. 6d. cloth.
    Charles Darwin. By Grant Allen. | Steele. By Austin Dobson.
    Shaftesbury (The First Earl). By | Ben Jonson. By J. A. Symonds.
      H. D. Traill. | George Canning. By Frank H. Hill.
    Admiral Blake. By David Hannay. | Claverhouse. By Mowbray Morris.
    Marlborough. By Geo. Saintsbury. |
Fox (Charles James) The Early History of. By Sir G. O. Trevelyan. Cr. 8vo. 6s.
Froude's Cæsar: a Sketch. Crown 8vo. 6s.
Hamilton's (Sir W. R.) Life, by Graves. 3 vols. 8vo. 15s. each.
Havelock's Life, by Marshman. Crown 8vo. 3s. 6d.
Jenkin's (Fleeming) Papers, Literary, Scientific, &c. With Memoir by R. L. Stevenson. 2 vols. 8vo. 32s.
Laughton's Studies in Naval History. 8vo. 10s. 6d.
Macaulay's (Lord) Life and Letters. By his Nephew, Sir G. O. Trevelyan, Bart. Popular Edition, 1 vol. cr. 8vo. 2s. 6d. Student's Edition, 1 vol. cr. 8vo. 6s. Cabinet Edition, 2 vols. post 8vo. 12s. Library Edition, 2 vols. 8vo. 36s.
Mendelssohn's Letters. Translated by Lady Wallace. 2 vols. cr. 8vo. 5s. each.
Müller's (Max) Biographical Essays. Crown 8vo. 7s. 6d.
Newman's Apologia pro Vitâ Suâ. Crown 8vo. 6s.
Pasteur (Louis) His Life and Labours. Crown 8vo. 7s. 6d.
Southey's Correspondence with Caroline Bowles. 8vo. 14s.
Stephen's Essays in Ecclesiastical Biography. Crown 8vo. 7s. 6d.
Vignoles' (C. B.) Life. By his Son. 8vo. 16s.
Wellington's Life, by Gleig. Crown 8vo. 6s.

MENTAL AND POLITICAL PHILOSOPHY, FINANCE, &c.

Adam's Public Debts; an Essay on the Science of Finance. 8vo. 12s. 6d.
Amos' View of the Science of Jurisprudence. 8vo. 18s.
— Primer of the English Constitution. Crown 8vo. 6s.
Bacon's Essays, with Annotations by Whately. 8vo. 10s. 6d.
— Works, edited by Spedding. 7 vols. 8vo. 73s. 6d.
Bagehot's Economic Studies, edited by Hutton. 8vo. 10s. 6d.
Bain's Logic, Deductive and Inductive. Crown 8vo. 10s. 6d.
    PART I. Deduction, 4s. | PART II. Induction, 6s. 6d.
— Mental and Moral Science. Crown 8vo. 10s. 6d.
— The Senses and the Intellect. 8vo. 15s.
— The Emotions and the Will. 8vo. 15s.
Barnett's Practicable Socialism. Crown 8vo. 2s. 6d.

LONGMANS, GREEN, & CO., London and New York.

Case's Physical Realism. 8vo. 15s.
Crump's Short Enquiry into the Formation of English Political Opinion. 8vo. 7s. 6d.
— Causes of the Great Fall in Prices. 8vo. 6s.
Dowell's A History of Taxation and Taxes in England. 8vo. Vols. 1 & 2, 21s. Vols. 3 & 4, 21s.
Green's (Thomas Hill) Works. (3 vols.) Vols. 1 & 2, Philosophical Works. 8vo. 16s. each. Vol. 3, Miscellanies. With Memoir. 8vo. 21s.
Hume's Essays, edited by Green & Grose. 2 vols. 8vo. 28s.
— Treatise of Human Nature, edited by Green & Grose. 2 vols. 8vo. 28s.
Kirkup's An Enquiry into Socialism. Crown 8vo. 5s.
Ladd's Elements of Physiological Psychology. 8vo. 21s.
Lang's Custom and Myth : Studies of Early Usage and Belief. Crown 8vo. 7s. 6d.
— Myth, Ritual, and Religion. 2 vols. crown 8vo. 21s.
Leslie's Essays in Political Economy. 8vo. 10s. 6d.
Lewes's History of Philosophy. 2 vols. 8vo. 32s.
Lubbock's Origin of Civilisation. 8vo. 18s.
Macleod's The Elements of Economics. 2 vols. crown 8vo. 7s. 6d. each.
— The Elements of Banking. Crown 8vo. 5s.
— The Theory and Practice of Banking. Vol. 1, 8vo. 12s. Vol. 2, 14s.
Max Müller's The Science of Thought. 8vo. 21s.
Mill's (James) Analysis of the Phenomena of the Human Mind. 2 vols. 8vo. 28s.
Mill (John Stuart) on Representative Government. Crown 8vo. 2s.
— — on Liberty. Crown 8vo. 1s. 4d.
— — Examination of Hamilton's Philosophy. 8vo. 16s.
— — Logic. Crown 8vo. 5s.
— — Principles of Political Economy. 2 vols. 8vo. 30s. People's Edition, 1 vol. crown 8vo. 5s.
— — Utilitarianism. 8vo. 5s.
— — Three Essays on Religion, &c. 8vo. 5s.
Mulhall's History of Prices since 1850. Crown 8vo. 6s.
Sandars' Institutes of Justinian, with English Notes. 8vo. 18s.
Seebohm's English Village Community. 8vo. 16s.
Sully's Outlines of Psychology. 8vo. 12s. 6d.
— Teacher's Handbook of Psychology. Crown 8vo. 6s. 6d.
Swinburne's Picture Logic. Post 8vo. 5s.
Thompson's A System of Psychology. 2 vols. 8vo. 36s.
— The Problem of Evil. 8vo. 10s. 6d.
— The Religious Sentiments of the Human Mind. 8vo. 7s. 6d.
— Social Progress : an Essay. 8vo. 7s. 6d.
Thomson's Outline of Necessary Laws of Thought. Crown 8vo. 6s.
Webb's The Veil of Isis. 8vo. 10s. 6d.
Whately's Elements of Logic. Crown 8vo. 4s. 6d.
— — — Rhetoric. Crown 8vo. 4s. 6d.
Zeller's History of Eclecticism in Greek Philosophy. Crown 8vo. 10s. 6d.
— Plato and the Older Academy. Crown 8vo. 18s.
— Pre-Socratic Schools. 2 vols. crown 8vo. 30s.
— Socrates and the Socratic Schools. Crown 8vo. 10s. 6d.
— Stoics, Epicureans, and Sceptics. Crown 8vo. 15s.
— Outlines of the History of Greek Philosophy. Crown 8vo. 10s. 6d.

LONGMANS, GREEN, & CO., London and New York.

CLASSICAL LANGUAGES AND LITERATURE.

Æschylus, The Eumenides of. Text, with Metrical English Translation, by J. F. Davies. 8vo. 7s.
Aristophanes' The Acharnians, translated by R. Y. Tyrrell. Crown 8vo. 2s. 6d.
Aristotle's The Ethics, Text and Notes, by Sir Alex. Grant, Bart. 2 vols. 8vo. 32s.
— The Nicomachean Ethics, translated by Williams, crown 8vo. 7s. 6d.
— The Politics, Books I. III. IV. (VII.) with Translation, &c. by Bolland and Lang. Crown 8vo. 7s. 6d.
Becker's *Charicles* and *Gallus*, by Metcalfe. Post 8vo. 7s. 6d. each.
Cicero's Correspondence, Text and Notes, by R. Y. Tyrrell. Vols. 1 & 2, 8vo. 12s. each.
Mahaffy's Classical Greek Literature. Crown 8vo. Vol. 1, The Poets, 7s. 6d. Vol. 2, The Prose Writers, 7s. 6d.
Plato's Parmenides, with Notes, &c. by J. Maguire. 8vo. 7s. 6d.
Virgil's Works, Latin Text, with Commentary, by Kennedy. Crown 8vo. 10s. 6d.
— Æneid, translated into English Verse, by Conington. Crown 8vo. 6s.
— — — — — by W. J. Thornhill. Cr. 8vo. 7s. 6d.
— Poems, — — — Prose, by Conington. Crown 8vo. 6s.
Witt's Myths of Hellas, translated by F. M. Younghusband. Crown 8vo. 3s. 6d.
— The Trojan War, — — Fcp. 8vo. 2s.
— The Wanderings of Ulysses, — Crown 8vo. 3s. 6d.

ENCYCLOPÆDIAS DICTIONARIES, AND BOOKS OF REFERENCE.

Acton's Modern Cookery for Private Families. Fcp. 8vo. 4s. 6d.
Ayre's Treasury of Bible Knowledge. Fcp. 8vo. 6s.
Gwilt's Encyclopædia of Architecture. 8vo. 52s. 6d.
Keith Johnston's Dictionary of Geography, or General Gazetteer. 8vo. 42s.
M'Culloch's Dictionary of Commerce and Commercial Navigation. 8vo. 63s.
Maunder's Biographical Treasury. Fcp. 8vo. 6s.
— Historical Treasury. Fcp. 8vo. 6s.
— Scientific and Literary Treasury. Fcp. 8vo. 6s.
— Treasury of Bible Knowledge, edited by Ayre. Fcp. 8vo. 6s.
— Treasury of Botany, edited by Lindley & Moore. Two Parts, 12s.
— Treasury of Geography. Fcp. 8vo. 6s.
— Treasury of Knowledge and Library of Reference. Fcp. 8vo. 6s.
— Treasury of Natural History. Fcp. 8vo. 6s.
Quain's Dictionary of Medicine. Medium 8vo. 31s. 6d., or in 2 vols. 34s.
Reeve's Cookery and Housekeeping. Crown 8vo. 5s.
Rich's Dictionary of Roman and Greek Antiquities. Crown 8vo. 7s. 6d.
Roget's Thesaurus of English Words and Phrases. Crown 8vo. 10s. 6d.
Willich's Popular Tables, by Marriott. Crown 8vo. 10s. 6d.

LONGMANS, GREEN, & CO., London and New York.

CHEMISTRY, ENGINEERING, & GENERAL SCIENCE.

Abbott's Elementary Theory of the Tides. Crown 8vo. 2*s*.
Allen's (Grant) Force and Energy: a Theory of Dynamics. 8vo. 7*s*. 6*d*.
Arnott's Elements of Physics or Natural Philosophy. Crown 8vo. 12*s*. 6*d*.
Bourne's Catechism of the Steam Engine. Crown 8vo. 7*s*. 6*d*.
— Handbook of the Steam Engine. Fcp. 8vo. 9*s*.
— Recent Improvements in the Steam Engine. Fcp. 8vo. 6*s*.
Clerk's The Gas Engine. With Illustrations. Crown 8vo. 7*s*. 6*d*.
Clodd's The Story of Creation. Illustrated. Crown 8vo. 6*s*.
Crookes's Select Methods in Chemical Analysis. 8vo. 24*s*.
Culley's Handbook of Practical Telegraphy. 8vo. 16*s*.
Fairbairn's Useful Information for Engineers. 3 vols. crown 8vo. 31*s*. 6*d*.
— Mills and Millwork. 1 vol. 8vo. 25*s*.
Forbes' Lectures on Electricity. Crown 8vo. 5*s*.
Galloway's Principles of Chemistry Practically Taught. Crown 8vo. 6*s*. 6*d*.
Ganot's Elementary Treatise on Physics, by Atkinson. Large crown 8vo. 15*s*.
— Natural Philosophy, by Atkinson. Crown 8vo. 7*s*. 6*d*.
Gibson's Text-Book of Elementary Biology. Crown 8vo. 6*s*.
Haughton's Six Lectures on Physical Geography. 8vo. 15*s*.
Helmholtz on the Sensations of Tone. Royal 8vo. 28*s*.
Helmholtz's Lectures on Scientific Subjects. 2 vols. crown 8vo. *s*. 6*d*. each.
Herschel's Outlines of Astronomy. Square crown 8vo. 12*s*.
Hudson and Gosse's The Rotifera or 'Wheel Animalcules.' With 30 Coloured Plates. 6 parts. 4to. 10*s*. 6*d*. each. Complete, 2 vols. 4to. £3. 10*s*. With Supplement, £4. 4*s*. Supplement separately, 12*s*. 6*d*.
Hullah's Lectures on the History of Modern Music. 8vo. 8*s*. 6*d*.
— Transition Period of Musical History. 8vo. 10*s*. 6*d*.
Jago's Inorganic Chemistry, Theoretical and Practical. Fcp. 8vo. 2*s*. 6*d*.
Jeans' Handbook for the Stars. Royal 8vo. 5*s*.
Kolbe's Short Text-Book of Inorganic Chemistry. Crown 8vo. 7*s*. 6*d*.
Lloyd's Treatise on Magnetism. 8vo. 10*s*. 6*d*.
Longmans' New Atlas. 56 Maps. Edited by G. G. Chisholm. 4to. or imperial 8vo. 12*s*. 6*d*.
Macalister's Zoology and Morphology of Vertebrate Animals. 8vo. 10*s*. 6*d*.
Macfarren's Lectures on Harmony. 8vo. 12*s*.
— Addresses and Lectures. Crown 8vo. 6*s*. 6*d*.
Martin's Navigation and Nautical Astronomy. Royal 8vo. 18*s*.
Meyer's Modern Theories of Chemistry. 8vo. 18*s*.
Miller's Elements of Chemistry, Theoretical and Practical. 3 vols. 8vo. Part I. Chemical Physics, 16*s*. Part II. Inorganic Chemistry, 24*s*. Part III. Organic Chemistry, price 31*s*. 6*d*.
Mitchell's Manual of Practical Assaying. 8vo. 31*s*. 6*d*.
— Dissolution and Evolution and the Science of Medicine. 8vo. 16*s*.
Noble's Hours with a Three-inch Telescope. Crown 8vo. 4*s*. 6*d*.
Northcott's Lathes and Turning. 8vo. 18*s*.
Oliver's Astronomy for Amateurs. Crown 8vo. 7*s*. 6*d*.
Owen's Comparative Anatomy and Physiology of the Vertebrate Animals. 3 vols. 8vo. 73*s*. 6*d*.

LONGMANS, GREEN, & CO., London and New York.

8 General Lists of Works.

Richardson's The Health of Nations; Works and Life of Edwin Chadwick, C.B. 2 vols. 8vo. 28*s*.
— The Commonhealth; a Series of Essays. Crown 8vo. 6*s*.
Schellen's Spectrum Analysis. 8vo. 31*s*. 6*d*.
Scott's Weather Charts and Storm Warnings. Crown 8vo. 6*s*.
Sennett's Treatise on the Marine Steam Engine. 8vo. 21*s*.
Smith's Graphics, or the Art of Calculation by Drawing Lines. Part I. with Atlas of Plates, 8vo. 15*s*.
Stoney's The Theory of the Stresses on Girders, &c. Royal 8vo. 36*s*.
Tilden's Practical Chemistry. Fcp. 8vo. 1*s*. 6*d*.
Tyndall's Faraday as a Discoverer. Crown 8vo. 3*s*. 6*d*.
— Floating Matter of the Air. Crown 8vo. 7*s*. 6*d*.
— Fragments of Science. 2 vols. post 8vo. 16*s*.
— Heat a Mode of Motion. Crown 8vo. 12*s*.
— Lectures on Light delivered in America. Crown 8vo. 5*s*.
— Lessons on Electricity. Crown 8vo. 2*s*. 6*d*.
— Notes on Electrical Phenomena. Crown 8vo. 1*s*. sewed, 1*s*. 6*d*. cloth.
— Notes of Lectures on Light. Crown 8vo. 1*s*. sewed, 1*s*. 6*d*. cloth.
— Researches on Diamagnetism and Magne-Crystallic Action. Cr. 8vo. 12*s*.
— Sound, with Frontispiece and 203 Woodcuts. Crown 8vo. 10*s*. 6*d*.
Unwin's The Testing of Materials of Construction. Illustrated. 8vo. 21*s*.
Watts' Dictionary of Chemistry. New Edition (4 vols.). Vols. 1 and 2, 8vo. 42*s*. each.
Webb's Celestial Objects for Common Telescopes. Crown 8vo. 9*s*.

NATURAL HISTORY, BOTANY & GARDENING.

Bennett and Murray's Handbook of Cryptogamic Botany. 8vo. 16*s*.
Dixon's Rural Bird Life. Crown 8vo. Illustrations, 5*s*.
Hartwig's Aerial World, 8vo. 10*s*. 6*d*.
— Polar World, 8vo. 10*s*. 6*d*.
— Sea and its Living Wonders. 8vo. 10*s*. 6*d*.
— Subterranean World, 8vo. 10*s*. 6*d*.
— Tropical World, 8vo. 10*s*. 6*d*.
Lindley's Treasury of Botany. 2 vols. fcp. 8vo. 12*s*.
London's Encyclopædia of Gardening. 8vo. 21*s*.
— — Plants. 8vo. 42*s*.
Rivers's Orchard House. Crown 8vo. 5*s*.
— Miniature Fruit Garden. Fcp. 8vo. 4*s*.
Stanley's Familiar History of British Birds. Crown 8vo. 6*s*.
Wood's Bible Animals. With 112 Vignettes. 8vo. 10*s*. 6*d*.
— Homes Without Hands, 8vo. 10*s*. 6*d*.
— Insects Abroad, 8vo. 10*s*. 6*d*.
— Insects at Home. With 700 Illustrations. 8vo. 10*s*. 6*d*.
— Out of Doors. Crown 8vo. 5*s*.
— Petland Revisited. Crown 8vo. 7*s*. 6*d*.
— Strange Dwellings. Crown 8vo. 5*s*.

LONGMANS, GREEN, & CO., London and New York.

THEOLOGICAL AND RELIGIOUS WORKS.

Arnold's (Rev. Dr. Thomas) Sermons. 6 vols. crown 8vo. 5s. each.
Boultbee's Commentary on the 39 Articles. Crown 8vo. 6s.
Browne's (Bishop) Exposition of the 39 Articles. 8vo. 16s.
Bullinger's Critical Lexicon and Concordance to the English and Greek New Testament. Royal 8vo. 15s.
Colenso on the Pentateuch and Book of Joshua. Crown 8vo. 6s.
Conder's Handbook of the Bible. Post 8vo. 7s. 6d.
Conybeare & Howson's Life and Letters of St. Paul :—
    Library Edition, with Maps, Plates, and Woodcuts. 2 vols. square crown 8vo. 21s.
    Student's Edition, revised and condensed, with 46 Illustrations and Maps. 1 vol. crown 8vo. 6s.
Davidson's Introduction to the Study of the New Testament. 2 vols. 8vo. 30s.
Edersheim's Life and Times of Jesus the Messiah. 2 vols. 8vo. 24s.
    — Prophecy and History in relation to the Messiah. 8vo. 12s.
Ellicott's (Bishop) Commentary on St. Paul's Epistles. 8vo. Corinthians I. 16s. Galatians, 8s. 6d. Ephesians, 8s. 6d. Pastoral Epistles, 10s. 6d. Philippians, Colossians and Philemon, 10s. 6d. Thessalonians, 7s. 6d.
    — — Lectures on the Life of our Lord. 8vo. 12s.
Ewald's Antiquities of Israel, translated by Solly. 8vo. 12s. 6d.
    — History of Israel, translated by Carpenter & Smith. 8 vols. 8vo. Vols. 1 & 2, 24s. Vols. 3 & 4, 21s. Vol. 5, 18s. Vol. 6, 16s. Vol. 7, 21s. Vol. 8, 18s.
Hobart's Medical Language of St. Luke. 8vo. 16s.
Hopkins's Christ the Consoler. Fcp. 8vo. 2s. 6d.
Hutchinson's The Record of a Human Soul. Fcp. 8vo. 3s. 6d.
Jameson's Sacred and Legendary Art. 6 vols. square 8vo.
    Legends of the Madonna. 1 vol. 21s.
    — — — Monastic Orders 1 vol. 21s.
    — — — Saints and Martyrs. 2 vols. 31s. 6d.
    — — — Saviour. Completed by Lady Eastlake. 2 vols. 42s.
Jukes's New Man and the Eternal Life. Crown 8vo. 6s.
    — Second Death and the Restitution of all Things. Crown 8vo. 3s. 6d.
    — Types of Genesis. Crown 8vo. 7s. 6d.
    — The Mystery of the Kingdom. Crown 8vo. 3s. 6d.
    — The Names of God in Holy Scripture. Crown 8vo. 4s. 6d.
Lyra Germanica : Hymns translated by Miss Winkworth. Fcp. 8vo. 5s.
Macdonald's (G.) Unspoken Sermons. First and Second Series. Crown 8vo, 3s. 6d. each. Third Series. Crown 8vo. 7s. 6d.
    — The Miracles of our Lord. Crown 8vo. 3s. 6d.
Manning's Temporal Mission of the Holy Ghost. Crown 8vo. 8s. 6d.
Martineau's Endeavours after the Christian Life. Crown 8vo. 7s. 6d.
    — Hymns of Praise and Prayer. Crown 8vo. 4s. 6d. 32mo. 1s. 6d.
    — Sermons, Hours of Thought on Sacred Things. 2 vols. 7s. 6d. each.
Max Müller's Origin and Growth of Religion. Crown 8vo. 7s. 6d.
    — — Science of Religion. Crown 8vo. 7s. 6d.
    — — Gifford Lectures on Natural Religion. Crown 8vo. 10s. 6d.
Monsell's Spiritual Songs for Sundays and Holidays. Fcp. 8vo. 5s. 18mo. 2s.

LONGMANS, GREEN, & CO., London and New York.

Newman's Apologia pro Vitâ Suâ. Crown 8vo. 6s.
— The Arians of the Fourth Century. Crown 8vo. 6s.
— The Idea of a University Defined and Illustrated. Crown 8vo. 7s.
— Historical Sketches. 3 vols. crown 8vo. 6s. each.
— Discussions and Arguments on Various Subjects. Crown 8vo. 6s.
— An Essay on the Development of Christian Doctrine. Crown 8vo. 6s.
— Certain Difficulties Felt by Anglicans in Catholic Teaching Considered. Vol. 1, crown 8vo. 7s. 6d. Vol. 2, crown 8vo. 5s. 6d.
— The Via Media of the Anglican Church, Illustrated in Lectures, &c. 2 vols. crown 8vo. 6s. each.
— Essays, Critical and Historical. 2 vols. crown 8vo. 12s.
— Essays on Biblical and on Ecclesiastical Miracles. Crown 8vo. 6s.
— An Essay in Aid of a Grammar of Assent. 7s. 6d.
— Select Treatises of St. Athanasius in Controversy with the Arians. Translated. 2 vols. crown 8vo. 15s.

Newnham's Thy Heart with My Heart: Four Letters on the Holy Communion. 18mo. 3d. sewed 6d. cloth limp; 8d. cloth.
— The All-Father. Sermons. With Preface by Edna Lyall. Crown 8vo. 4s. 6d.

Roberts' Greek the Language of Christ and His Apostles. 8vo. 18s.
Son of Man (The) in His Relation to the Race. Crown 8vo. 2s. 6d.
Supernatural Religion. Complete Edition. 3 vols. 8vo. 36s.
Twells' Colloquies on Preaching. Crown 8vo. 5s
Younghusband's The Story of Our Lord told in Simple Language for Children. Illustrated. Crown 8vo. 2s. 6d. cloth.
— The Story of Genesis. Crown 8vo. 2s. 6d. cloth.

TRAVELS, ADVENTURES &c.

Baker's Eight Years in Ceylon. Crown 8vo. 5s.
— Rifle and Hound in Ceylon. Crown 8vo. 5s.
Brassey's Sunshine and Storm in the East. Library Edition, 8vo. 21s. Cabinet Edition, crown 8vo. 7s. 6d. Popular Edition, 4to. 6d.
— Voyage in the 'Sunbeam.' Library Edition, 8vo. 21s. Cabinet Edition, crown 8vo. 7s. 6d. School Edition, fcp. 8vo. 2s. Popular Edition, 4to. 6d.
— In the Trades, the Tropics, and the 'Roaring Forties.' Cabinet Edition, crown 8vo. 17s. 6d. Popular Edition, 4to. 6d.
— Last Journals, 1886–7. Illustrated. 8vo. 21s.
Cecil's Notes of my Journey Round the World. 8vo. 12s. 6d.
Coolidge's Swiss Travel and Swiss Guide-Books. Crown 8vo. 10s. 6d.
Crawford's Reminiscences of Foreign Travel. Crown 8vo. 5s.
Firth's Our Kin Across the Sea. With Preface by J. A. Froude. Fcp. 8vo. 6s.
Froude's Oceana; or, England and her Colonies. Cr. 8vo. 2s. boards; 2s. 6d. cloth.
— The English in the West Indies. Crown 8vo. 2s. boards; 2s. 6d. cloth.
Howitt's Visits to Remarkable Places. Crown 8vo. 5s.
James's The Long White Mountain; or, a Journey in Manchuria. 8vo. 24s.
Lees and Clutterbuck's B.C. 1887: a Ramble in British Columbia. Cr. 8vo. 10s. 6d.
Lindt's Picturesque New Guinea. 4to. 42s.
Pennell's Our Sentimental Journey through France and Italy. Illustrated. Crown 8vo. 6s.
Riley's Athos; or, The Mountain of the Monks. 8vo. 21s.
Smith's The White Umbrella in Mexico. Fcp. 8vo. 6s. 6d.
Three in Norway. By Two of Them. Illustrated. Crown 8vo. 2s. boards; 2s. 6d. cloth.

LONGMANS, GREEN, & CO., London and New York.

WORKS BY RICHARD A PROCTOR.

Old and New Astronomy. 12 Parts, 2*s.* 6*d.* each. Supplementary Section, 1*s.* Complete in 1 vol. 4to. 36*s.* [*In course of publication.*
The Orbs Around Us. With Chart and Diagrams. Crown 8vo. 5*s.*
Other Worlds than Ours. With 14 Illustrations. Crown 8vo. 5*s.*
The Moon. With Plates, Charts, Woodcuts, and Photographs. Crown 8vo. 5*s.*
Universe of Stars. With 22 Charts and 22 Diagrams. 8vo. 10*s.* 6*d.*
Light Science for Leisure Hours. 3 vols. crown 8vo. 5*s.* each.
Chance and Luck. Crown 8vo. 2*s.* boards; 2*s.* 6*d.* cloth.
Larger Star Atlas for the Library, in 12 Circular Maps. Folio, 15*s.*
New Star Atlas, in 12 Circular Maps (with 2 Index Plates). Crown 8vo. 5*s.*
The Student's Atlas. 12 Circular Maps. 8vo. 5*s.*
Transits of Venus. With 20 Lithographic Plates and 38 Illustrations. 8vo. 8*s.* 6*d.*
Studies of Venus-Transits. With Diagrams and 10 Plates. 8vo. 5*s.*
Elementary Physical Geography. With 33 Maps and Woodcuts. Fcp. 8vo. 1*s.* 6*d.*
Lessons in Elementary Astronomy. With 47 Woodcuts. Fcp. 8vo. 1*s.* 6*d.*
First Steps in Geometry. Fcp. 8vo. 3*s.* 6*d.*
Easy Lessons in the Differential Calculus. Fcp. 8vo. 2*s.* 6*d.*
How to Play Whist, with the Laws and Etiquette of Whist. Crown 8vo. 3*s.* 6*d.*
Home Whist: an Easy Guide to Correct Play. 16mo. 1*s.*
The Poetry of Astronomy. Crown 8vo. 5*s.*
The Stars in their Seasons. Imperial 8vo. 5*s.*
Strength. Crown 8vo. 2*s.*
Strength and Happiness. With 9 Illustrations. Crown 8vo. 5*s.*
The Seasons Pictured in Forty-eight Sun-Views of the Earth, and Twenty-four Zodiacal Maps and other Drawings. Demy 4to. 6*s.*
The Star Primer; showing the Starry Sky, week by week. Crown 4to. 2*s.* 6*d.*
Nature Studies. By Grant Allen, A.Wilson, E. Clodd, and R. A. Proctor. Cr. 8vo. 5*s.*
Leisure Readings. By E. Clodd, A. Wilson, and R. A. Proctor, &c. Cr. 8vo. 5*s.*
Rough Ways Made Smooth. Crown 8vo. 5*s.*
Our Place Among Infinities. Crown 8vo. 5*s.*
The Expanse of Heaven: Essays on the Wonders of the Firmament. Crown 8vo. 5*s.*
Pleasant Ways in Science. Crown 8vo. 5*s.*
Myths and Marvels of Astronomy. Crown 8vo. 5*s.*
The Great Pyramid: Observatory, Tomb, and Temple. Crown 8vo. 5*s.*

AGRICULTURE, HORSES, DOGS, AND CATTLE.

Fitzwygram's Horses and Stables. 8vo. 5*s.*
Lloyd's The Science of Agriculture. 8vo. 12*s.*
Loudon's Encyclopædia of Agriculture. 21*s.*
Prothero's Pioneers and Progress of English Farming. Crown 8vo. 5*s.*
Steel's Diseases of the Ox, a Manual of Bovine Pathology. 8vo. 15*s.*
— — — Dog. 8vo. 10*s.* 6*d.*
Stonehenge's Dog in Health and Disease. Square crown 8vo. 7*s.* 6*d.*
Taylor's Agricultural Note Book. Fcp. 8vo. 2*s.* 6*d.*
Ville on Artificial Manures, by Crookes. 8vo. 21*s.*
Youatt's Work on the Dog. 8vo. 6*s.*
— — — — Horse. 8vo. 7*s.* 6*d.*

LONGMANS, GREEN, & CO., London and New York.

WORKS OF FICTION.

By H. RIDER HAGGARD.
She : a History of Adventure. Illustrated. Crown 8vo. 3s. 6d.
Allan Quatermain. Illustrated. Crown 8vo. 3s. 6d.
Maiwa's Revenge. 2s. bds.; 2s. 6d. cl.
Colonel Quaritch. Crown 8vo. 6s.
Cleopatra. Illustrated. 6s.

By the EARL OF BEACONSFIELD.
Vivian Grey. | Tancred.
Venetia. | Sybil.
Coningsby. | Alroy, Ixion, &c.
Lothair. | Endymion.
The Young Duke, &c.
Contarini Fleming, &c.
Henrietta Temple.
Price 1s. each, bds. ; 1s. 6d. each, cloth .
The HUGHENDEN EDITION. With 2 Portraits and 11 Vignettes. 11 vols. Crown 8vo. 42s.

By G. J. WHYTE-MELVILLE.
The Gladiators. | Kate Coventry.
The Interpreter. | Digby Grand.
Holmby House. | General Bounce.
Good for Nothing.
The Queen's Maries.
Price 1s. each, bds.; 1s. 6d. each, cloth.

By ELIZABETH M. SEWELL.
Amy Herbert. | Cleve Hall.
Gertrude. | Ivors.
Ursula. | Earl's Daughter.
The Experience of Life.
A Glimpse of the World.
Katharine Ashton.
Margaret Percival.
Laneton Parsonage.
Price 1s. 6d. each, cloth ; 2s. 6d. each, gilt edges.

By Mrs. MOLESWORTH.
Marrying and Giving in Marriage. Price 2s. 6d. cloth.

By DOROTHEA GERARD.
Orthodox. Price 6s.

By Mrs. OLIPHANT.
In Trust. | Madam.
Price 1s. each, bds. ; 1s. 6d. each, cloth.
Lady Car. 6s.

By G. H. JESSOP.
Judge Lynch. 6s.

By A. C. DOYLE.
Micah Clarke. Crown 8vo. 6s.

By JAMES PAYN.
The Luck of the Darrells.
Thicker than Water.
Price 1s. each, boards; 1s. 6d. each, cloth.

By ANTHONY TROLLOPE.
The Warden.
Barchester Towers.
Price 1s. each, boards ; 1s. 6d. each, cloth.

By BRET HARTE.
In the Carquinez Woods.
Price 1s. boards ; 1s. 6d. cloth.
On the Frontier.
By Shore and Sedge.
Price 1s. each, sewed.

By ROBERT L. STEVENSON.
The Dynamiter.
Strange Case of Dr. Jekyll and Mr. Hyde.
Price 1s. each, sewed ; 1s. 6d. each, cloth.

By R. L. STEVENSON and L. OSBOURNE.
The Wrong Box. 5s.

By EDNA LYALL.
The Autobiography of a Slander. Price 1s. sewed.

By F. ANSTEY.
The Black Poodle, and other Stories. Price 2s. boards ; 2s. 6d. cloth.

By the AUTHOR OF THE 'ATELIER DU LYS.'
The Atelier du Lys; or, an Art Student in the Reign of Terror. 2s. 6d.
Mademoiselle Mori : a Tale of Modern Rome. 2s. 6d.
In the Olden Time : a Tale of the Peasant War in Germany. 2s. 6d.
Hester's Venture. 2s. 6d.

By Mrs. DELAND.
John Ward, Preacher. Crown 8vo. 2s. boards : 2s. 6d. cloth.

By W. HERRIES POLLOCK.
A Nine Men's Morrice, &c. Crown 8vo. 6s.

By D. CHRISTIE MURRAY and HENRY MURRAY.
A Dangerous Catspaw. Cr. 8vo. 6s.

By J. A. FROUDE.
The Two Chiefs of Dunboy. Crown 8vo. 6s.

LONGMANS, GREEN, & CO., London and New York.

POETRY AND THE DRAMA.

Armstrong's (Ed. J.) Poetical Works. Fcp. 8vo. 5s.
— (G. F.) Poetical Works :—
Poems, Lyrical and Dramatic. Fcp. 8vo. 6s.
Ugone: a Tragedy. Fcp. 8vo. 6s.
A Garland from Greece. Fcp. 8vo. 9s.
King Saul. Fcp. 8vo. 5s.
King David. Fcp. 8vo. 6s.
King Solomon. Fcp. 8vo. 6s.
Stories of Wicklow. Fcp. 8vo. 9s.
Mephistopheles in Broadcloth: a Satire. Fcp. 8vo. 4s.
Victoria Regina et Imperatrix: a Jubilee Song from Ireland, 1887. 4to. 2s. 6d.

Ballads of Books. Edited by Andrew Lang. Fcp. 8vo. 6s.
Bowen's Harrow Songs and other Verses. Fcp. 8v , 2s. 6d.
Bowdler's Family Shakespeare. Medium 8vo. 14s. - 6 vols. fcp. 8vo. 21s.
Deland's The Old Garden, and other Verses. Fcp. 8vo. 5s.
Fletcher's Character Studies in Macbeth. Crown vo. 2s. 6d.
Goethe's Faust, translated by Birds. Crown 8vo. Part I. 6s.; Part II. 6s.
— — translated by Webb. 8vo. 12s. 6d.
— — edited by Selss. Crown 8vo. 5s.
Higginson's The Afternoon Landscape. Fcp. 8vo. 5s.
Ingelow's Poems. 2 Vols. fcp. 8vo. 12s.; Vol. 3, fcp. 8vo. 5s.
— Lyrical and other Poems. Fcp. 8vo. 2s. 6d. cloth, plain ; 3s. cloth, gilt edges.
Kendall's (May) Dreams to Sell. Fcp. 8vo. 6s.
Lang's Grass of Parnassus. Fcp. 8vo. 6s.
Macaulay's Lays of Ancient Rome. Illustrated by Scharf. 4to. 10s. 6d. Bijou Edition, fcp. 8vo. 2s. 6d. Popular Edit., fcp. 4to. 6d. swd., 1s. cloth.
— Lays of Ancient Rome, with Ivry and the Armada. Illustrated by Weguelin. Crown 8vo. 3s. 6d. gilt edges.
Nesbit's Lays and Legends. Crown 8vo. 5s.
— Leaves of Life. Crown 8vo. 5s.
Newman's The Dream of Gerontius. 16mo. 6d. sewed ; 1s. cloth.
— Verses on Various Occasions. Fcp. 8vo. 6s.
Reader's Voices from Flowerland : a Birthday Book. 2s. 6d. cloth, 3s. 6d. roan.
Riley's Old-Fashioned Roses. Fcp. 8vo. 5s.
Southey's Poetical Works. Medium 8vo. 14s.
Stevenson's A Child's Garden of Verses. Fcp. 8vo. 5s.
Sumner's The Besom Maker, and other Country Folk Songs. 4to. 2s. 6d.
Tomson's The Bird Bride. Fcp. 8vo. 6s.
Virgil's Æneid, translated by Conington. Crown 8vo. 6s.
— Poems, translated into English Prose. Crown 8vo. 6s.

SPORTS AND PASTIMES.

Campbell-Walker's Correct Card, or How to Play at Whist. Fcp. 8vo. 2s. 6d.
Ford's Theory and Practice of Archery, revised by W. Butt. 8vo. 14s.
Francis's Treatise on Fishing in all its Branches. Post 8vo. 15s.
Longman's Chess Openings. Fcp. 8vo. 2s. 6d.
Pole's Theory of the Modern Scientific Game of Whist. Fcp. 8vo. 2s. 6d.
Proctor s How to Play Whist. Crown 8vo. 3s. 6d.
— Home Whist. 18mo. 1s. sewed.
Ronalds's Fly-Fisher's Entomology. 8vo. 14s.
Wilcocks's Sea-Fisherman. Post 8vo. 6s.

LONGMANS, GREEN, & CO., London and New York.

MISCELLANEOUS WORKS.

A. K. H. B., The Essays and Contributions of. Crown 8vo.
    Autumn Holidays of a Country Parson. 3s. 6d.
    Changed Aspects of Unchanged Truths. 3s. 6d.
    Common-Place Philosopher in Town and Country. 3s. 6d.
    Critical Essays of a Country Parson. 3s. 6d.
    Counsel and Comfort spoken from a City Pulpit. 3s. 6d.
    Graver Thoughts of a Country Parson. Three Series. 3s. 6d. each.
    Landscapes, Churches, and Moralities. 3s. 6d.
    Leisure Hours in Town. 3s. 6d. Lessons of Middle Age. 3s. 6d.
    Our Homely Comedy; and Tragedy. 3s. 6d.
    Our Little Life. Essays Consolatory and Domestic. Two Series. 3s. 6d.
    Present-day Thoughts. 3s. 6d.   [each.
    Recreations of a Country Parson. Three Series. 3s. 6d. each.
    Seaside Musings on Sundays and Week-Days. 3s. 6d.
    Sunday Afternoons in the Parish Church of a University City. 3s. 6d.
Archer's Masks or Faces? A Study in the Psychology of Acting. Crown 8vo. 6s. 6d.
Armstrong's (Ed. J.) Essays and Sketches. Fcp. 8vo. 5s.
Arnold's (Dr. Thomas) Miscellaneous Works. 8vo 7s. 6d.
Bagehot's Literary Studies, edited by Hutton. 2 vols. 8vo. 28s.
Baker's War with Crime. Reprinted Papers. 8vo. 12s. 6d.
Farrar's Language and Languages. Crown 8vo. 6s.
Hargreave's Literary Workers; or, Pilgrims to the Temple of Honour. Small 4to. 7s. 6d.
Huth's The Marriage of Near Kin. Royal 8vo. 21s.
Jefferies' Field and Hedgerow: Last Essays. Crown 8vo. 6s.
Lang's Letters to Dead Authors. Fcp. 8vo. 6s. 6d.
    — Books and Bookmen. Crown 8vo. 6s. 6d.
    — Letters on Literature. Fcp. 8vo. 6s. 6d.
Matthews' (Brander) Pen and Ink. Reprinted Papers. Crown 8vo. 5s.
Max Müller's Lectures on the Science of Language. 2 vols. crown 8vo. 16s.
    — — Lectures on India. 8vo. 12s. 6d.
    — — Biographies of Words and the Home of the Aryas. Crown 8vo. 7s. 6d.
Rendle and Norman's Inns of Old Southwark. Illustrated. Royal 8vo. 28s.
Wendt's Papers on Maritime Legislation. Royal 8vo. £1. 11s. 6d.

WORKS BY MRS. DE SALIS.

Savouries à la Mode. Fcp. 8vo. 1s.	Cakes and Confections. 1s. 6d.
Entrées à la Mode. Fcp. 8vo. 1s. 6d.	Sweets & Supper Dishes à la Mode. 1s. 6d.
Soups and Dressed Fish à la Mode. Fcp. 8vo. 1s. 6d.	Oysters à la Mode. Fcp. 8vo. 1s. 6d.
	Vegetables à la Mode. Fcp. 8vo. 1s. 6d.
Puddings and Pastry à la Mode. 1s. 6d.	Game and Poultry à la Mode. 1s. 6d.

LONGMANS, GREEN, & CO., London and New York.

MEDICAL AND SURGICAL WORKS.

Ashby's Notes on Physiology for the Use of Students. 120 Illustrations. 18mo. 5*s*.
Ashby and Wright's The Diseases of Children, Medical and Surgical. 8vo. 21*s*.
Barker's Short Manual of Surgical Operations. With 61 Woodcuts. Cr. 8vo. 12*s*. 6*d*.
Bentley's Text-book of Organic Materia Medica. 62 Illustrations. Cr. 8vo. 7*s*. 6*d*.
Coats's Manual of Pathology. With 339 Illustrations. 8vo. 31*s*. 6*d*.
Cooke's Tablets of Anatomy. Post 4to. 7*s*. 6*d*.
Dickinson's Renal and Urinary Affections. Complete in Three Parts, 8vo. with 12 Plates and 122 Woodcuts. £3. 4*s*. 6*d*. cloth.
— The Tongue as an Indication of Disease. 8vo. 7*s*. 6*d*.
Erichsen's Science and Art of Surgery. 1,025 Engravings. 2 vols. 8vo. 48*s*.
— Concussion of the Spine, &c. Crown 8vo. 10*s*. 6*d*.
Gairdner and Coats's Lectures on Tabes Mesenterica. 28 Illustrations. 8vo. 12*s*. 6*d*.
Garrod's (Sir Alfred) Treatise on Gout and Rheumatic Gout. 8vo. 21*s*.
— Materia Medica and Therapeutics. Crown 8vo. 12*s*. 6*d*.
Garrod's (A. G.) Use of the Laryngoscope. With Illustrations. 8vo. 3*s*. 6*d*.
Gray's Anatomy. With 569 Illustrations. Royal 8vo. 36*s*.
Hassall's San Remo Climatically and Medically Considered. Crown 8vo. 5*s*.
— The Inhalation Treatment of Disease. Crown 8vo. 12*s*. 6*d*.
Hewitt's The Diseases of Women. With 211 Engravings. 8vo. 24*s*.
Holmes's System of Surgery. 3 vols. royal 8vo. £4. 4*s*.
Ladd's Elements of Physiological Psychology. With 113 Illustrations. 8vo. 21*s*.
Little's In-Knee Distortion (Genu Valgum). With 40 Illustrations. 8vo. 7*s*. 6*d*.
Liveing's Handbook on Diseases of the Skin. Fcp. 8vo. 5*s*.
— Notes on the Treatment of Skin Diseases. 18mo. 3*s*.
— Elephantiasis Græcorum, or True Leprosy. Crown 8vo. 4*s*. 6*d*.
Longmore's The Illustrated Optical Manual. With 74 Illustrations. 8vo. 14*s*.
— Gunshot Injuries. With 58 Illustrations. 8vo. 31*s*. 6*d*.
Mitchell's Dissolution and Evolution and the Science of Medicine. 8vo. 16*s*.
Munk's Euthanasia; or, Medical Treatment in Aid of an Easy Death. Cr. 8vo. 4*s*. 6*d*.
Murchison's Continued Fevers of Great Britain. 8vo. 25*s*.
— Diseases of the Liver, Jaundice, and Abdominal Dropsy. 8vo. 24*s*.
Paget's Lectures on Surgical Pathology. With 131 Woodcuts. 8vo. 21*s*.
— Clinical Lectures and Essays. 8vo. 15*s*.
Quain's (Jones) Elements of Anatomy. 1,000 Illustrations. 2 vols. 8vo. 18*s*. each.
Quain's (Dr. Richard) Dictionary of Medicine. With 138 Illustrations. 1 vol. 8vo. 31*s*. 6*d*. cloth, or 40*s*. half-russia. To be had also in 2 vols. 34*s*. cloth.
Salter's Dental Pathology and Surgery. With 133 Illustrations. 8vo. 18*s*.
Schäfer's The Essentials of Histology. With 283 Illustrations. 8vo. 6*s*.
Smith's (H. F.) The Handbook for Midwives. With 41 Woodcuts. Cr. 8vo. 5*s*.
Smith's (T.) Manual of Operative Surgery on the Dead Body. 46 Illus. 8vo. 12*s*.
Thomson's Conspectus adapted to the British Pharmacopœia of 1885. 18mo. 6*s*.
West's Lectures on the Diseases of Infancy and Childhood. 8vo. 18*s*.
— The Mother's Manual of Children's Diseases. Fcp. 8vo. 2*s*. 6*d*.
Wilks and Moxon's Lectures on Pathological Anatomy. 8vo. 18*s*.
Williams's Pulmonary Consumption. With 4 Plates and 10 Woodcuts. 8vo. 16*s*.
Wright's Hip Disease in Childhood. With 48 Woodcuts. 8vo. 10*s*. 6*d*.

LONGMANS, GREEN, & CO., London and New York.

16 General Lists of Works.

THE BADMINTON LIBRARY.
Edited by the DUKE OF BEAUFORT, K.G. and A. E. T. WATSON.

Hunting. By the Duke of Beaufort, K.G. and Mowbray Morris. With Contributions by the Earl of Suffolk and Berkshire, Rev. E. W. L. Davies, Digby Collins, and Alfred E. T. Watson. With Coloured Frontispiece and 53 Illustrations on Wood by J. Sturgess, J. Charlton, and Agnes M. Biddulph Fourth Edition. Crown 8vo. 10s. 6d.

Fishing. By H. Cholmondeley-Pennell. With Contributions by the Marquis of Exeter, Henry R. Francis, M.A. Major John P. Traherne, G. Christopher Davies, R. B. Marston, &c.
Vol. I. Salmon, Trout, and Grayling. With Frontispiece, and 150 Illustrations of Tackle, &c. Fourth Edition. Crown 8vo. 10s. 6d.
Vol. II. Pike and other Coarse Fish. With Frontispiece, and 58 Illustrations of Tackle, &c. Third Edition. Crown 8vo. 10s. 6d.

Racing and Steeple-Chasing. Racing: By the Earl of Suffolk and W. G. Craven. With a Contribution by the Hon. F. Lawley. Steeple-chasing: By Arthur Coventry and Alfred E. T. Watson. With Coloured Frontispiece and 56 Illustrations by J. Sturgess. Second Edition. Crown 8vo. 10s. 6d.

Shooting. By Lord Walsingham and Sir Ralph Payne-Gallwey. With Contributions by Lord Lovat, Lord Charles Lennox Kerr, the Hon. G. Lascelles, and A. J. Stuart-Wortley. With 21 Full-page Illustrations, and 149 Woodcuts in the Text, by A. J. Stuart-Wortley, Harper Pennington, C. Whymper, J. G. Millais, G. E. Lodge, and J. H. Oswald Brown.
Vol. I. Field and Covert. Second Edition. Crown 8vo. 10s. 6d.
Vol. II. Moor and Marsh. Second Edition. Crown 8vo. 10s. 6d.

Cycling. By Viscount Bury, K.C.M.G. and G. Lacy Hillier. With 19 Plates, and 61 Woodcuts in the Text, by Viscount Bury and Joseph Pennell. Second Edition. Crown 8vo. 10s. 6d.

Athletics and Football. By Montague Shearman. With an Introduction by Sir Richard Webster, Q.C. M.P. and a Contribution on 'Paper Chasing' by Walter Rye. With 6 Full-page Illustrations, and 45 Woodcuts in the Text, from Drawings by Stanley Berkeley, and from Instantaneous Photographs by G. Mitchell. Second Edition. Crown 8vo. 10s. 6d.

Boating. By W. B. Woodgate. With an Introduction by the Rev. Edmond Warre, D.D. And a Chapter on 'Rowing at Eton' by R. Harvey Mason. With 10 Full-page Illustrations, 39 Woodcuts in the Text, after Drawings by Frank Dadd, and from Instantaneous Photographs, and 4 Maps of the Rowing Courses at Oxford, Cambridge, Henley, and Putney. Second Edition. Crown 8vo. 10s. 6d.

Cricket. By A. G. Steel and the Hon. R. H. Lyttelton. With Contributions by Andrew Lang, R. A. H. Mitchell, W. G. Grace, and F. Gale. With 11 Full-page Illustrations, and 52 Woodcuts in the Text, after Drawings by Lucien Davis, and from Instantaneous Photographs. Second Edition. Crown 8vo. 10s. 6d.

Driving. By the Duke of Beaufort, K.G.; with Contributions by other Authorities. Photogravure Intaglio Portrait of his Grace the Duke of Beaufort, 11 full-page Illustrations, and 54 Woodcuts in the Text, after Drawing by G. D. Giles and J. Sturgess, and from Photographs. Second Edition. Crown 8vo. 10s. 6d.

In Preparation.

Riding. By the Earl of Suffolk and Berkshire and W. R. Weir. Crown 8vo. 10s. 6d.
Fencing, Boxing, and Wrestling. By F. C. Grove, Walter H. Pollock, Walter Armstrong, and M. Prévost.
Tennis, Lawn Tennis, Racquets, and Fives. By Julian Marshall.
Golf. By Horace Hutchinson and other writers.
Yachting. By Lord Brassey, Lord Dunraven, and other writers.

LONGMANS, GREEN, & CO., London and New York.

Spottiswoode & Co. Printers, New-street Square, London.

www.ingramcontent.com/pod-product-compliance
Lightning Source LLC
Chambersburg PA
CBHW031954230426
43672CB00010B/2146